THE KALININGRAD QUESTION

New International Relations of Europe
Series Editor: Ronald H. Linden

THE KALININGRAD QUESTION

Richard J. Krickus

ROWMAN & LITTLEFIELD PUBLISHERS, INC.
Lanham • Boulder • New York • Oxford

For Valentina

ROWMAN & LITTLEFIELD PUBLISHERS, INC.

Published in the United States of America
by Rowman & Littlefield Publishers, Inc.
4720 Boston Way, Lanham, Maryland 20706
www.rowmanlittlefield.com

12 Hid's Copse Road, Cumnor Hill, Oxford OX2 9JJ, England

British Library Cataloguing in Publication Information Available

Library of Congress Cataloging-in-Publication Data

Krickus, Richard J.
　　The Kaliningrad question / Richard J. Krickus.
　　　　p.　cm. — (New international relations)
　　Includes bibliographical references and index.
　　ISBN 0-7425-1704-7 (alk. paper) — ISBN 0-7425-1705-5 (pbk. : alk. paper)
　　1. Kaliningradskaëi oblast§'(Russia)—Relations—Foreign countires.
　　2. Kaliningradskaëi oblast§'(Russia)—Politics and government.
　　3. Kaliningradskaëi oblast§'(Russia)—Strategic aspects.　I. Title.　II. Series.
DK511.K157 K75　2002
327.47'24—dc21　　　　　　　　　　　　　　　　　　　2001048485

Printed in the United States of America

♾ ™ The paper used in this publication meets the minimum requirements of American
National Standard for Information Sciences—Permanence of Paper for Printed Library
Materials, ANSI/NISO Z39.48-1992.

Contents

Acknowledgments

THE SMITH-RICHARDSON FOUNDATION provided a grant to conduct research on this book. Since I first served as an international monitor to the Lithuanian elections in 1990, Mary Washington College has been generous in providing me with grants to travel throughout the Baltic Sea region.

The following individuals helped make this book possible although they are not accountable for any of its flaws. Ron Asmus, Steve Blank, Per Carlson, Darius Degutis, Stephen Dewar, Algirdas Gureckas, Bertel Heurlin, Raimundas Lopata, Marek Karp, Kestutas Jankauskas, Rolandas Kacinskas, Rita Kazragiene, Jack Kramer, Steve Larrabee, Marius Laurinavicius, Genadijus Mackelis, Johnathan Moore, Arkady Moshes, Bob Nurick, Ingmar Oldberg, Witold Rodkiewics, Ricardas Slepavicius, Keith Smith, Henryk Szlajfer, Dmitri Trenin, Conrad Trible, Christian Wellmann, Vytautas Usackas, and Vytautas Zalys.

I would also like to thank the participants attending presentations that I made at the Danish Institute of International Affairs, Hudson Institute, the Polish Foreign Ministry and the U.S. Foreign Service Institute.

My wife, Valentina, is deserving of special mention since she read the entire manuscript, provided research assistance, and did the lion's share of the Lithuanian, Polish, and Russian translations.

EU member states

Candidate states negotiating accession

Candidate state, not negotiating

Possible Dates of Accession

2003–2007	Cyprus
	Czech Republic
	Estonia
	Hungary
	Latvia
	Lithuania
	Malta
	Poland
	Slovakia
	Slovenia
2008–2010	Bulgaria
	Romania
2010–?	Turkey

FINLAND

SWEDEN

Helsinki

Stockholm · Tallinn · ESTONIA

BALTIC
SEA

LATVIA

Riga

KALININGRAD LITHUANIA

Copenhagen Vilnius

Berlin · Warsaw

POLAND

Prague

CZECH. REPUBLIC

SLOVAKIA

Vienna · Bratislava

Budapest

AUSTRIA HUNGARY

SLOVENIA

Ljubljana

Zagreb CROATIA

BOSNIA Belgrade

Sarajevo SERBIA

ADRIATIC MONTENEGRO
SEA

Rome Skopje

Tirana MACEDONIA

ALBANIA

GREECE AEGEAN
SEA

Athens

SICILY

Valletta IONIAN SEA
· MALTA

Moscow

RUSSIA

BELARUS

Minsk

Kiev

UKRAINE

Moldova
Chisinau

ROMANIA

Bucharest

BLACK SEA

BULGARIA

Sofia

Ankara

TURKEY

Nicosia

CYPRUS LEBANON
Beirut

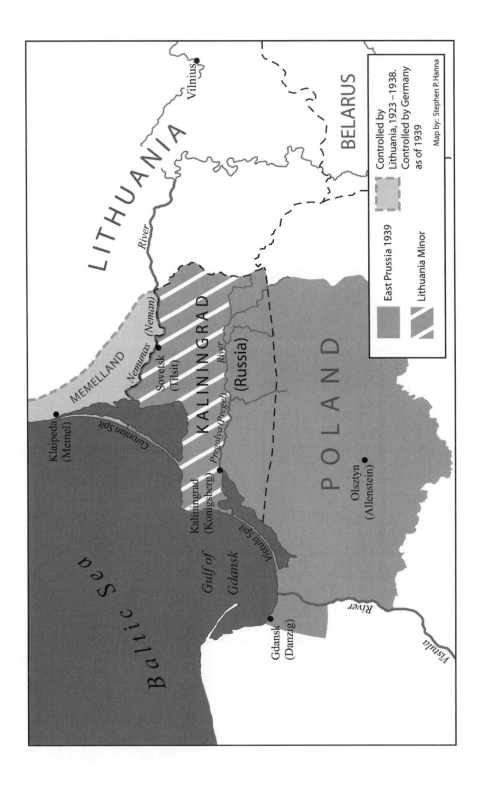

VILNIUS

LITHUANIA

BELARUS

River

Neman (Neman)

Nemunas (Neman)

MEMELLAND

Klaipeda (Memel)

Sovetsk (Tilsit)

KALININGRAD

(Russia)

Curonian Spit

Pregolya (Pregel) River

Kaliningrad (Konigsberg)

POLAND

Olsztyn (Allenstein)

Vistula Spit

Gulf of Gdansk

Gdansk (Danzig)

Vistula River

Baltic Sea

Map by: Stephen P. Hanna

Controlled by Lithuania, 1923–1938.
Controlled by Germany as of 1939

East Prussia 1939

Lithuania Minor

Introduction

D URING THE SPRING 1998 Senate debate over NATO enlargement, Senator Daniel Patrick Moynihan, a leading opponent of the initiative,
pointed to a map over his shoulder and warned that if Poland became a
member, NATO's border would extend to Russian territory. As the TV cam-
era zoomed in for a close-up, the former Harvard professor pointed to Kaliningrad, Russia's westernmost oblast. It shares a border with Poland and
Lithuania—another state seeking NATO membership. If that small Baltic
democracy joined the alliance, NATO forces would surround Kaliningrad.
Under such circumstances, Moynihan said, Russia would have to defend
itself by deploying nuclear weapons there. Other analysts opposed to enlargement went further and warned that Russia would have to scrap its strategic
doctrine of "no first use" to protect its security. This meant the United States
would be subject to attack from Russian strategic weapons on hair-trigger
status.[1]

For most Americans, this was the first time they had ever heard of Kaliningrad. That was not surprising because most foreign policy analysts in the
United States were also ignorant about the area, and the knowledge they possessed was sketchy and often false.

They knew the following: before World War II, Kaliningrad belonged to
Germany for centuries and was called East Prussia. At the 1945 Potsdam
Conference, Poland was given two-thirds of the territory to the south and
the Soviet Union got the remaining northern portion. But there was a caveat
to this exchange of territory. It would be finalized only after a peace treaty
resolving World War II was signed by the allied and axis powers—Great Britain, France, the Soviet Union, the United States, and Germany.

That settlement never occurred, but in 1990 the newly reunified German government asserted that it no longer claimed East Prussia. The Soviets cited this, and other international agreements, to bolster their claim that the area clearly belonged to them.

Stalin had incorporated his portion of East Prussia into the Soviet Union and henceforth called the oblast Kaliningrad to honor the recently deceased Soviet President Mikhail Kalinin. It was about the size of Northern Ireland, and by the mid-1990s had a population of 930,000; most of the people there were ethnic Russians who entered the area after it had been emptied of German inhabitants. Stalin gave the same name to the region's capital, which had been known as Konigsberg before the war. Those Germans who remained in the area, and survived the war after the victorious Red Army entered it in 1945, were later expelled from it abruptly and brutally. In 1946 the first wave of displaced Russian, Ukrainian, and Belarussian settlers arrived. They worked in the region's fields and rebuilt its cities, transportation infrastructure, and factories. During the Cold War it was a closed territory with a heavy military presence; the Soviet Union's Baltic Fleet was located there along with contingents of ground and air defense forces. It was the USSR's first line of defense against an attack from the West and could be used simultaneously for offensive operations in a westward coup d'main.

After the USSR's implosion, Kaliningrad became an oblast in the Russian Federation. Since it existed outside of Russian territory and was surrounded by the Baltic Sea, Poland, and Lithuania, it became an exclave, a geopolitical anomaly. Kaliningrad remained a Russian political entity, but geographically it was in Europe. Its future relied as much upon the good will of Kaliningrad's neighbors as upon Moscow's capability to nurture Russia's westernmost enclave. All land and rail routes to the oblast henceforth had to cross foreign borders.

Publicly, governments that had some interest in Kaliningrad—its Baltic Sea neighbors, the rest of Europe, the United States, as well as Russia itself—remained relatively silent about its fate. In private, however, "Kaliningrad watchers" from Bonn, Moscow, Vilnius, Warsaw, and Washington indicated that the "Kaliningrad Question" needed to be addressed.[2] It was a potential source of conflict between Russia and the Euro-Atlantic community, not only the oblast's closest neighbors.

Interested countries have perceived the Kaliningrad Question as follows:

The United States

After the Potsdam agreement, some non-Russian scholars and politicians argued that the Soviet Union did not enjoy de jure control over the territory and neither did Russia, which replaced the USSR in December 1991. This was—and is—the position of the U.S. government, which claims that Russia, like the USSR before it, enjoys only administrative (not de jure) control of the area. Kaliningrad's status therefore remains to be decided. Washington, however, has not pressed the issue.

By the mid-1990s, the Clinton administration began to look at the oblast as a potential flash point of conflict, although it did not speak about this in public. Kaliningrad's uncertain legal status and a heavy military presence there were cause of potential friction between the oblast and its neighbors. NATO enlargement, which was one of Washington's major post–Cold War objectives in Europe, could lead to even greater friction with Russia because Poland, a new alliance member, shared a common border with the Russian oblast. This was the position of Senator Moynihan and many former U.S. officials who feared enlargement would place Russian–American relations at risk.

Some analysts in the State Department believed, however, that Kaliningrad might serve a second major U.S. objective in post–Cold War Europe: to integrate Russia into the Euro-Atlantic community. Also, through joint Russian–Western efforts to revitalize Kaliningrad's economy, Moscow and Washington might foster a culture of cooperation in Northeastern Europe and improve U.S.–Russian relations, which were discordant on many fronts—for example, over arms transfers to Iran and Iraq and access to the Caspian Sea's gas and oil wealth. But the U.S. foreign policy community at large saw little reason to devote much time to the Baltic Sea region; after all it was one of the most stable areas in Europe. Defense experts felt much the same way.

The consensus was that Europe's most dangerous trouble-spot was in the Balkans. Since Yugoslavia began to unravel in 1991, bloody fighting and the evil practice of ethnic cleansing there had required close and immediate attention. NATO's failure to address the Balkans' crisis henceforth contributed to further killings and ethnic cleansing, most recently typified by Slobodan Milosevic's 1999 anti-Albanian campaign in Kosovo; albeit reluctantly, NATO finally responded to his brutal policies with bombs.

When pressed, however, some administration officials conceded that the Kaliningrad Question could become a source of friction between the United States and Russia. Even if Moscow reluctantly accepted Polish membership in the alliance, Russian officials and generals warned that if Lithuania joined NATO, Russia might respond by deploying tactical nuclear weapons in the oblast.[3] Given the highly publicized and much admired role of the Lithuanians in helping bring down the Soviet empire in the early 1990s, Lithuania had strong support in the U.S. Congress, the media, and among the American people. Any threat to Lithuania from Russia would place relations between Moscow and Washington at risk.

Relations between both capitals slipped badly after NATO bombed Serbia and the issue of Russian corruption was inserted into the 2000 U.S. presidential campaign. After he was elected president, George W. Bush persisted in his pledge to build a National Missile Defense (NMD) system that would protect the United States against missile attacks from "rogue states"—even if this meant scrapping the 1972 ABM Treaty. Russia's president, Vladimir Putin, said that would spell the end of existing arms control agreements. "As soon as we pull out (of) that axis, the (other agreements) will automatically fall apart."[4]

Levelheaded officials in Moscow and Washington realized, however, that while the honeymoon between the Americans and Russians of the 1990s was over, it was in the vital interest of presidents Bush and Putin to prevent a truly hostile relationship from developing in the twenty-first century.

A major goal of this book is to consider how Kaliningrad might serve as an area of U.S.–Russian cooperation. Unlike nuclear weapons and international terrorism, it is not uppermost in the minds of leaders in either country, but efforts to deal with the Kaliningrad Question may serve as a confidence-building measure.

First, however, U.S. policy makers need to gain a better understanding of the Kaliningrad Question. The EU and its member states, and Kaliningrad's neighbors, of course, are central to any Western effort directed at the oblast's revitalization. What has been their perception of the Kaliningrad Question? And, even more important, how does Russia feel about such cooperative efforts?

Russia

After Kaliningrad became an exclave, officials in Kaliningrad and Western analysts alike complained that Moscow had no Kaliningrad policy. Members of the Russian Foreign Ministry and Duma said there was no need for one, or claimed that Moscow had one in place. Those in the first category proclaimed that the oblast was only one of eighty-nine Russian regions and undeserving of special attention. Besides, any foreign program directed at Russia's region would first go through Moscow, the "Center" of the Russian Federation.

But President Boris Yeltsin, by virtue of his actions, had conceded Kaliningrad's exclave status meant it be treated differently than other Russian regions. Consequently, in the early 1990s, Kaliningrad was provided special economic concessions, most particularly to be a free economic zone. Moscow opponents of the free economic zone, however, prevented it from fully operating as it was intended to function—to attract foreign investors. Some other regions, such as St. Petersburg, deemed it a source of competition and lobbied against its receiving special privileges.

Meanwhile, Russian officials denied that troops in the oblast represented a threat to Kaliningrad's neighbors. Also they were wary of any suggestion from the West that Russia engage in a special development project there with the cooperation of neighboring states. Moscow's wariness on this matter was compounded by the propensity of some "foreign provocateurs" to question Kaliningrad's legal state—in other words, Russia's right to hold the territory—and the fear of Moscow elites about separatism in Russia. The humiliating 1994–96 war with Chechnya, and the resumption of fighting there in 1999 abetted fears among federation officials that Russia could split apart.

Furthermore, Yeltsin and his prime ministers treated the Kaliningrad Question as a pawn to be used in its foreign relations with the West: "Yes, we will work with the West, even the Americans, in joint efforts to revitalize Kaliningrad but only after the Balts are denied membership in NATO."

In October 1999, Prime Minister Putin seemed to suggest that Kaliningrad was a special case, but the situation in the oblast was problematic. Among other things the popularly elected governor, Leonid Gorbenko, remained at odds with the Kaliningrad Duma, which has sought his impeachment. His predecessor, Yuri Matochkin—a Yeltsin appointee—favored both a free economic zone in the oblast and close cooperation with the West, the EU in particular. Gorbenko did not cooperate with the EU experts in Kaliningrad and his opponents claimed his corrupt governance had contributed to the region's plight.

Polls first indicated that his prospects for reelection were good. But Gorbenko's political prospects took a turn for the worse in 2000, and in the November elections he lost his bid for reelection. He was replaced by Vladimir Yegorov, the former commander of Russia's Baltic Sea Fleet. Kaliningraders hoped that the "admiral," who was supported by Putin, would glean the kind of assistance from Moscow that the oblast needed and would allow it to accept foreign offers of help as well.

Kaliningrad's residents in the 1990s, while welcoming help from any quarter, remained wary of the West. While NATO was raining bombs on Serbia in the spring of 1999, they displayed solidarity with their fellow Russians in protesting the "aggression." For example, one bar in Kaliningrad displayed the following message. "No beer for customers from NATO countries!"

Poland

Poland received two-thirds of East Prussia at Potsdam, and after it gained independence and the Soviet Union collapsed, the Poles found themselves sharing a border with Russia's exclave. Warsaw expressed concern about the concentration of Russian troops there and even after their numbers declined, the Poles continued to grouse about them in private. At one point in the mid-1990s, Yeltsin proposed that Warsaw agree to a corridor that would run from Kaliningrad through Poland to Belarus. This heightened Polish fears that Russia intended to use the oblast as a card to be played at Warsaw's expense—not to mention their anger about Yeltsin making such an insensitive proposal in the first place.

After NATO announced that Poland would be one of the three former Soviet satellites to join the alliance, Russian officials responded in anger. They noted that once Poland entered the alliance, NATO would share a border with Russia via Kaliningrad and compel Moscow to take countermilitary actions. This threat had the expected result of arousing opposition to NATO enlargement in the U.S. Senate.

Rhetorical threats and perceived slights aside, the Poles have cooperated with the authorities in Kaliningrad and have been forthcoming in addressing common economic, communications, and transportation problems. Furthermore, Polish investment in the oblast has been considerable and Kaliningrad's residents rely heavily upon food products and other consumer goods imported from Poland. Politicians in Kaliningrad therefore responded with anger when Warsaw, in anticipation of becoming an EU member, adopted a new strict visa regime in January 1998. But Kaliningraders welcome close cooperation with Poland, and authorities in the oblast have publicly praised the Poles' positive attitude toward their region.

Although the Russians have accepted Polish membership in NATO—and authorities in Warsaw talk openly about Kaliningrad serving as a point of cooperation—the Poles concede in private that at some future date the oblast could become a flash point of conflict with Russia. Early in January 2001, the *Washington Times* claimed that Russia had deployed tactical nuclear weapons in Kaliningrad in 2000, and many Poles assumed their fears had become a reality even though Moscow denied the claim.[5]

Lithuania

Lithuania, the second foreign country that shares a border with Kaliningrad, is much smaller than Poland and therefore the Kaliningrad Question is one of its major foreign policy preoccupations. Fewer than four million people live in Lithuania while more than thirty million people reside in Poland. Not aligned with NATO, Lithuania is much more vulnerable to developments in Russia than is Poland. Like officials in Warsaw, those in Vilnius have expressed concern about the heavy Russian military presence in the oblast and the Lithuanian government has been subjected to pressure from Moscow to grant it special transit rights through Lithuania to Kaliningrad. At one point, after Vilnius said it would not grant any single country special transit rights, Moscow threatened to impose economic sanctions upon the former Soviet Republic if it did change its transit policies.

Moscow and Vilnius have since resolved the transit issue but it may be reopened like a raw wound at some future date—most specifically when Lithuania is considered for NATO membership. This is what Lithuania fears and what officials in Russia have indicated may be one of their countermeasures should NATO welcome Lithuania into the alliance in the next round of enlargement.

Lithuania has made a concerted effort to cooperate with Kaliningrad's authorities, and even Russian officials have conceded that the Lithuanians have acted as a good neighbor. Indeed, after the August 17, 1998, economic meltdown in Russia, Lithuania was the first country to provide humanitarian assistance to Kaliningrad's needy residents. It amounted to more than a million dollars, a considerable sum for a small, poor country.

Lithuanian entrepreneurs also have invested in the oblast, and Lithuania is one of Kaliningrad's major trading partners. The Lithuanians, through government-to-government exchanges and nongovernmental organizations (NGOs), have helped officials in Kaliningrad—among other things—to develop their public administration skills and rationalize border traffic. In the summer of 1999 Lithuania and Russia signed an agreement of cooperation and resolved the last remaining areas of dispute over border demarcations. The next year, representatives from both governments signed an agreement of cooperation to enhance Kaliningrad's developmental prospects.

Vilnius–Moscow relations, however, will continue to be marred by Lithuania's quest to gain membership in NATO in the second round of enlargement scheduled for 2002. Russian officials and military leaders have noted that with Lithuania in NATO, Kaliningrad will be surrounded by NATO member states. This means Moscow will have to take countermeasures; for example, as indicated earlier, some Russian generals have suggested tactical nuclear weapons be deployed in the oblast. Such threats may be mere bluster, but Moscow is likely to exert economic pressure upon its smaller neighbor and as a result, Lithuanian–Russian relations will take a turn for the worse; U.S.–Russian relations, of course, also will suffer as a consequence. The Balts have many staunch supporters in the United States at all levels of government, in the media, and among the general population.

Like their counterparts in Warsaw, the future of Kaliningrad is a major Lithuanian foreign policy concern. Officials in Vilnius are eager to work through the Council of Baltic Sea States (CBSS) and with the EU, to prevent the Kaliningrad Question from becoming a point of discord between Lithuania and Russia.

Germany

After Kaliningrad became an exclave, there were expressions of concern that "the Germans" would return to their lost territory, economically if not militarily, and once again dominate the region. This specter was not restricted to residents of Kaliningrad or to officials in Moscow; similar fears surfaced in Lithuania and Poland. But the Germans have not returned to Kaliningrad in a big way; instead they have adopted a low economic and political profile there. The German government insists that its relations with the oblast will be canalized through the European Union, or subregional bodies such as the CBSS.

On occasion, former residents of East Prussia have expressed interest in their old homeland through émigré organizations but they do not constitute a significant political force and, given their age, Mother Nature is rapidly depleting their ranks. At the same time, the residents of the western half of Germany continue to grumble about the awesome burden that reunification has imposed upon them as their tax dollars are interjected into the former German Democratic Republic to help Germans there revitalize a society devastated by Communism. One can assume therefore that a majority of Germans are ill disposed to adopt another socialist welfare case even farther to their east.

In an attempt to assuage Moscow's fears about German revanchism, the German government has favored the position of officials in Moscow that any help provided to Russia should be funneled through the Center and not its peripheral—regional—entities. This posture is in keeping with the reluctance of many German politicians, left, center and right, to integrate all of the former communist lands of Europe into the EU and NATO even though they may make public pronouncements to that effect. Doubts about EU enlargement eastward have been fueled in Berlin by the poor performance of the Euro vis-à-vis the U.S. dollar.

The Scandinavians

The Scandinavians see a new opportunity to develop a range of cooperative programs in the Baltic Sea region now that it is no longer artificially divided by the Cold War. They have been generous in helping the Estonians, Latvians, and Lithuanians in their collective campaigns to transit to open societies with democratic polities and free market economies. Individually they have supported a range of programs in Kaliningrad to help it with its daunting problems. They have pragmatic reasons for doing so. What they fear most is that the EU experts working in Kaliningrad's TACIS (technical assistance to the Commonwealth of Independent States) program may be right about situation there; in other words, without outside help the oblast will become a "black hole" in the Baltic Sea region and export its varied problems to neighboring states; violent crime, AIDS, drugs and weapons contraband are samples of the exportable problems uppermost in their minds.

The Nordics therefore are anxious to work with Kaliningrad and in cooperation with the EU to prevent it from becoming a bastion for criminal gangs and corrupt politicians such as those found in some parts of Latin America. They welcome U.S. economic aid but some fear the Americans—by dint of their awesome military power—may interject hard security questions into any such effort or, by adopting a large profile, spook the Russians, who are wary of U.S. interest in Kaliningrad.

The Danes are of the opinion that eventually hard security questions will arise in any international effort to address the Kaliningrad Question, and that means a significant U.S. role in whatever policies are crafted to deal with it. After all, it was the enlargement of NATO that prompted many Western governments to consider the Kaliningrad Question in the first place. Moreover, recall what Russians have told American Kaliningrad watchers pointblank: "Sure, we will join you in efforts to address the Kaliningrad Question but only after you state categorically that you will not support Baltic membership in NATO."

The European Union

In spite of lobbying efforts by the Kaliningrad watchers, who advocate the EU development of a special assistance program for Kaliningrad, the bureaucracy in Brussels and European Commission experts in Moscow have been cool toward any such initiative. They have done so even though TACIS experts working there have warned that extensive economic assistance must be provided to the oblast lest it become a black hole in Europe and exports its crime, drug, ecology, and AIDS problems to neighboring states.

Also, behind the fig leaf of "we must first deepen the EU before we widen it," some EU officials, and politicians from member states, really have no stomach for major developmental efforts to their east. Poorer members like Portugal and Greece also do not relish the prospect of sharing EU development funds with the needy countries in Central and Eastern Europe.[6]

But in summer of 1999, the EU announced that it had formed a commission to study its eastward enlargement activities. This measure, along with pressure from states in the Baltic Sea region in 2000 that the EU address the Kaliningrad Question, suggested to Kaliningrad watchers that the EU henceforth would be more forthcoming in opening its doors to the new democracies in the east.

One of the major problems that the EU will encounter is the pervasive ignorance among its own officials and influential political elites in the member states about the Kaliningrad Question. This justifies a second goal of this book, that is, to provide both international relations scholars and practitioners alike with some basic information about Kaliningrad's history, its relationship with Moscow and its neighbors, and the key economic, political, and social indicators within the oblast. Both European and American policy makers are in desperate need of such information because the Kaliningrad Question remains a source of much confusion and misinformation on the part of even sophisticated international relations analysts.

Implications for U.S. Policy

What should U.S. policy be toward Kaliningrad? Can Kaliningrad provide Moscow and Washington with the opportunity to work in harmony in the Baltic Sea region and improve overall relations between Russia and the United States at a time when they are in discord on so many other fronts? Should the assistance from the international community be filtered through Moscow, or might it make more sense to provide direct assistance to Russia's disparate regions? How can Washington work effectively with Moscow to prevent latent points of conflict in Kaliningrad from becoming manifest? Under what circumstances might the Kaliningrad Question once again become a security issue? U.S. policy makers, who are in the process of developing programs for Washington's Northern European initiative, must address these questions; all will be in the chapters that follow.

Finally an assessment of a single Russian region will provide insight into two pivotal questions that challenge U.S. policy makers today. First, what are the problems and prospects of Russia's building an open society early in the twenty-first century? And second, what can the West in general, and the United States in particular, do to help the Russians achieve this objective? If Russia lapses once again into autocracy then the Euro-Atlantic community will have to live with the world's second-largest nuclear power returning to past policies that are doomed to fail once again. This is a formula for disaster for both Russia and the Western democracies.

The Center Versus the Regions

Yevgeni Primakov was appointed prime minister in the wake of the August 1998 ruble devaluation. A month later he said to Duma deputies: "The new government must first and foremost pay special attention to preserving Russia as a single state. We are facing a serious threat of disintegration of our country."[7] For many other Moscow-centric elites in Russia, the rise of regional political power was deemed ominous and gave substance to the nightmarish prospect that the diffusion of power outward from the Center would end in disaster. On the eve of the twenty-first century, a number of danger signals could be cited:

- The war in Chechnya witnessed a reduction in the level of fighting by the fall of 2000, but the rebels continued to impose casualties upon the Russian troops operating there.
- Tatarstan and other ethnic republics, which already enjoyed extensive "home rule" powers, were demanding new privileges—including the right to veto where Muslim military personnel could be deployed.
- Eduard Rossel, the governor of Yekaterinburg, had proposed that his region develop its own currency.
- Governors, and even mayors in Russia's Far East, were snubbing Moscow and demanding greater control over tax collection: residents on one of the Kurile Islands even supported a referendum that would lease their territory to Japan.
- The Federation Council—the upper branch of the Federal Duma composed of regional officials—refused to fire Yuri Skuratov in the spring of 1999 even though Yeltsin favored his removal. Skuratov was the prosecutor who claimed that he had evidence of corruption emanating from the president's office in the Kremlin.
- Military units in many parts of Russia depended on regional political and economic elites to feed their troops and provide gasoline to keep their vehicles running.

Some pundits in Moscow characterized the confrontation between Yeltsin and regional leaders throughout the 1990s as the "czar versus the Boyars." Then in the spring of 1999, Yeltsin dismissed Primakov's replacement, Sergei Stepashin, after Stepashin would not, or could not, prevent the appearance of a new power bloc that was hatched not in the Kremlin but outside its walls. Moscow's powerful mayor, Yuri Luzhkov, merged his Fatherland party to the All Russia bloc that was composed of many powerful regional leaders—led by Tatarstan's president, Mintimer Shaimiev. Furthermore, Vladimir Gusinsky, owner of the Most Group, was said to be a financial supporter of the bloc.

Putin, who served in the KGB in East Germany during the Cold War, replaced Stepashin. A relatively young man in his mid-forties without any real political experience, Putin's prospects for remaining in office for more than several months were deemed poor. The idea that he would guard Yeltsin's Kremlin from further deadly political assaults was also considered ludicrous. The Communists might not do well in the December 1999 Duma elections, but the All Russia–Fatherland bloc was expected to match if not exceed the Communist seats in the Duma. It might prove to be a more difficult source of opposition than that represented by the Communists.

To make matters worse, Primakov joined the new alliance and immediately was characterized as the man most likely to win the Russian presidential elections in the summer of 2000. By joining it, Primakov—then the frontrunner for the 2000 presidential race—was perhaps acknowledging that the regions had become a powerful political force in Russia, and an accommodation had to be made for them. If elected president, Primakov would reassert Moscow's control of the regions, but as many Russia watchers indicated, the days of Moscow dictating to the regions were over. What Yeltsin had failed to anticipate was that the privatization program, championed by his young reformers after the USSR's collapse, was one of the major reasons that the regions with new-found wealth soon became a political force that Moscow could not ignore. Also, free economic markets create conditions for the dispersal, not the concentration, of political power.

In the summer of 1999, a new war erupted in the Northern Caucasus— first in Dagestan and later in Chechnya. Claiming they would expel the Russians from the area, the Chechen fighters provided new fears in Moscow that Russia might flake off into many parts. Clearly, Moscow had to pay close attention to what was happening in all of the regions. The Chechens, who humiliated the Russian army in the mid-1990s war, demonstrated that neither the region's size nor its economic status mattered. After all, who could forget that tiny Lithuania in 1990–91 set into motion the forces that eventually led to the Soviet Union's demise. Geography mattered a lot, however, for Russian regions that bordered on foreign lands were much more susceptible to foreign interference and revanchist movements than those entombed in Russia's heartland.

The specter of growing regional power in Russia caused some observers, both in and outside of the country, to doubt the military's loyalty to the Center in places where it had become dependent upon regional authorities and not officials in Moscow to provide for the needs of military units. Many officers were working with criminal elements as they embraced the crude materialistic impulses prevalent among warlords, not professional soldiers.

To the surprise of both Russian and foreign analysts, however, the fighting in Chechnya this time deeply angered the Russian people. The deaths of hundreds of civilians who were victimized when their apartments were bombed—allegedly by Chechen terrorists—prompted them to support Prime Minister Putin's hard-line policies. They cheered when he sent more than 100,000 troops with awesome air, artillery, and tank assets to the south to crush the Chechen "bandits." As a consequence, Putin soared ahead of Primakov as the most popular politician in Russia. His support for the quickly organized pro-Kremlin voting bloc, Unity, helped win it second place in the quest for Duma seats in the December 1999 elections.

With a Duma inclined to support his government and riding the crest of mass popular support for his tough policies in Chechnya, Putin was deemed the man to beat in the summer 2000 presidential elections. On New Year's Eve 1999, Yeltsin shocked the world when he announced his retirement. In his place, Putin would serve as acting president until the elections could be held in the summer of 2000.

Putin's popularity soared and regional leaders immediately jumped on his bandwagon. Soon men presumed to be presidential candidates—the former prime minister, Primakov, and Moscow's powerful mayor, Luzhkov—said they had withdrawn from the race.

On March 26, 2000—the Kremlin had fast-forwarded the election to exploit Putin's popularity—Putin was elected president on the first round when he captured 52 percent of the vote. His principal opponent, the communist Gennady Zyuganov, came in second with 23 percent of the votes cast.

In contrast to his predecessor, Putin henceforth enjoyed the support of the Duma and he began to reassert the Center's control over the regions. By the end of his first year as president, the Kremlin's campaign to undercut the power of the regional economic and political barons met with some but not complete success. Recalcitrant governors like Kursk's Alexander Rutskoi were denied reelection but the Kremlin's effort to oust St. Petersburg's governor Vladimir Yakovlev failed. Putin did pass a decree, however, that subjected governors to removal if they violated federal law and denied them a seat on the Federation Council.

A major conclusion of this study is that Russia's quest to build a democratic polity with a free-market economy will be advanced by empowering Russia's regions and by enabling them to develop close commercial ties with foreign investors. Kaliningrad may serve as a text case showing how this can be done. It is noteworthy that influential politicians such as Moscow's Mayor Yuri Luzhkov and former Prime Minister Yevgeni Primakov oppose the direct election of regional governors and favor their being appointed by the Russian Federation's president instead. In other words, they oppose the devolution of power to regional entities even though this reorientation in power has become a prominent part of all European societies—including two once-mighty empires, Spain and the United Kingdom. Trends indicate, however, that the Moscow "centrists" are unlikely to enjoy the same centralized power that the czars possessed for centuries and their Soviet successors did for much of the twentieth century.

Putin may persist in his campaign to undercut the power of regional authorities but ultimately his more pragmatic instincts may suggest he reach an accommodation with them. As developments in Kaliningrad suggest, both local elites—political and economic—and a growing number of ordinary Russians, have begun to challenge the centuries-old domination of Moscow. This is a historical development of major proportions because if Russia is going to develop a democracy after centuries of autocracy, people there must be empowered at the grass roots. Only in this setting can capitalism and civil society survive.

Kaliningrad is neither a large nor a rich Russian region. Nonetheless, by assessing economic, political, and social trends there, we may also gain insight into the problems and prospects of Russia's developing a federal system based upon the rule of law and not of political clans who exploit political authority to enrich themselves.

If Putin fails to create a democratic Russia with a viable free market economy and federal system, his successors may revisit Russian autocracy. The restoration of a reactionary Russia, with imperialistic tendencies, would not only be a disaster for the Russian people, it could be a source of grave instability for their neighbors as well.

President Bush is right that only Russians have the key to Russia's future but preventing the disintegration of Russia is a vital U.S. interest—recognizing, of course, that the United States has only limited ability to prevent this disaster.

Notes

1. See, for example, Stanley Kober, "NATO Expansion Flashpoints No. 3 Kaliningrad," CATO Institute Paper no. 46, Washington, 11 February 1998.

2. The term *Kaliningrad watchers* refers to diplomats, academics, and analysts in Europe, the United States, and Russia who have displayed a special interest in Kaliningrad—for example, the men and women belonging to the Kaliningrad Roundtable that the Lithuanian Ministry of Foreign Affairs first organized in the late 1990s.

3. Ingmar Oldberg, "Kaliningrad: Problems and Prospects," in *Kaliningrad: The*

European Amber Region, ed. Pertti Joenniemi and Jan Prawitz (Aldershot, England: Ashgate Publishing, 1998), 6.

4. Peter Baker and Susan B. Glasser, "Putin Vows to Preserve Democracy," *Washington Post* (7 March 2001), 17.

5. Bill Gertz, "Russia Transfers Nuclear Arms to Baltics," *Washington Times* (3 January 2001).

6. For a cogent discussion of the EU's approach to expansion toward the East, see Elizabeth Pond, *The Rebirth of Europe* (Washington, D.C.: The Brookings Institution Press, 1999), 108–57.

7. Mikhail Alexseev, "Challenges to the Russian Federation," in *Center Periphery Conflict in Post-Soviet Russia,* ed. Mikhail Alexseev (New York: St. Martin's Press, 1999), 2.

1

Kaliningrad: A Historical Overview

The German Invasion

IN 1226, with the signing of the Bull of Rimini, the Teutonic Knights were ordered to conquer the heathens who lived in territories running along the northeastern shore of the Baltic Sea. The Knights arrived in 1231 and clashed with the Prussians, the original inhabitants of that territory who spoke a language similar to Latvian and Lithuanian. The Germans earlier occupied what is the present-day Riga area and henceforth established forts and castles in the Baltic region, covering territory from Danzig to Narva. Supported by the emperor of the Holy Roman Empire and the Pope, the Knights eliminated or assimilated the local peoples over several centuries of colonial occupation. By the close of the seventeenth century, the Prussians had lost both their ancient tongue and their national existence. What's more, the German invaders took the local's name and henceforth called themselves "Prussians."

Before World War I, a Lithuanian short-story writer presumably revealed the date of the Prussians' extinction while reading a Prussian catechism in a Saint Petersburg library. She spotted the following notation in German script on the title page, which was made in 1700: "This old Prussian language has now completely disappeared. The only old man who had lived on the Curonian Isthmus and still knew some Prussian died in 1677, although there are still some like him."[1] The narrow isthmus referred to runs from present-day Lithuania to the Kaliningrad oblast and is known as the Curonian Spit. A similar swordlike isthmus runs from the oblast to Gdansk in Poland and is called the Vistula Spit.

In 1255, the king of Bohemia, Ottokar II, joined the Prussian crusade and founded the city of Konigsberg on the Pregel River, one of East Prussia's major waterways that runs east to west through the territory. Konigsberg attracted German settlers to its walls and the surrounding countryside. The city's prosperity grew apace with the development of agriculture in the hinterland and, in 1340, Konigsberg became a Hanseatic city, a center of trade linking Western Europe to Russia. Duke Albrecht, who had been the Teutonic Order's Grand Master, established the University of Konigsberg in 1544. Later one of the giants of Western philosophy, Emanuel Kant, would teach there for many years. His tomb, embedded in the bombed-out shell of the Konigsberg Cathedral—now being reconstructed—is one of the few tourist attractions in that blighted city today.

In their raids along the Baltic, the Germans encountered stiff resistance from the local peoples and often bested them in battle. As is frequently the case when outsiders overrun a divided indigenous population, the divided people coalesced, and this is what the disparate Lithuanian tribes did under the leadership of King Mindaugas. In 1251, Mindaugas converted to Christianity to protect his kingdom from the German invaders. In 1386, the Lithuanian pagan king, Jogaila, married the Polish queen, Jadwiga, beginning a long union between the two peoples. Facing the danger of Germans from the west, and Russians from the east, Lithuanians and Poles would have a dual incentive to enhance their security through a union that endured for several centuries. In 1569, the Polish–Lithuanian Commonwealth was established in Lublin in an act of union. It would extend its influence over vast areas of what is central Europe today. The commonwealth would survive until the "third" partition of Poland in 1795.

The German expansion eastward was halted in 1410, when a combined Polish–Lithuanian army (led by the Lithuanian Grand Duke Vytautas and supported by Russians, Tatars, and Czechs) defeated them at the Battle of Tannenberg. In 1454–56, the Poles defeated the Knights again, although this time the Lithuanians remained neutral. A century later, the Germans would fall to the Poles with even greater political significance as they wrested Western Prussia from the Germans. But in 1525 the Polish king allowed the Grand Master of the Knights to establish the Duchy of Prussia. It would, however, remain subject to the Polish crown.

The early seventeenth century would be a high point for Polish power, because in 1610 the Poles occupied Moscow and ensconced themselves in the Kremlin. The Polish pretender to the Russian throne, Dmitry, entered the Kremlin in triumph but a year later left that fortress in ignominy when the remains of his body (according to legend) were fired from a cannon into a bog beyond the Kremlin's walls.[2]

Poland's fortunes slumped in 1656, when German forces from Brandenburg, along with Swedes, joined the Prussian Germans and crushed a Polish army at the Battle of Warsaw. In 1701, Prussia became a kingdom under Frederick I, who established his capital in Konigsberg. After he died in 1713, his shoes were filled by his son, Frederick William I. Unlike his father, Frederick William I did not relish the splendor of the court and he imposed austerity upon the kingdom of two million people to establish a strong state perched on a firm financial base. By the time he died in 1740, Prussia had acquired an army of 60,000; it was fourth in size in Europe, but first in quality.

In 1740, Frederick William I was replaced by his son Frederick the Great, a man of many talents; he demonstrated a genius for military affairs and also was an accomplished musician. Even today music lovers listen to his compositions. Under Frederick, Prussia added new territory to the kingdom and each victory inspired him to seek new conquests. Among other things, he wrested control of vast areas of Silesia from the German Catholics of Austria. Prussia's military threat to its neighbors east and west, however, earned Frederick many enemies, and in 1756 the Seven Years War began.

The Russians in particular hoped to extend their power westward at Prussia's expense. In 1757, while the Prussians defeated a French army at Rossbach, the Russians overwhelmed Frederick's forces in East Prussia. In 1758 the Russians took the city of Konigsberg and held parts of East Prussia for several years. No significant colony of Russians, however, existed in the area until after World War II.

Over the next several years the fortunes of Frederick's army suffered other significant setbacks. It was on the brink of further reversals when Czarina Elizabeth died on January 5, 1762, and Frederick was spared what could have been total defeat. Czar Peter III, who was a longtime admirer of Frederick, replaced her and he persuaded his allies to achieve a peace with Prussia. Frederick's fortunes took a turn for the better in 1772 with the first division of Poland and he received West Prussia, including the prominent port of Gdansk that the Germans called Danzig. The Polish peasants enjoyed more liberal policies under the rule of their German masters than the far harsher conditions they had endured under their Polish lords. Now Brandenburg via West Prussia was joined with East Prussia thereby relieving the latter of its isolation.

The Partition of Poland

In 1793, Poland was partitioned again, inspiring Polish and Lithuanian uprisings in Warsaw and Vilnius. Tadeusz Kosciuszko, who had fought on the side of the colonists in the U.S. war for independence, led the resistance, but Prussian and Russian forces crushed the Polish and Lithuanian rebels. Two years later, the Third Partition of Poland occurred and neither the Poles nor the Lithuanians lived in an independent state of their own again until after World War I. Most of the Poles became subjects of German rule, although a smaller number endured Russian hegemony.

The Lithuanians, who lived along the Baltic Sea coast, resided in "Lithuania Minor" under German domination. Those in the hinterland of Lithuania, "Lithuania Major" were incorporated into the Russian empire. When the Lithuanian national movement appeared in the last half of the nineteenth century, therefore, many Lithuanians dreamed of joining the divided Lithuanian peoples into one country; hence, the claim of some Lithuanian nationalists today that much of East Prussia belongs to them.

East Prussia would flourish in the last quarter of the eighteenth century but in 1806, in face of Napoleon's advancing army numbering 600,000, the Prussian King Frederick William III moved his court from Berlin to Konigsberg. And in February 1807, as Napoleon's army poured across the plains of western Prussia, Frederick William III retreated again to the very eastern borders of East Prussia where he sought refuge in the port city of Memel. On June 2, 1807, on a raft in the middle of the Memel River, Napoleon and Czar Alexander of Russia signed a peace treaty, the outcome of which was a disaster for Prussia. In addition to having to pay enormous financial reparations, Prussia lost half of its territory, and from 1807 to 1815 Danzig was a city-state.

The little man from Corsica provided the monarchs of Europe with an enlightening, twofold lesson. First, the ranks of armies filled with men, who had experienced the enthralling social-psychological impact of nationalism, would fight and—unlike their opponents who were forced into service—not run in the face of stiff resistance or flee under the shadow of nightfall. This phenomenon much impressed the reactionary Junkers but it also struck fear in their hearts; if the German liberals, who advocated the consolidation of Europe's Germans into a unified state, were successful, the liberated peasantry would spell doom for their rule. Consequently the German aristocracy would resist that move for more than fifty years.

But Prussia was spared further humiliation when a popular uprising in Spain forced Napoleon to redeploy troops from northeast Europe to the Iberian Peninsula. And in 1809, Austria went to war against France with the hope that Europe's Germans would rise up as one and crush Napoleon. But Frederick Wilhelm balked lest the German masses became aroused. The whole purpose of the alliance against Napoleon was to prevent him from establishing a social order in which common folk would have some voice. The outcome was a humiliating defeat for Austria.

In February 1812, the Prussian king was forced into an alliance with Napoleon, who was poised to attack Russia once again. On June 22, 1812, Napoleon with a large contingent of German troops in his army crossed Lithuania and attacked Russia. During a short stay in Vilnius, he would help reignite the flames of Lithuanian nationalism, albeit they would burn bright for only a brief time. Napoleon's invasion of Russia would prove to be his undoing as the Russian generals demonstrated their strategic acumen. They coaxed Napoleon's army into Russia's vast hinterland, and as its lifeline became attenuated and could not resupply its units, the Russians attacked. Soon they were the ones who were advancing as Napoleon's troops, broken and demoralized, fled west in defeat. Some German soldiers, like Carl von Clausewitz, who would gain fame as a military strategist in the twentieth century, fought alongside the Russians.

By March 1813, Frederick William III now deemed it prudent to join Russia in fighting Napoleon, and Germans everywhere joined the War of Liberation against France. It was in the crucible of the War of Liberation that the German national ideal was advanced, but the reactionary Junkers of Prussia continued to oppose reunification for fear that it would ultimately result in the diminution of their power and privileges. During the 1860s, Prussia, under the stewardship of Chancellor Otto von Bismarck, expanded its control over large chunks of territory inhabited by German speakers. Prussian armies defeated the Danes in 1864 and the Austrians in 1866. But Bismarck ignored the pleas of the German general staff that urged him to march into Vienna and crush Austrian power. His reasoning was trenchant: to destroy Austria was to leave the center of Europe with a political vacuum, one that the Russians would only be too happy to fill.

German reunification was achieved at long last in 1871 under the brilliant stewardship of Prussia's "Iron Chancellor." Henceforth most of Europe's Germans would live in a single state, except those who continued to reside in the multiethnic Austro-Hungarian Empire that was soon to vanish from the world stage. In the next quarter century, Germany would become an industrial giant, and as its economy grew so did its military prowess.

The First World War

In July 1914, East Prussia became the focus of Russia's August invasion of Germany after the czar's generals scrapped their plans to attack Berlin and Austria simultaneously. First they would destroy the German defenses in East

Prussia, then they would drive toward Berlin. Initially the Russian forces enjoyed good fortune as German Commanding General Freidrich von Prittwitz panicked after his army was badly mauled and requested to withdraw from East Prussia. His advice was ignored as the German high command felt that a virtual German surrender would gravely damage troop morale. Prittwitz was relieved of his post and replaced by General Paul von Hindenburg. With the help of his chief of staff, Erich Ludendorff, the German forces regained their composure and on August 31 they lured the Russian General Aleksandr Sansonev into a trap and killed or wounded 70,000 Russians and captured almost 100,000 of their compatriots. A despondent Sansonev committed suicide.

The Baltic German General Paul-Georg von Rennenkamp was the next victim when the Germans crushed his forces on September 9; in that battle, the Russians suffered an additional 60,000 casualties. Richard Pipes writes, "The East Prussian victory greatly bolstered the morale of the Germans: for they had not only inflicted heavy losses on the Russians and saved their homeland from invasion but succeeded, with inferior forces and relatively small casualties, in stopping dead the Russian hordes."[3] The next summer the Germans attacked Russia from their East Prussian bases and pushed the czar's troops deeper into the country's hinterland, destroying the morale of the Russian soldiers on the way. By the end of the year the Germans and Austrians had devastated the Russian army. One million Russian fighting men were captured and forced to work in the fields to nurture their captors.

After World War I, Russian, and later Soviet military thinkers would associate their country's security with Russia occupying territory as far westward into the European continent as possible. Control of such territory would serve as a two-edged sword. On defense it would serve as a buffer against an attack from western aggressors, and on the offense, it would allow Russia to simultaneously attack its enemies in central and western Europe.

In the aftermath of World War I, Poland regained its status as an independent state. The Treaty of Versailles awarded the Poles parts of West Prussia, which historically belonged to Poland but had been lost to Germany more than a century earlier. After Germany's defeat, the Poles believed they would receive the Baltic port city of Gdansk-Danzig along with the rest of West Prussia. But since ethnic Germans populated it, Britain's David Lloyd George thought it best to make it a free city and he convinced his colleagues of the wisdom of that decision.[4] However, the allies allocated a short coastline west of the city to Warsaw, because without it, Poland would be landlocked. By awarding Warsaw a "Polish Corridor," however, Prussia became physically separated from the rest of Germany. Under the pretext that the Poles were mistreating the Germans in Danzig, Hitler would attack Poland late in 1939 and start the most destructive war in history.

Soviet Russia's displeasure with the post–World War I Polish–Russian border also would prove a point of friction between Warsaw and Moscow. In March 1919, the Allied Supreme Council in Paris asked the Commission on Polish Affairs to recommend an eastern frontier for Poland. This request was consistent with President Woodrow Wilson's Fourteen Points, which he promulgated on January 8, 1918. The thirteenth point read, "An independent Polish State should be erected which should include territories inhabited by indisputably Polish populations and which should be assured a free and secure access to the sea. . . ." At that time the Poles were fighting Lithuanian, Soviet, and Ukrainian units for control of territory that the authorities in Warsaw claimed as "historical Polish territory," for example, the Lithuania's ancient capital of Wilno/Vilnius and the Ukrainian city of Lwow/Lviv.

"For six months the Commission on Polish Affairs considered the eastern frontier problem. They issued their recommendation in a series of reports, of which the first (March 12, 1919) dealt with the Polish–German frontier. A second report (April 22, 1919) proposed a frontier running from the border of East Prussia as far south as a point on the River Bug in the latitude of Chelm. This frontier, with its southern extension to the Carpathians across the former Austrian Crownland of Galicia, subsequently became known as the Curzon Line."[5]

After several years of fighting, the Polish–Russian border was finally settled with the Treaty of Riga in 1921. It was fixed much further east than the Curzon Line and corresponded roughly with Poland's eastern border that existed during the Second Partition of Poland. The Poles acquired territory Moscow deemed traditionally Russian covering 70,000 square miles with a population of six million largely Ukrainian, Belarussian, and Lithuanian, and only a relatively small number Polish speakers.[6]

While Poland blocked German access to East Prussia from the west, territory would be taken from the Germans by the newly independent Lithuanian state to its east. After the war, Memelland, which included the city of Memel and surrounding territory, was put under French trusteeship. But the Lithuanians claimed Memel—in the northernmost extremity of East Prussia—was rightfully theirs, even though most of the citizens of the city they called Klaipeda were Germans. The Germans called it and the surrounding territory inhabited primarily by ethnic Lithuanians Memelland, but it was called Lithuania Minor by the Lithuanians. (With the exception of Klaipeda, the territory designated Lithuania Minor was located between the Pregel and Memel Rivers in East Prussia.) The authorities in the Lithuanian capital of Kaunas claimed their brethren had always occupied this territory and to return it to their descendants was consistent with Wilson's Fourteen Points.

In January 1923, armed Lithuanians forced the French troops to flee as they occupied the city of approximately 36,000. In the greater Klaipeda area there was a total population of 140,000 people. As a consequence, they gained a port facility for their newly independent country. The Lithuanians had calculated correctly that the Germans in the city were too weak to oppose them and their countrymen in Germany were too preoccupied with their own problems to assist the Memelites.

World War II

After Hitler wrested power in Berlin, the Germans in Memel, who fumed at their subject status, anticipated that the Nazi dictator would release them from Lithuanian control. But Hitler did not move for six years lest he drive the Lithuanians into the arms of the Poles or the Russians. The Soviets, meanwhile, advised the Lithuanians not to resist the Germans in their effort to retake the city. One Soviet envoy to Lithuania said, "Give up Klaipeda now. There will come a time when we will return it to you and even add Konigsberg."[7]

In March 1939, Hitler finally decided to recapture the city from the Lithuanians after the British and French allowed him to absorb Czechoslovakia. On March 23, he boarded the German battleship *Deutschland,* which steamed for the port of Klaipeda. A poor sailor, he endured physical discomfort to personally retake Memel. Three days earlier, Hitler had presented the Lithuanians with an ultimatum—surrender the city voluntarily or Germany would take it by force. Without the military assets to resist, the authorities in Kaunas had acceded to his demands. Hitler was greeted by the German residents of the city in wild exultation when he addressed an adoring crowd at the city's main square.

Upon returning to Berlin, he immediately made plans to settle the Polish question by demanding that the government in Warsaw allow Germany to control a corridor through Polish territory to the German port city of Danzig. Hitler anticipated that the allies would not "die for Danzig." During a debate at the Oxford Union this question had been put to the gathering of students and their dons. Unlike World War I, this time the country's best and brightest were not anxious to go to war. After all, many in the audience believed that Hitler was a western bulwark against the spread of Communism into the heartland of Europe and Germany prevented the Bolsheviks from leapfrogging the choppy English Channel to conquer the British Isles.

The Molotov–Ribbentrop Pact, which had been signed a month prior to Hitler's September 1, 1939, attack on Poland, spelled doom for both an independent Poland and its smaller Baltic neighbors, Estonia, Latvia, and Lithuania. After Polish resistance against the invading Germans was crushed, the Red Army entered Poland on September 17. Stalin received a portion of Poland as stipulated by the Non-Aggression Pact and occupied territory it had lost to Poland with the Treaty of Riga. In an agreement with the Nazis on September 28, 1939, the Soviets received an area of Poland that was 77,606 square miles with a population of 13 million. In turn, the Soviet Union ceded 2,750 square miles of Lithuanian territory that included a population of 457,500.[8]

But Stalin returned Vilnius to the Lithuanians in 1939, preferring that the ancient city be populated by the smaller Lithuanian nation and not the larger, recalcitrant Polish nation. The Lithuanians had lost their ancient capital in 1920 when Polish General Lucjan Zeligowski's troops seized it and surrounding territory from Poland's smaller neighbor. Enmity between the Poles and Lithuanians would prevent them from joining forces to forestall the eventual Nazi, and then Soviet, occupation of their countries for a half-century. Acknowledging the fighting prowess of the Poles, even against overwhelming odds, Stalin welcomed the flight of ethnic Poles from Eastern Lithuania in 1944 and encouraged others to leave in face of his draconian occupation policies. The Poles who remained in Eastern Lithuania were largely peasants, whom the Lithuanians claimed were Polanized Lithuanians who spoke neither Lithuanian nor Polish but a local tongue that reflected many lingual influences. The Polish-Lithuanians called themselves by the Polish word *Tutejszi*—locals—and even though some of their number would join the Lithuanian drive for independence in the late 1980s, most of their Soviet-era leaders remained loyal to Moscow until the USSR collapsed in 1991.

German troops attacked the Soviet Union in June 1941 with the intent of occupying both Leningrad and Moscow in a blistering blitzkrieg attack. The German Army Group North, commanded by Field Marshall Wilhelm von Leeb, orchestrated an attack from East Prussia through the Baltic States to capture Leningrad. With Operation Barbarosa, the center of gravity of the German war machine shifted from Berlin to East Prussia. The Germany Navy dominated most of the Baltic Sea and forced the Soviet Navy to remain bottled up in and around the ports of Leningrad. To direct Operation Barbarosa, Hitler established his headquarters, the Wolf's Lair, near the Prussian City of Rastenburg.

The Lithuanians would greet the Germans with some foreboding but also as liberators from Stalin's brutal occupation of their country. Immediately after they were occupied by the Red Army in June 1940, tens of thousands of their citizens would be arrested, killed or sent via cattle cars to the Soviet Gulag. Among their number was Menachem Begin, a Jew from Poland who was arrested in Lithuania and who decades later would become the Prime Minister of Israel. After the Germans demonstrated that they were oppressors and not liberators, some Lithuanians took to the forests to forcibly resist Hitler's minions. Among those in the Lithuanian resistance was the teen-age Valdas Adamkus, a Lithuanian Catholic, who helped edit an underground youth newspaper. More than fifty years later, Adamkus would return to Lithuania and become president of his homeland.

After massive victories against an out-matched Red Army in the summer of 1941, the cruel Russian winter and the bravery of the Soviet troops stopped the advancing German units. And Hitler, rather than striking at the heart of the Soviet empire, Moscow, halted his forces on the outskirts of the city (with the help of a Soviet counteroffensive) and embarked upon a major strategic strike toward the southern part of the USSR. It was a fateful mistake, and after the bruising battle of Stalingrad in early 1943, the German fortunes took a decisive turn for the worse. Hence, the Red Army crushed German units in an impressive display of military prowess over a broad front but with the final objective always in mind, a coup de main against Germany via Berlin.

By early October 1944 Army Group North had been forced by an advancing Red Army to retreat westward with the Baltic Sea to its back, desperately clinging to the port cities there—Riga, Memel, Konigsberg, and Danzig. All of these cities were now subject to attack from the British and Russian air forces. To lift the morale of their troops and people, German propagandists at this time spoke often about Frederick the Great's ability to maintain control of Baltic port cities during the Seven Years War. But the German commanders deemed their positions indefensible and urged Hitler to allow them to retreat and consolidate their forces. He refused their pleas. On several occasions Army Group North faced the prospect of being overwhelmed by Soviet forces led by the Soviet General of the Army, Commander Ivan Bagramyan. By this time, the Soviet Union's troops enjoyed an enormous majority in fighting men (and women) and weapons. The Red offensive failed to split Army Group North, but it reduced the battlefront from 240 miles to 20 miles and inadvertently made the German positions more compact and defensible.

The Third Belarussian Front was poised to cross the Nemunas River and attack Tilsit the last week in September 1944. Early the following month, the First Baltic Front launched an attack directed at Memel and the German line of defense along the Baltic shrank even further. On October 7, the Third Panzer Army command post was overrun and XXVIII Corps was forced into a small pocket around the port of Memel—where Hitler in March 1939 had been greeted by a cheering throng of triumphant Germans.

Several days later the Germans deserted Riga, and other units were pulled back to block a Soviet offensive toward East Prussia. Russian conquest of East Prussia, "the heartland of Prussian militarism," would represent a great moral victory for the Red Army. It would constitute the first time during the war that Soviet soldiers trod German soil. But the Third Panzer Army launched a counterattack across the Nemunas River on October 19, and soon the Russian campaign to overrun East Prussia was halted.

German troop morale received a serious blow on October 10, however, when Hitler left Rastenburg for the Western Front and in the process conceded that the Eastern campaign was hopeless. The Soviets entering East Prussia clearly indicated something even more horrific: Germany proper was at grave risk.

In the last weeks of 1944, harsh winter conditions and the requirements of sustaining the Soviet campaign in its westward drive forced a halt in Soviet operations. The High Command of the Soviet Armed Forces, STAVKA, was not on holiday but busy planning a massive offensive to begin in January 1945. It would end, the planners calculated, forty-five days later with the collapse of the German army in the rubble of the Third Reich.

In the Baltic area, one major objective was to split the Third Panzer Army off from Army Group Central by advancing on Konigsberg. In preparation for this push, the Red Army propagandists shifted the focus of their political indoctrination from one of "liberating Soviet territory" to a single word—"vengeance!" The word was highlighted on road signs, in pamphlets, and in articles written by prominent Soviet literary figures like Ilya Ehrenburg. But by mid-January the offensive stalled as the Red Army's lines of transportation became attenuated.

In late January, Hitler gave command of the newly created Army Group Vistula to Heinrich Himmler, Reichsfeuhrer and head of the SS. One of the Army Group's tasks was to open a corridor through East Prussia, but by the time Himmler arrived on the scene in his palatial railway train, the Russians were sealing the corridor. Although Hitler badly wanted to maintain control of East Prussia, and the city of Konigsberg in particular, heavy guns were stripped from the city's concrete redoubtments and shipped to the Western front along with five panzer divisions.

On January 21, the Soviet offensive in East Prussia accelerated as the Soviets overran defending German units; by January 23 the East Prussia city of Elbing was in their gun sights. At this point, Hitler redeployed two divisions from Memel to East Prussia, but by January 25, Colonel General Chernyakhovsky's troops were twelve miles from Konigsberg, poised to attack the city from the southeast. The Germans lost even more territory in the next week and this was accompanied by a massive flight of civilians from East Prussia. "During the succeeding days the flood of civilian refugees out of East Prussia reached its peak. Some were taken out by boat, most walked across the Frische Nehrung and the Vistula delta. By mid-February 1,300,000 of the 2,300,000 total population were evacuated; of those who stayed behind about half were Volkssturm and others absorbed into the Wehrmacht."[9]

The January offensive, of course, was coordinated with Stalin's planned meeting with Roosevelt and Churchill at Yalta in February. It would serve Stalin well at the summit if the Red Army occupied Poland and Germany was about to expire before the advancing Soviet forces. By February, his troops were fifty miles from Berlin, but to the dismay of his commanders, he ordered them to halt the final drive on Hitler's capital. Adam Ulam claims Stalin feared that some unanticipated setback for the Red Army would deny him the high hand that he intended to flash before Roosevelt and Churchill at the conference.[10]

By February 1945, Konigsberg was cut off but the Soviet troops concentrated their attention on overrunning West Prussia instead. The Red Army Commander, Colonel General Chernyakhovsky was killed in East Prussia and replaced by Colonel General Vasilevsky, who led his troops to new attacks in East Prussia. But the offensive was stalled first by heavy snows and then by roads choked with deep mud after a sudden and dramatic thaw. Toward the end of the third week in February, STAVKA told General of the Army Ivan Bagramyan to disregard Konigsberg and to concentrate on cleaning up the German units on the Samland Peninsula.

On February 20, the Germans counterattacked and forestalled a quick Russian victory in East Prussia. At this time the Great Soviet offensive stalled once again as the Red Army paused to regroup. The January offensive had been costly for the Red Army as it suffered 680,000 casualties. But the Soviets possessed a vast numerical advantage over the Germans who in January 1945 had total troop strength of two million men. About a fourth of that total, 556,000, was bottled up in Courland and East Prussia—the result of Hitler's foolish policy of holding onto the Third Reich's Baltic colonies.

In late February, German intelligence discovered Soviet forces were poised to strike the pockets of German resistance that clung to the Baltic Sea littoral. This action was meant to protect their flanks as they embarked upon their final drive toward Berlin. On March 30, Danzig fell. On April 6, after four days of vicious fighting and bombing by the British air force, Vasilevsky with the power of four armies attacked Konigsberg and it fell on April 9.[11]

After the advancing Red Army overwhelmed the Germans, Western commentators claimed that Stalin would kill, starve, or deport the remaining residents of East Prussia. But only 25,000 remained in the city of Konigsberg, so many German lives were spared. The only significant and protracted resistance to the USSR in the region would occur in Lithuania and persist until the early 1950s.

A large number of Lithuanians retreated to the forests to resist Soviet reoccupation of their country. The Forest Brethren held out until 1953 when the Lithuanian resistance movement was destroyed in a number of small battles. The brave fighters believed that in spite of the odds against them, the West would eventually confront Stalin in a new war. In their resisting the Soviet army and security services, "some 20,200 partisans were killed, 140,000 people were sent to concentration camps and 118,000 deported."[12] One result of their resistance was that Russian settlers were much more reluctant to move to Lithuania than to Estonia and Latvia where they migrated in significant numbers. Stalin's propagandists portrayed the Forest Brethren as fascists and the charge stuck. Consequently, in the late 1990s, when the Balts were seeking access to NATO, even democratic-minded Russians characterized them as such in an attempt to remind Westerners that the Balts were not deserving of membership.

The Aftermath of World War II

In December 1941, Antony Eden, the British foreign minister, met Stalin in Moscow and the Soviet leader brought up the subject of East Prussia. He demanded that "the portion of Germany containing Tilsit and to the North of the Nemen River should be added to the Lithuanian Republic of the USSR." This territory was traditionally known as Lithuania Minor and presumably Stalin believed that since Russia had no historical claims on the area but Lithuania did, the allies would be more likely to accept this proposal. The rest of East Prussia, and additional German territory, would be given to Poland in exchange for Warsaw's surrendering land east of the Curzon Line to Russia. Two years transpired before the subject was aired again and according to a British account, "It appeared to be assumed by all that Poland would be compensated with the whole of East Prussia."[13]

After the Soviet–British Defense Alliance was signed on July 12, 1941, the British urged the Polish government in exile to reach an accommodation with the Soviet Union. The Poles accepted this move as in keeping with a common struggle against Hitler. "However, the Polish condition sin qua non was that the Soviets had to nullify the Ribbentrop–Molotov line of Poland's partition and should guarantee the interwar Polish–Soviet border, established by the Treaty of Riga in 1921 and confirmed by the Polish–Soviet Non-Aggression Treaty of 1932."[14]

Winston Churchill was intent upon denying Stalin territory after the war ended but he did not have sufficient clout to influence the "old Khan's" thinking unilaterally. Britain needed U.S. support, for without it, there was no way that the British could force Stalin to surrender his ambitious postwar territorial claims.

President Franklin Delano Roosevelt did have considerable influence, which he could bring to bear in his negotiations with Stalin, but FDR's leverage would decline in the last stages of the war when Stalin's capacity to get his way was markedly improved each time the Red Army routed the Germans. In addition, Roosevelt, as both his wartime aides and postwar historians have noted, was naive about the Soviet Union and his ability to build a grand alliance with Stalin in the war's aftermath—a United Nations, which would henceforth maintain global peace.

Moreover, there is no question, as John Lewis Gaddis has indicated in his masterful history on the origins of the Cold War, that FDR found himself in a bind:

> In contrast to their confusion over Germany, Washington officials knew what they wanted in Eastern Europe: maximum possible self-determination for the people of that region without impairing the unity of the Grand Alliance. Unfortunately these two goals—both fundamental elements in the American program for preventing future wars—conflicted with each other. Stalin had made it clear since the summer of 1941 that he would not tolerate hostile states along his western border, yet in most of Eastern Europe free elections, if held, would produce governments unfriendly to Moscow."[15]

FDR tried to convince Polish leaders, who had fled their homeland after Hitler and Stalin attacked their country in 1939 and established a government in exile in London, that they need not fear Moscow. He said that after the war, they could participate in a Polish government that would be acceptable to Stalin. Naturally, the Poles greeted FDR's words in stunned disbelief; later many East Europeans, and their brethren in the New World, would cite FDR's behavior as evidence of his naiveté if not outright duplicity. Of course, in Roosevelt's defense, once the Red Army began to defeat the Wehrmacht in successive battles on the "Russian front," the United States had little chance of influencing Moscow short of using force, which was out of the question. FDR needed Russia to help the allies defeat Japan in Asia and to establish a postwar United Nations that would keep the peace.

In a meeting with the British Foreign Minister Anthony Eden on March 14, 1943, FDR supported Polish claims to East Prussia and exclaimed: "We should make arrangements to move the Prussians out of East Prussia the same way the Greeks were moved out of Turkey after the last war; while this is a harsh procedure, it is the only way to maintain peace, and in any circumstances the Prussians cannot be trusted."[16]

At Tehran in November 1943, the allied powers met specifically to discuss the opening of the second front in France, but Stalin used the occasion to submit his postwar territorial demands. Churchill had indicated that "the home of the Polish State and nation should be between the so-called Curzon Line and the Line of the Oder, including for Poland East Prussia and Oppeln." Stalin responded: "The Russians have no ice-free ports on the Baltic. That is why the Russians would need the ice-free ports of Konigsberg and Memel and the corresponding part of the territory of Eastern Prussia. . . . If the British agree to the transfer of the said territory to us, we shall agree to the formula proposed by Churchill."[17]

It did not escape U.S. officials, such as George Kennan, that Stalin was demanding an ice-free port on the Baltic even though there were several such ports under his control in Estonia, Latvia, and Lithuania. Stalin also argued that after having suffered millions of casualties at the hands of the Wehrmacht, the Soviet peoples deserved to wrench territory from the Germans as small compensation for the terrible casualties they suffered. In light of the twenty-seven million people the Soviet Union lost during the war, who could deny the USSR some retribution?

President Roosevelt's position on the post–World War II frontier question was that no decision should be reached until after the Nazis were defeated and a peace treaty was signed. He candidly shared with Stalin, however, that he was running for reelection in November 1944 and needed the Polish vote, so he preferred to stay out of the debate over Poland's frontiers. He told Stalin, in effect, that the USSR could have the territories Moscow wanted after the war but that the United States could not appear as if it were supporting such a move at this time. His opponent in 1944, Thomas E. Dewey, also courted the Poles but about nine out of ten of them voted for FDR because they feared a Republican victory would mean the end of the New Deal, which had helped all working Americans.

According to his Russian translator, Charles (Chip) E. Bohlen, Roosevelt and Stalin discussed the Baltic countries. "The President pointed out that because there were Balts in the United States, their independence was a moral issue for Americans, and he felt that public opinion would demand some expression of the wishes of the Baltic peoples before action was taken." But then, "at one point Roosevelt jokingly remarked that when the Soviet troops reoccupied the Baltic states, he did not intend to go to war with the Soviet Union."[18] A bad joke indeed.

Afterward, Eden hoped that if the Poles agreed to the Curzon Line, Britain could prevail upon Stalin to drop his demand for Konigsberg, which the Foreign Office considered "would take most of the gilt off the East Prussian gingerbread for Poland."[19] But Stalin informed the British that without Soviet possession of Konigsberg, "the Soviet Union's concession in recognizing the Curzon Line becomes entirely pointless, as I told you at Teheran."[20]

In 1944, Roosevelt told Polish leaders that he did not believe that they needed to worry about the question of territory. The losses they incurred vis-à-vis the Soviet Union would be compensated for by the gains they got at Germany's expense; and Stalin's demand for Konigsberg should not be regarded as final. He also seemed to believe that Stalin would allow free elections to be conducted in Poland, another reason that the Poles need not worry about their postwar relations with the USSR.

At the Yalta Conference in February 1945, the Polish Question was settled as far as Stalin was concerned. President Roosevelt, whose illness concerned his aides and the British, told Stalin that the United States accepted his demands concerning Poland's eastern borders which would be delineated by the Curzon line but suggested (to placate Polish concerns) Stalin might allow them to keep the Ukrainian city of Lvov and oil producing territory within the line. Stalin rejected the advice. He knew precisely what he wanted but as George Kennan noted in a letter to Chip Bohlen on the eve of the conference, "We have consistently refused to make clear what our interests and our wishes were, in eastern and central Europe."[21] Kennan missed the point, FDR was really not interested in border questions nor did he fight hard for the right of the London Poles to share power with the Soviet-backed Lublin-Poles in forming a new government in Warsaw. His major goal at Yalta was to get Stalin to honor his promise to enter the war against Japan once Hitler's armies were crushed in Europe.

Churchill was more insistent in pressing Stalin on including the London-Poles in the new provisional government in Warsaw—which had been formed by the pro-Soviet Lublin-Poles—but he did not have any luck on this score, either. The allies should have known that Stalin would reject their advice. In April 1943, he broke relations with the London-Poles when they asked the Red Cross to investigate German charges that the Soviets had slaughtered thousands of Polish army officers in the Katyn Woods in 1940. Nor could Churchill deny Stalin his firm plans to set Poland's boundaries east and west in a manner that best served the USSR's postwar objectives. By the conference's close, Soviet possession of Konigsberg was deemed pretty much a done deal.

Harry Hopkins, FDR's most trusted aide, summarized the Roosevelt administration's positive view of Yalta. "The Russians had proved that they could be reasonable and farseeing and there wasn't any doubt in the minds of the President or any of us that we could live with them and get along with them peacefully for as far into the future as any of us could imagine."[22] Protestations from victims of Stalin's Gulag who escaped to the West and argued that the democracies could not do business with the Old Georgian were discarded. After all, "how could these people be objective in their analysis of the Soviet Union." This practice of ignoring the assessments of victims of Soviet oppression helps explain why both U.S. policy makers and their Soviet counterparts failed to anticipate the collapse of the Soviet Union in 1991.

Not many months after the Yalta Conference, FDR died and was replaced by his vice president, Harry Truman. The senator from Missouri had little foreign policy experience. Like his predecessor and the American people, Truman took office in the belief that while Stalin got what he wanted in the way of postwar territorial claims, he would permit free elections to take place as consistent with the Atlantic Charter. But as Gaddis writes, "The peculiar mixture of naiveté and realism which characterized Roosevelt's East European policy had created a painful dilemma, which it would now be up to Harry S. Truman to resolve."[23]

Truman would get that chance in the summer of 1945, after Hitler's armies were crushed into submission and the allies met at Potsdam—a city in the midst of the Russian zone of Germany. On the second day of the conference, when substantive issues were first mentioned, the three allied leaders adopted President Truman's proposal that Germany's border as of December 1937 would be the point of reference. Stalin then introduced the Soviet proposal on the Polish Question. It contended that the Polish government in exile, which was located in London, would be replaced by the provisional government in Warsaw. Truman, in keeping with his predecessor's belief, interjected that free elections had to be conducted in Poland as agreed by the Big Three during the Tehran Conference.

At the fifth session on July 21, U.S. Secretary of State James Byrnes reported that the foreign ministers—who met through the conference to deal with the specifics of the broad issues that the three heads of state discussed—had reached an impasse on the Polish Question. Truman balked at the idea that German territory was being given to Poland without the authority of the Big Three. Poland, in effect, was getting a zone of Germany that had not been discussed at the Yalta Conference. Stalin responded that both Germans and Poles had lived in the area but after Hitler's defeat, the Poles had stayed behind while the Germans fled the territory. Truman and Churchill complained that taking this land from Germany would make it difficult for the

Americans and British to care for the Germans who had relocated in their zones.

The Czechs and Poles attended the conference eager to enlist the allied powers' help in expelling the Germans who had occupied their territory. They got what they wanted, for Article XIII of the Potsdam agreement reads: "The three Governments having considered the question in all of its aspects, recognize that the transfer to Germany of German populations, or elements thereof, remaining in Poland, Czechoslovakia, and Hungary, will have to be undertaken. They agree that any transfers that take place should be effected in an orderly and humane manner."[24]

The Soviets at the conference made a formal case for acquiring Konigsberg and areas surrounding it. East Prussia would be cleaved in two with the Poles securing the southern two-thirds of the territory and the Soviets the northern one-third.

Both President Truman and British Prime Minister Winston Churchill were inclined to concede to Stalin's wishes and they said in the Potsdam Protocol that they would support the transfer of territory to the USSR "at the forthcoming peace conference." U.S. commentators would argue that since a peace conference, providing a de jure termination of World War II, never occurred, that pledge was never acted upon. Henceforth the United States would concede Soviet administrative control of the territory but not Moscow's de jure possession of it. The final protocol to the Potsdam Conference stated the following:

> The Conference examined a proposal by the Soviet Government to the effect that pending the final determination of territorial questions at the peace settlement, the section of the western frontier of the Union of Soviet Socialist Republics, which is adjacent to the Baltic Sea should pass from a point on the eastern shore of the Bay of Danzig to the east, north of Braunsberg–Goldap, to the meeting point of the frontiers of Lithuania, the Polish Republic and East Prussia. The Conference has agreed in principle to the proposal of the Soviet Government concerning the ultimate transfer to the Soviet Union of the City of Konigsberg and the area adjacent to it as described above subject to expert examination of the actual frontier. The President of the United States and the British Prime Minister have declared that they will support the proposal of the Conference at the forthcoming peace settlement.[25]

Truman and Churchill originally noted that the initial Soviet proposal stated in effect that the Baltic countries belonged to the USSR, a position that neither the British nor the Americans accepted. That is why the offending words were struck from the text. But it is noteworthy that in his memoirs, Truman states that the most controversial issues discussed at Potsdam were

Poland's western frontier (but not Russia getting a chunk of Konigsberg) and German reparations.

Afterward, when the Poles complained that Molotov had provided the Polish representatives with a map that gave the Russians more territory than was granted at Potsdam, Moscow sought to placate them. The Soviet Foreign Minister promised that Polish ships from the Polish port of Elbing could use the channel through the Vistula Lagoon to the Gulf of Gdansk, the only access point to the open sea. Stalin later rejected the idea, not wishing "to have foreign spies spying on Konigsberg." This proscription against Polish shipping would prevail throughout the Cold War, except in those instances where the Poles first received permission from Moscow to use the existing channel on a case-by-case basis. The Poles were denied access to the Kaliningrad oblast even after a pro-Soviet Polish-Communist government gained power.[26]

Notes

1. See Algirdas Sabaliauskas, *We the Balts* (Vilnius: Science and Encyclopedia Publishing, 1993), 70.

2. James H. Billington, *The Icon and the Axe* (New York: Alfred A. Knopf, 1968), 105.

3. Richard Pipes, *The Russian Revolution* (New York: Alfred A. Knopf, 1990), 214.

4. Anthony Reed and David Fisher, *The Deadly Embrace* (New York: W. W. Norton, 1988), 33.

5. Llewellyn Woodward, *British Foreign Policy in the Second World War,* vol. 2 (London: British Foreign Office, 1971), 658.

6. Sarah M. Terry, *Poland's Place in Europe* (Princeton, N.J.: Princeton University Press, 1983), 3.

7. Zenonas Butkus, "The Diplomatic Cooperation between Germany and the USSR in the Baltic States in 1920–1940," in *Lithuanian Foreign Policy Review,* no. 3 (fall 1999): 146.

8. Joseph B. Schechtman, *Postwar Population Transfers in Europe* (Philadelphia: University of Pennsylvania Press, 1962), 153.

9. This discussion of the battle for East Prussia borrows heavily from Earl F. Ziemke's *Stalingrad to Berlin: The German Defeat in the East* (Washington: U.S. Government Printing Office, 1968), 432. Note also that in 1939, according to Nazi Party data, the population of East Prussia was 3,338,978, so presumably about one million people had already fled the area before the German resistance collapsed. Of course, in citing such data, we must take into account that scholars are often not in agreement about East Prussia's population because, from after World War I until 1939, revisions were made in East Prussia's boundaries. See Tim Kirk, *The Longman's Companion to Nazi Germany* (London: Longman, 1995), 62. Also, during the war, large

numbers of military personnel entered the area and Algirdas Gureckas has observed that after the Nazis defeated Poland in 1939, Polish territory was annexed by East Prussia, which may explain why Kirk's population figures exceed those of other writers (private correspondence with Gureckas).

10. Adam Ulam, *Stalin: The Man and His Era* (Boston: Beacon Press, 1989), 156.

11. Ziemke, *Stalingrad to Berlin,* 470.

12. Nijole Gaskaite Zematiene, "The Partisan War in Lithuania 1944 to 1953," in *The Anti-Soviet Resistance in the Baltic States,* ed. Arvydas Anusauskas (Vilnius: Genocide and Resistance Research Centre, 1999), 44.

13. Tony Sharp, "The Russian Annexation of the Konigsberg Area 1941–1945," *Survey* 23, no. 4 (1977–78): 156.

14. Piotr Wrobel, "The Catastrophe: The Impact of World War II in Poland," *SIEC Special Report Part II* (30 September 1999), 3.

15. John Lewis Gaddis, *The United States and the Origins of the Cold War* (New York: Columbia University Press, 1972), 133.

16. Schechtman, *Post-War Population Transfers in Europe,* 36.

17. Sharp, "The Russian Annexation," 156.

18. Charles Bohlen, *Witness to History 1929–69* (New York: W. W. Norton, 1973), 151.

19. Sharp, "The Russian Annexation," 157.

20. Sharp, "The Russian Annexation," 158.

21. Bohlen, *Witness to History,* 175.

22. Gaddis, *The United States,* 164.

23. Gaddis, *The United States,* 164.

24. Schechtman, *Post-War Population Transfers,* 36.

25. *Documents on Germany, 1944–1961,* U.S. Senate Committee on Foreign Relations (Washington: U.S. Government Printing Office, 1961), 37.

26. Interview with Ambassador Henryk Szlajfir, Polish Foreign Ministry, spring 1998.

2

Kaliningrad under Soviet and Russian Rule

The New Migrants

A CCORDING TO ONE SCHOLAR of post–World War II European migrations, East Prussia's prewar population of 2,470,000 swelled to 2,653,000 during the war after it became the strategic base from which the invasion of the USSR was launched. Later, when the Red Army invaded in April 1945, the population shrank to 600,000; most of East Prussia's residents fled over land and sea at the urging of German authorities.[1] They needed no prompting however, since they had heard about the atrocities that the Soviet troops were committing as they moved into German territory, and many knew that the German Army had committed atrocities of its own in Russia. Soviet occupation of German territory would be brutal and no German could feel safe after Stalin's troops arrived.

The out-migration of German civilians therefore continued as Hitler's forces and the Red Army struggled to dominate the area. But after Germany surrendered in May 1945, about 200,000 former residents of East Prussia returned to their homes and farms out of desperation—they simply had no other place to go and they were prepared to take their chances with their Soviet captors.[2]

The German out-migration from the war-ravaged territory resumed, and at one point as many as 50,000 former Prussian residents sought safety in Lithuania. In 1946, the Soviet MVD estimated the population in the area of Soviet-occupied East Prussia to be 170,019. An estimated 100,000 were Germans; most were women, 57,683; children younger than fifteen, 38,286; and the rest were men—1,375 of that number were older than sixty. The head of the MVD in Kaliningrad informed his superiors in Moscow that most of the Germans were too weak or sick to work. For this reason, and given their anti-Soviet attitude, he recommended that they be deported. Between 1945 and 1947, 35,000 civilians died in East Prussia presumably as a result of disease and malnutrition. An estimated 32,514 people were deemed capable of working and about 20,000 thereafter labored on Kolkhozes.

The NKVD provided a different estimate of East Prussia's population under Soviet administration; it arrived at a figure of 250,000. It claimed that during 1947–48, 102,125 Germans were deported and in 1951, 3,386 Germans were expelled from Lithuania.[3]

It is uncertain how many of those who remained in East Prussia died from disease and starvation or were killed by Soviet forces, but all the area's residents eventually were expelled to Germany or sent to labor camps in the USSR. In April 1945, only 30,000 citizens remained in the city of Konigsberg and during the next year about 10,000 more Germans relocated there.[4]

By June 1947, the population of the Polish sector of East Prussia known as the voyevodship of Olsztyn was 484,000. This included 452,000 Poles and 32,000 Germans.[5] For all intents and purposes, the allied policy of ridding East Prussia of Germans was a success.

East Prussia's cities were devastated by the fighting, Konigsberg in particular. The Red Army's artillery and air attacks and the British air force's bombing raids in the final days of battle destroyed most of its dwellings; one Soviet estimate held that 90 percent of Konigsberg's buildings were demolished. Consequently, few of the majestic structures that the Germans had constructed over the centuries—churches, castles, cathedrals, bridges, commercial structures, and residential dwellings—survived World War II. The ports, railways, roads, and airdromes throughout East Prussia were similarly devastated.

In the 1960s, the West German government in a gesture of good will proposed that it be allowed the honor of rebuilding the old castle that once stood in the heart of Kaliningrad City. Leonid Brezhnev refused the offer. Instead, he ordered the remnants of the castle be removed and a new structure, the House of Soviets, be constructed on the site. Today visitors to the city marvel at that architectural monstrosity, which never has been occupied. Some Kaliningrader's claim its foundation—under which the cellars of the castle remained intact—is unsafe, while others contend the massive concrete structure is unfinished. It does not escape the attention of anyone standing in proximity to Brezhnev's "gift" that in contrast to the old bombed-out, yet still majestic and graceful cathedral that is situated close to it, the Soviet leviathan is one of the major sources of eye pollution in the city. Brezhnev called the cathedral, the home of Immanuel Kant's tomb, a "rotten tooth," but today it stands on an island in the Pregel River and is being restored. Kaliningraders hope that once it regains its old majesty, the House of Soviets will be destroyed and German tourists, their wallets bursting with hard currency, will visit the city.

During the early stages of World War II, when the Soviet Union was still reeling from the awful blows it received from Hitler's Wehrmacht, Lithuanians were informed over Moscow radio that Lithuania Minor would be returned to their country after Hitler's legions were driven from Soviet territory. Stalin could have integrated all of East Prussia that came under the USSR's administration into Soviet Lithuania as he had suggested in his discussions with Antony Eden in 1941. Instead, on October 17, 1945, he made it an oblast of the Russian Soviet Federation. Why had Stalin changed his mind about ceding the territory to Lithuania? The answer presumably is that while the Western allies had refused to recognize his 1940 annexation of Lithuania, they had diplomatic relations with the USSR and they could not complain about Kaliningrad being incorporated into the Russian Federation.

On July 4 of the following year, Konigsberg was renamed Kaliningrad to honor the recently deceased Soviet President Mikhail Ivanovich Kalinin, who never visited the place. Soon afterward, Soviet "scholars" and writers would refer to it as being part of Russia's patrimony. In 1947, *Izvestia* wrote: "Slavs are again settling on this ancestral Slavic soil. Kolkhozians from Belorussia, Smolensk, Pskov, and Vladimir transport hither their livestock, poultry, farm implements, and seeds."[6] And in 1953, Fedor Vedin wrote, "By all laws these lands belong to us . . . we are traversing Russian land. We settled accounts with the fascists and retook our land."[7]

The Soviets consigned German name-places to the memory hole of history with Orwellian zeal and replaced them with Russian names and designations. Tilsit was renamed Sovietsk, Gumbinnen was called Gusevo, and so on. In Kaliningrad's schools, little or no mention was made of the areas in the German past except in discussions of how it figured into the "Great Patriotic War," and the Soviet Union's successful campaign against Hitler's forces in the area. Students were taught that East Prussia had been a Slavic homeland for centuries.

Later, Nikita Khrushchev suggested—as part of a reorganization scheme—that Lithuania might take control of the territory, but the Lithuanian Communist Party leader, Antanas Snieckus, refused the offer.[8] His action was based upon the fear of the authorities in Vilnius that to add almost one million Russian-speakers into Lithuania would be to invite the same kind of thorny problem that Estonia and Latvia faced as their countries absorbed large numbers of Russians in the late 1940s and 1950s.

Unlike his counterparts in Riga and Tallinn, Snieckus had used his influence with Stalin to minimize the massive transfer of Russians to Lithuania. It was considerable, since the Old Georgian admired the way Snieckus ruled Lithuania with "Stalinlike" ruthlessness. The heroic resistance of the Forest Brethren in Lithuania, which fought the Soviet occupiers until 1953, also served as a potent disincentive to Russians moving to the country for almost a decade after World War II.

All the original Lithuanian residents of East Prussia, who lived in Lithuania Minor, suffered the same fate as their German neighbors but, over time, about 20,000 Lithuanians from outside of Lithuania Minor would relocate in the oblast. During the Soviet era, Lithuania had the responsibility for meeting much of Kaliningrad's nonmilitary needs. Among other things, all civilian flights to and from the oblast were handled by air traffic controllers in Lithuania, and the most direct way to travel to Moscow by car, bus, train, or truck was through Lithuania. About 80 percent of Kaliningrad's electricity was received from power grids from Lithuania, and Lithuania processed crude oil extracted from Kaliningrad's wells. Lithuania was a favorite resort area for both civilian and military personnel stationed in the region. For vacationers from other parts of Russia, the Curonian Spit and the Baltic resort town of Palanga were favored holiday destinations. For Soviet citizens who sought respite from the drabness of Russia, spending a vacation in Palanga was like traveling to Europe. Kaliningrad, like Lithuania and its sister Baltic republics, Latvia and Estonia, were deemed security-sensitive areas of the USSR and non-Soviet citizens had a hard time getting permission to visit them as well.

Simultaneously, given their proximity and Soviet affiliation, Lithuanians experienced less difficulty gaining permission to enter the oblast for business, cultural, and tourist reasons, than other prospective visitors. The border between Poland and Kaliningrad, by contrast, was closed; besides, Poland was in the USSR's "outer Empire" and its people were spared deep immersion into the culture and mores of the Soviet Union. Like the Kaliningraders, the Lithuanians were citizens of the USSR's "inner empire." Most spoke Russian and all were members of the Soviet cultural complex—Homo Sovieticus. Consequently, in no small part because of this shared cultural experience, the Lithuanians after the USSR's demise would demonstrate greater acumen in relating to officials and residents of Kaliningrad than the Poles.

The Soviet Union embarked upon a campaign of ethnic resettlement soon after the Germans were expelled from East Prussia. The tide of settlers from elsewhere in the USSR was at first slow but by the second half of 1946, about 200,000, mostly Russians, settled in East Prussia, peoples whose homes and villages had been destroyed by the war. In the last years of the decade, and the early years of the 1950s, several hundred thousand additional migrants arrived in the region. By 1959, Kaliningrad had a population of 611,000, in

1970 it was 732,000, in 1989, 913,000 and in 1996, 926,000. About 80 percent of the population was Russian, 10 percent Belarussian, 6 percent Ukrainian, 2 percent Lithuanian, and less than 1 percent German. The urban population grew from 395,000 in 1959 to 726,000 in 1996, while the rural population slumped from 216,000 in 1959 to 182,000 in 1989. It rebounded in 1994 to 189,000 and reached 206,000 in 1996.[9]

A large number of these new settlers found work in the region's major economic enterprises, mostly defense-oriented industries that serviced the military units in Kaliningrad—such as ship building and repair—while others found employment in amber mining, fishing, and the production of wood pulp and paper. Of course, for many years, construction was a major source of employment at military bases throughout the oblast. The outer port on the Baltic Sea, the naval base at Baltijsk, and military installations in Kaliningrad and other cities throughout the region were reconstructed or built from scratch. Likewise, considerable manpower was expended to revitalize roads, rail transit facilities, and civilian airports, and to build flats for the settlers—thousands of ugly, poorly constructed Soviet-style apartments—similar to those that mushroomed elsewhere throughout the vastness of the USSR. Most took on the aspect of slums soon after they were occupied.

Kaliningrad's residents maintained close relations with their families and friends back home and it was a fluid population; especially mobile were the military personnel and their dependents that served in the oblast. No large ethnic minority lived there and claimed the territory as their own so Kaliningraders were not subjected to the cross-pressures of conflicting ethnic loyalties. Since the vast majority of the population was Russian (or Russian-speaking), non-Russians were under pressure to adopt a Russian identity. By contrast in the Soviet Union, in those places where Russians were in a minority, the pressure was the other way around. For example, in Lithuania the children of a mixed Lithuanian–Russian marriage almost always identified with the Lithuanian parent, learned Lithuanian, and felt comfortable celebrating Lithuanian culture.[10]

The residents of Kaliningrad deemed themselves Soviet-Russian or Soviet-Ukrainian citizens who accepted the Soviet Union as their home and remained loyal to it. Although physically removed from Russia proper, they thought much the same way other Russians did. A good example of this phenomenon occurred during NATO's war with Serbia in 1999 when Kaliningraders, like Russians elsewhere in the country, vocally protested the action. In one bar in Kaliningrad City a sign read "No beer will be served to customers from NATO countries."

The formation of a Soviet identity among the residents of Kaliningrad—perhaps to a far larger degree than elsewhere in the USSR—was given impetus by its serving as the Soviet Union's westernmost military outpost. The Baltic Fleet had facilities at Klaipeda, Liepaja, Ventspils, Riga, Tallinn, and Leningrad. At Baltijsk, it had a full complement of combat ships and support vessels that enabled the Soviet Navy to deny enemy naval units the opportunity to strike targets in the northwestern quadrant of the USSR. From Kaliningrad, Soviet and air units could attack targets in the Baltic Sea littoral in Denmark, Germany, and Sweden. Air wings were attached to the 11th Guard Army, which had armor, anti-aircraft, logistic, artillery, and infantry units capable of supporting Soviet forces in East Germany and Poland.

It was from the port of Baltijsk that Soviet subs would probe the waters of southern Sweden and during the Cold War, Western newspaper readers would come upon stories that claimed "unidentified subs" were detected in the territorial waters of Sweden. Some of them—sunk by accidents or poor maintenance—remain in their Baltic Sea tombs today. And on one occasion the captain of a Soviet sub, an ethnic Lithuanian, landed his vessel at Sweden's shores and sought and received political asylum from Stockholm. Later Tom Clancy would write a book—*The Hunt for Red October*—which was based on the exploits of this Lithuanian officer.

The Soviet military units in Kaliningrad served as command headquarters and maintained prepositioned weapons—including nuclear arms—that would be used by Soviet reinforcements sent there in event of war. These units could engage in either defensive or offensive operations and they attracted some of the most talented members of the Soviet military establishment to the oblast—which many officers, men and their families spoke of as "the West."

At least 100,000 troops were regularly stationed in Kaliningrad during the Soviet era although some estimates ran as high as 200,000 to 300,000.[11] By the 1970s, if military families and military retirees were included, a significant proportion of the population was associated with the armed forces. Not included in these numbers were engineers, scientists, technicians, and unskilled workers who maintained all of the military installations there. To call Kaliningrad a "military bastion" then was appropriate.

Other Kaliningraders not directly engaged in military-related activities provided support to those who were and so it was fair to argue that a majority of the people who resided in the oblast depended upon the military for their livelihoods.

The Economic Picture

During the centuries when the Germans controlled East Prussia, the area's agricultural output was impressive. Indeed, Konigsberg became a major city and Hanseatic trading center because of East Prussia's agricultural wealth. But after the Soviet occupation, the area's "agriculture was reorganized from small and medium-size farms into large-scale collective and state-farms." In the area of Polesk (Labiau) located northeast of Kaliningrad City, for example, "about 5,000 pre-war farms were reorganized into 8 gigantic farms—4 collective farms and 4 state farms." Like the status of agriculture in other areas of the USSR, farming was extensive rather than intensive in magnitude, "lacking regular crop rotation, and with a strong emphasis on grain and feed crops."[12] In contrast to the rural areas of East Prussia under the Germans, many small communities under Russian control shrank in population and some settlements were abandoned altogether.

By contrast, while prewar villages and settlements in the Soviet half of East Prussia disappeared, those along the Polish–Kaliningrad boundary prospered in the Olsztyn district of Poland. The same held true for agricultural areas of Soviet Lithuania.[13]

Under Soviet rule, regions—indeed entire republics—performed relatively narrow specialized economic functions to meet the needs of the Soviet economy at large. There remained some economic diversity, but Kaliningrad's primary purpose was to serve as a military bastion and all other economic activities were secondary to that function. Consequently, to a greater degree than other regions of the USSR, the residents of Kaliningrad were even more dependent upon subsidies from Moscow than were their fellow countrymen.

As long as the Soviet Union endured, Kaliningrad was guaranteed subsidies from the Center and the troops stationed in the oblast and the people living there thought themselves fortunate. Their prospects and their assessment of their situation, however, would change dramatically after the collapse of the Soviet Union in December 1991.

After the Soviet Union disappeared, Kaliningrad became an exclave, bounded by the Baltic Sea to its west and by Lithuania and Poland on its other three sides. The region was separated from the Russian Federation by a distance exceeding five hundred kilometers, and its isolation henceforth became a political and administrative burden for the authorities in the region and those in Moscow more than a thousand kilometers away.

Henceforth, like other exclaves, Kaliningrad's road, rail, and waterway transportation systems were disengaged from the infrastructure of the mainland territory. The oblast's isolation complicated relations with Moscow and required close cooperation with foreign political authorities. Consequently, if officials in Kaliningrad decided to build a network of roadways to upgrade its underdeveloped infrastructure, and provide overland connections with neighboring states, they first needed the permission and funds from Moscow. Then they had to secure the cooperation of authorities in Warsaw and Vilnius lest the new roads or rail lines be inadequately calibrated to neighboring highways and railroads. Poland, for example, refused to build a road through its Suwalki district—the Suwalki Corridor—that would link ground traffic from Kaliningrad through Poland, south to Belarus.

Additionally, goods being transported across the territory of Lithuania and Poland were henceforth subjected to visa regimes, tariffs, duties, and insurance requirements that added cost to the price of the goods being exported from Kaliningrad. At the same time, the area's residents benefited from having access to higher quality food and consumer goods made available by their two neighbors along with liberal visa regimes; that Kaliningraders were allowed to enter Poland and Lithuania without visas was seen as a highly valued privilege. Such access also facilitated trading between the oblast and the adjacent countries.

After it became an exclave, official statistics indicated that Kaliningrad's industrial output declined. Industrial production fell by 61 percent from 1990 to 1995, and the dip in agriculture was 50 percent during the same period.[14] The manufacture of machinery represented 27.9 percent of industrial output in 1989, but it accounted for only 8.7 percent of industrial output in 1995. Also, in 1991, Kaliningrad produced 1.6 million metric tons of crude oil, but by 1996 output declined to 700,000 tons of that commodity.[15] Even the fishing industry showed a decline. During the Soviet period, Kaliningrad-based fishing vessels caught much of the fish eaten by Soviet citizens in Northwest Russia and vast numbers of tins of fish processed in the oblast were shipped to customers beyond the Soviet Union's borders. By the mid-1990s, the catching and processing of fish had become unprofitable because the price of fuel rose sharply while federal subsidies to the industry fell.

Three ports are located in Kaliningrad: a commercial port in Kaliningrad, which is accessed by a twenty-mile-long canal to the Baltic Sea through the Straits of Baltijsk, and fishing and naval ports at Baltijsk. The amount of cargo being processed through Kaliningrad's ports has declined since the collapse of the USSR and the economic downturn that followed. Kaliningrad's commercial port also has lost business to competitors in other countries on the Baltic Sea: Gdansk, Klaipeda, Liepaja, Ventspils, Riga, and Tallinn, as well as Russia's ports in St. Petersburg. The oblast's authorities are unfamiliar with a free market and personnel operating the port remain wedded to bureaucratic practices that private entrepreneurs find intolerable. According to the account of one TACIS consultant, it takes so long to process a ship in Kaliningrad that many shipping companies off-load their vessels at St. Petersburg ports instead; presumably the Mafia controlling them is more efficient than their counterparts in Kaliningrad. The bribes ship owners pay are worth the expense because it costs them more to unload cargo in Kaliningrad, where red tape made the process much slower than in St. Petersburg. The longer ships remain in port, the higher the costs incurred by their owners.

Equally significant, Russian analysts discovered that Kaliningrad's economic decline was even worse than that suffered by the Russian Federation at large. "For the period of 1990–1995, production sharply declined and the rates of recession became higher, as compared with the rates in the Russian Federation as a whole. According to official statistics, industrial production fell by 61 percent, agricultural production by 50 percent compared to 51 percent and 29 percent respectively in Russia as a whole."[16]

A plunge in Kaliningrad's agricultural output is significant because the inability of any society with a large agricultural sector to feed its people suggests it is a seriously flawed economy. The following figures are suggestive: In 1990, Kaliningrad produced 50,000 tons of meat, but by 1995 that figure plunged to 11,000 tons. Milk production nose-dived from 143,000 tons in 1990 to 51,000 tons in 1995. And the respective figures for flour were 270,000 tons and 54,000 tons. These figures also account for the fact that residents of Kaliningrad are burdened with a lion's share of their budgets being devoted to food purchases. "Price liberalization has forced a considerable number of the inhabitants to spend their whole income on food, while those with the lowest income are threatened with malnutrition."[17]

The plight of Kaliningrad's farmers, which was bad during the Soviet era, got even worse with the collapse of the USSR. With the lifting of prices and subsidies, the oblast's farmers could not purchase the implements, seeds, fertilizers, and other materials needed to maintain agricultural output. And Kaliningrad's agricultural sector was also stricken by the inability of federal authorities to develop a coherent law that facilitated the selling and buying of land.

Throughout the 1990s, President Yelstin and the Russian Duma remained deadlocked over the issue. Yeltsin claimed, "I have said and I will never get tired of repeating: land in Russia should be bought and sold. That is how it is in the entire civilized world. It should be the property of the peasantry, and they themselves should decide what to do with it."[18] The Communist-dominated Duma, however, opposed the sale of agricultural land and imposed such onerous restrictions upon land sales that not much land was sold. Russia's reactionary agricultural elite—whose interests and association with land stems from their running Soviet-era agricultural enterprises—supported this policy. They claimed if land were freely sold in Russia, foreigners would buy it all up.

Land can be bought in Russia, but with many restrictions. For example, land controlled by former collective and state farms is difficult to sell. Only land held by private owners and used for small-scale agricultural purposes can be sold; for example, garden plots that are held by individual families on collective farms or the Dacha plots that existed even under Soviet rule. But as late as 1998, less than 10 percent of agricultural land was "owned by private farmers, private plot operators and owners of land plots in collective fruit and vegetable gardens."[19] Land development has been hampered by questions about who really owns the land and complications associated with the purchase and sale of land. Most important, neither state nor municipal controlled land can be sold to private agricultural interests.

"Even though collective farms had completed reorganizations by 1994, the vast majority of them or their legal successors still control most of their land or have obtained land through post-reorganization lease arrangements."[20] In most cases people capable of selling land have assigned their land shares back to the collective and not to individuals. Moreover, land continues to be seen by the Russian peasant as insurance against hard times. Consequently, one of the greatest deterrents to peasants selling their land rights is that afterward they must leave the farm on which they have worked for most of their lives. This is an especially powerful incentive against selling for pensioners or people approaching their retirement years. When Russia was stricken by the August 1998 economic meltdown, many Russians took comfort in the fact that they had relatives or friends who continued to own or operate farms and they could be counted upon to provide city dwellers' food during hard times.

In their assessment of the Russian agricultural scene in 1998, two Polish researchers concluded their study with the following words: "The hostile economic climate confronting private farming is reflected in increasing farm bankruptcies, declining numbers of private farms, falling farm productivity, and the general unpopularity of private farming among the rural population."[21]

After the collapse of the Soviet Union, high levels of unemployment struck Kaliningrad; the official level was calculated at 10 percent but the real rate undoubtedly exceeded that figure. From 1980 to 1994, the number of workers in industry dropped from 136,000 to 100,000 and in agricultural from 57,000 to 35,000.[22] To make matters worse, after the oblast became an exclave, workers there, like their counterparts elsewhere in Russia, were not paid on time—waiting months in some cases for their pay. Pensioners, who represented at least 20 percent of the population, also had to wait for their money. This meant great hardship for old folks with little or no savings.

Kaliningrad's economic decline had its sources in four major explanations:[23]

1. As had been the case throughout the former Soviet Union, Kaliningrad's large enterprises were no longer economically viable and many

did not survive the transition to a market economy and needed subsidies to operate. Given the economic difficulties plaguing Russia and the subsequent dip in revenues, Moscow could not send the same level of subsidies to Kaliningrad that it did during the Soviet era.

2. An estimated 35 percent to 40 percent of the oblast's economy had been linked to the Soviet military-industrial complex, but with dramatic cuts in the defense budget, military-related activities were dramatically curtailed.

3. The region had to rely upon locally generated revenue, not just funding from the Russian Federation. Of course, as regional economic activity declined, Kaliningrad's revenue base became attenuated as well.

4. Being cut off from the rest of Russia had become a costly burden for Kaliningrad, and its exclave status complicated administration of the oblast. "The complete change in the geopolitical location of the district after the dissolution of the USSR has transferred many previously domestic problems to international issues. Many traditional relations with the Baltic States have been severed. The Kaliningrad district thus has to enter two markets simultaneously; the Russian market and the Baltic regional market."[24]

Achieving a Free Economic Zone

In the face of existing and projected economic problems, authorities in Kaliningrad lobbied Moscow for the formation of a free economic zone in the oblast. This was not a new idea. Soviet economic planners, who were encouraged by Gorbachev to find ways to revitalize the Leninist system, had hoped to attract foreign investment, trade, and technological and managerial know-how to Kaliningrad—and indirectly to the USSR—by establishing a free economic zone there.

"The idea was to exploit its favorable geographical position close to Western Europe with ice-free ports at the Baltic and railways with both European and Russian widths. Foreign investments were to be attracted by favorable taxation and customs rates, free profit export, a good industrial and social infrastructure, and a cheap and well-trained work force."[25]

In 1990, the first resolution was issued to create a free economic zone (FEZ) in the oblast. It provided investors, foreign and domestic, with tax breaks and other incentives to create joint ventures and to provide new avenues of capital for local enterprises. The zone could become a test case for reforming the Soviet economy and a magnet for foreign investment. At this time, Yuri Matochkin represented Kaliningrad in the Supreme Soviet of the

USSR and he was an articulate advocate of the zone. In September 1991 it was officially established and was one of six free zones in the Soviet Union at that time. Later in that year, local goods were exempted from export tariffs, and imported goods that remained in the region were exempted from customs duties. Thus consumers could buy goods much more cheaply in the region than in the rest of Russia. Having several ports, which attracted ships from Russia and beyond, Kaliningrader's gained access to scare items, or those in short supply elsewhere in the federation, such as foreign cars, trucks, and other highly prized consumer goods such as alcohol and tobacco products. In 1992, 76 percent of Kaliningrad's residents favored the zone.[26]

Under FEZ, a modest amount of foreign investment was attracted to the oblast: $10 million in 1994 and $27 million in 1995. Moscow provided Kaliningrad with other privileges in recognition of—and compensation for—transit and customs expenses imposed upon entrepreneurs in the exclave. The region was allowed to keep a growing share of tax revenues, from 45 percent in 1992 to 70 percent in 1995.[27] In an attempt to attract new commercial activities—tourism in particular—the military vacated the Vistula Spit, which has extensive and wide beaches on both the Baltic Sea and lagoon side of the spit.

After he was appointed by Yeltsin to be the oblast's governor, Matochkin continued to press the Russian president to provide Kaliningrad with more autonomous powers, something in line with those enjoyed by the ethnic republics like Tatarstan. Yeltsin responded that the federation was unstable and it was not the time to make such a move. The FEZ however would provide Kaliningrad with most of the special economic rights for which Matochkin was lobbying.[28]

In 1993, the Communist chairman of the regional Soviet, Yuri Semionov, "agreed to propose a referendum on making the oblast a republic within the Russian Federation like the ethnic ones. This meant that the region should have its own constitution, laws, and representation in the federal bodies."[29]

In March 1995, however, the Yantar (the old Russian name for *amber*) free zone's customs exemptions were eliminated, according to some accounts by an accidental presidential decree. Citing Russian commentators, Lyndelle Fairlie says that the mistake was a result of conflict between the International Monetary Fund (IMF) and EU. "Fyodorov and Zverev start from the position that the FEZ was ended in response to IMF guidelines, which required Moscow to cut expenses such as the revenue loss due to customs exemptions of the FEZ."[30] Another, perhaps more accurate, explanation is that the FEZ had attracted the attention of opponents in Moscow who complained that it contributed to massive smuggling and tax dodging. Such accusations were by no means groundless. For example, entire railroad cars began their journey across Lithuania with oil tanks destined for Kaliningrad but never arrived; their cargo had been off-loaded in transit and sold in Lithuania or had been shipped outside of the country. The perpetrators of such "hijacking" gleaned huge profits and the governments in Kaliningrad and Moscow, in turn, were denied vital revenues.

To cope with this problem, shippers were compelled to pay for export duties "up front" so that the appropriate jurisdictions were not denied tax revenues. If the shipment did not reach the final destination indicated on the routing papers, the shippers lost their deposits. But the shippers complained that this procedure was an unfair burden, since they had to pay the money beforehand and only after the goods were delivered were their deposits reimbursed to them. It was just such "additional expenses," they complained, that accounted for the failure of FEZ to achieve the goals established for it.

Meanwhile, lobbyists in St. Petersburg—specifically the Mafia and its friends in government—also used their political influence in the Russian Duma to cancel Kaliningrad's FEZ. And it did not escape the attention of tight-fisted authorities in Moscow, either, that unlike regions like Tatarstan, Kaliningrad was not a net contributor to Russia's budget but a recipient of alms from the Center.

In 1996, Tamara Poluektova, Yeltsin's representative in Kaliningrad, indicated that many powerful people in Moscow did not accept the argument that, given its location, the oblast experienced unique disadvantages and deserved special compensation. According to Fairlie, "This argument has been especially hard to sell in the Federation Council where representatives of other regions are trying to look after their own interests and can argue that any expense which Kaliningrad causes for the federal budget may be disadvantageous to their own regions."[31]

Finally, there were political concerns that contributed to the FEZ's demise. Some officials in Moscow feared that by enhancing the economic prospects of the region's population, the forces of separatism would be encouraged. Consequently, opponents of Kaliningrad's receiving special privileges cited the same argument that supporters of those privileges did to disband the zone—its location outside of Russia.

After the FEZ was canceled, politicians in Kaliningrad, who reasoned that Moscow could not provide the oblast the investment it required, lobbied officials at the federal level to provide them with a new vehicle to attract foreign investment. Under pressure from the man he had appointed governor, Matochkin, Yeltsin created a new special economic zone (SEZ) in 1996. It would last for three years but with a more restrictive charter than FEZ and was designed to placate "separatist" fears in Moscow. It did not grant the oblast the kind of extensive rights that republics like Tatarstan enjoyed—including the power to develop commercial relations with foreign governments. Officials in Kaliningrad could arrange transactions with cities and regions in Lithuania and Poland and private entrepreneurs, but not with other central governments. Such agreements had to be sanctioned by the Russian Foreign Ministry, which had its own representation in the oblast.

Regional Power

In the Soviet Union, Moscow made most of the important strategic economic and political decisions for the republics and regions. Since "real power," sovereign power, was centered in Moscow, ambitious politicians struggled to be posted there so they could advance their careers. Regional party bosses, of course, enjoyed power and privileges in the republics and regions where they were in charge, but with the onset of perestroika, Mikhail Gorbachev sought to undercut the influence of the party "hacks" who opposed the reforms he deemed necessary to revitalize the Soviet system. In the 1990 elections, conducted at all levels of government in the USSR, he sought to shift power from the party to the government and had himself appointed president of the USSR. But he was not entirely successful in this gambit: "Following the election to regional legislators in 1990, the majority of first secretaries of the regional party committees became heads of executive committees of the soviets. In 1991, they safely moved into the chairs of regional governors."[32]

At the same time, Russian president Boris Yeltsin decentralized power by stripping the party of its influence and thereby advanced his own influence at Gorbachev's expense. "The open rivalry between Mikhail Gorbachev and Boris Yeltsin and then between the latter and the Russian parliament as well as Yeltsin's conscious decision to decentralize political and economic decision making, led to an unprecedented increase in the autonomy and power of regional and republican elites in Russia."[33] Indeed, Yeltsin urged the regional officials to grab as much power as they could and in early 1991, he "introduced the first economic concessions, such as giving some regional and republican leaders the right to grant export licenses to enterprises and to play an important role in the allocation of export quotas for strategic resources."[34]

In March 1992, treaties were signed between the Center and the regions that gave them greater authority to manage their own economic affairs and resources. During the 1993 power struggle between Yeltsin and the Russian Duma, both sides courted the regional elites. In the process they became so emboldened that "On 30 September, leaders of 70 percent of the constituent units of the Russian Federation set up the Council of Members of the Federation. The Council stated that the central government in Moscow had discredited itself and therefore should step down." The council would govern Russia until new elections were held.[35]

Yeltsin ignored the council's power grab, but after directing tanks under his command to blast his opponents in the Duma from their White House redoubt, he dismissed some of the council members. The 1993 Constitution he crafted left little power in the hands of the regional leaders and gave the president, not the Constitutional Court, the power to suspend regional legislation. The electoral success of the "Reds" and "Browns" in the December 1993 Duma elections, however, encouraged the federal government to court the regions once again—giving them greater inputs into budgetary and tax matters. In the fall of 1993, the governors secured more power after the abolition of the Soviets and the constitution of that year increased their influence vis-á-vis their legislators. "Governors obtained the right to make the final decision on the regional budget, veto laws passed by the regional legislatures and, according to a Yeltsin decree of November 1994, could appoint executives at the municipal level."[36]

A unique feature of Russian federalism was that local and regional administrators could hold offices in regional and local legislatures. Furthermore, in 1995–96 the regions acquired the power to sign treaties with the federal government—a privilege that only the republics had previously enjoyed—and this enhanced their control over their natural resources and gave them wider budgetary and taxing powers. The theory behind this unconventional arrangement—"asymmetrical federalism"—was that no strict federal law could possibly allow for the disparate arrangements between the Center and the regions in such a large and diverse society, even though the treaties were extra-constitutional.[37]

Kaliningrad was one of the first regions to sign a bilateral treaty with Moscow in large part because Yeltsin had appointed a man to be governor there who was a Yeltsin supporter—the academic, Yuri Matochkin. Yeltsin appointed him to that post in September 1991. Matochkin, a member of Our Home Is Russia Bloc, was supported by the All-Russian Coordinating Council and in 1993 was elected to the Federation Council where he served on the International Affairs Committee.

After the USSR's demise, Yeltsin acquired the power to appoint and dismiss governors and ignored requests from the regions that their governors be popularly elected, not appointed by the Russian president. The election of regional officials, after all, was consistent with Yeltsin's efforts to democratize Russia and build a free market economy there. A federal system where the Center dominated all strategic political and economic decisions was inconsistent with both democracy and capitalism.

According to Leonid Smirnyagin, a former adviser to Yeltsin, "The majority of governors were against being elected in the first place and they accepted it only under pressure from Moscow and the 'Kremlin team,' because the direct election of governors was deemed essential to democratic government." In the 1996 elections, the voters rejected half of the appointed governors. "As one member of the Federation Council explained, it is much easier to lick one boot clean than 400,000. Russia's regional elites were always adroit in the ways of the Czar's court and had mastered the Byzantine skills of saving their posts."[38]

Yeltsin himself was reluctant to concede power to appoint and dismiss governors because he rightly feared that the communists, and other enemies of his reforms, would replace his appointees through elections. This was the reason that no popular election took place in Kaliningrad until October 1996. In the 1993 Duma elections, Vladimir Zhirinovsky's crypto-fascist Liberal Democratic Party of Russia gained the most votes cast in Kaliningrad, 29.9 percent, while the Communist Party came in third with 10.5 percent. In the 1995 Duma elections, the Communists captured 19.3 percent of the votes and the Liberal Democratic Party came in second with 11.4 percent in Kaliningrad.

The Political Picture

In the 1991 presidential election, Kaliningrad gave Yeltsin 39 percent of the ballots; he ran first there with Nikolai Ryzkov in second place with 23.7 percent. In 1996, the voters in Kaliningrad continued to prefer him to his opponents.

In the October 1996 gubernatorial elections in Kaliningrad, Yeltsin's man

TABLE 2.1
1996 Presidential Elections

Candidate	Percent Turnout First Round	Percent Turnout Second Round
Yeltsin	33.4	57.6
Zyuganov	23	35.3
Lebed	19.3	NA
Yavlinski	12.8	NA
Zhirinovsky	7.2	NA
Turnout Kaliningrad	71.7	69.1
Turnout Russia	69.6	68.7

Source: "OMRI Russian Regional Report: Kaliningrad Oblast":
www.omri.cz/Elections/Russia/Regions/About/Kaliningrad.html, 1996.

Matochkin ran against several opponents in the election's first round and achieved 31.3 percent of the votes. The man who ran second place, Leonid Gorbenko, received 22.3 percent. Gorbenko was supported by economic interests associated with Moscow's Mayor Yuri Luzhkov and associates of General Aleksandr Lebed. Gorbenko had been the manager of Kaliningrad's fishing port and in the second round he bested Matochkin by gaining 40.6 percent of the votes to Matochkin's 40.4 percent.

Ideological differences did not explain the outcome of the election. Journalists observed that it was not a matter of Communists versus reformers because both Matochkin and Gorbenko actively sought the support of Kaliningrad's Communist Party. It was headed by Yuri Semionov who ran third in the gubernatorial race. In the runoff, Semionov supported Gorbenko, who appointed Semionov deputy governor; but several months later he fired him.

In the final analysis, the election's outcome was a matter of one economic clan clashing with another one. In this connection, Yeltsin's prime minister, Viktor Chernomyrdin (for Matochkin) and Moscow's Mayor Yuri Luzhkov (for Gorbenko) were mentioned. In post-election evaluations several factors were cited to explain why Matochkin lost the election:

- The primary reason was the electorate's unhappiness with economic conditions in the oblast, declining living standards and grim economic prospects in particular.
- The voters deemed Matochkin ill-equipped for the job of governing because he was an academic with "little practical" experience. Gorbenko, by contrast, was "a man of the world" who managed a major economic enterprise in the oblast. Studies of regional elections in other parts of Russia indicate voters have employed pragmatic not ideological criteria in choosing candidates; those viewed as "economic managers" have been most popular with the electorate.[39]
- Many of Matochkin's supporters did not bother to go to the polls because they deemed his election preordained; they no doubt felt this way, in part, because they still perceived elections through the prism of their Soviet past where incumbents always were reelected.
- Because Yeltsin's key aides were divided among themselves over whom to support—for example, Anatoli Chubais and Vicktor Chernomyrdin—regional candidates favored by Yeltsin did not get as much help from Moscow as they could have received were the Moscow election team unified.
- Matochkin received the support of major economic interests, such as Lukoil, but Gorbenko was favored by local economic elites and the military establishment as well. In addition to Lebed's support, Russian

Defense Minister Igor Radionov visited Kaliningrad two days before the election and apparently helped capture thousands of military votes for Gorbenko.[40]

- Both candidates courted voters who closely identified with the Communist Party, but Gorbenko conceivably secured more ballots from them than Matochkin because he was seen by the voters as hostile to the special economic zone that the governor had championed. Editors at *Kaliningradskya Pravda* also saw Matochkin's support of the SEZ losing him votes among ordinary people who did not think it was an economic asset to them. Finally, Matochkin's failure to defend his economic policies, and to acknowledge that some of them had been mistaken, was cited as a vote loser for him.

- Matochkin turned off some voters because "he spent too much time in Moscow" where he tried to exploit his contacts. What some of his advisers had believed to be an electoral asset proved to be a liability. Conversely, Gorbenko's slashing attacks on SEZ seemed to resonate with nationalists who characterized it as a device to open the door to "foreign influence." Gorbenko, by contrast, spoke forcefully in favor of Kaliningrad becoming self-sufficient and relying upon its own resources.

Upon taking office, Gorbenko immediately clashed with the Kaliningrad Duma when he sought to remove its chairman, Valery Ustyugov, from power. His opponents led by the tart-tongued Solomon Ginzburg—a Matochkin confident—accused Gorbenko of appointing people to high office in his administration who lacked both political and professional experience. But by far the most serious charge that the reformers leveled against him was that he opposed the special economic zone and his claim that he would rely upon Kaliningrad's own resources to fuel its economic recovery.[41]

Gorbenko's critics of course accused him of policy failures, which were not of his making, such as Moscow's failure to pass enabling legislation for the special economic zone. But like his counterparts in other areas of Russia, Gorbenko ran the oblast to promote his own welfare and that of his economic cronies; the population got secondary consideration. And Gorbenko, like the old Communists in Moscow, had little or no idea how a free-market economy operated.

Notes

1. Joseph B. Schechtman, *Postwar Population Transfers in Europe* (Philadelphia: University of Pennsylvania Press, 1962), 196.

2. Schechtman, *Postwar Population Transfers*, 196.

3. Arthur Hermann, "Karaliaučiaus Srities Rytprusiečių Likimas Po 1945 Metu (The Destiny of East Prussians in Karaliauciaus After 1945)," in *Sugriautų Namų Vaikai (The Children of Destroyed Homes)*, ed. Silvija Peleckienė (Klaipėda: Rytas, 1995), 180–86.

4. Hermann, "Karaliaučiaus," 187.

5. Schechtman, *Postwar Population Transfers*, 217.

6. Eugene M. Kulischer, *Europe on the Move: War and Population Changes, 1917–47* (New York: Columbia University Press, 1948), 300.

7. Romuald J. Misiunas and Rein Taagerpera, *The Baltic States: Years of Dependence, 1940–1990* (Berkeley: University of California, 1993), 339.

8. Interviews in Lithuanian Foreign Ministry, spring 1998.

9. Steven Main, "The Prospects Posed by the Kaliningrad Oblast and Possible Solutions for the Future," paper, June 1997, 5.

10. For a comprehensive and insightful discussion of Soviet nationalities policy in theory and practice, see Rasma Karkin's *Ethnic Relations in the USSR* (Boston: Unwin Hyman, 1986).

11. Malgorzata Pacuk and Tadeusz Palmowski, "Changes and Perspectives for the Economic Development of the Kaliningrad District in the Light of Regional Baltic Co-Operation," in *The Yearbook of North European and Baltic Integration*, ed. Bjorne Lindstrom and Lars Hedegaard (Berlin: Springer Verlag, 1997), 270.

12. Chauncy D. Harris, "Europa Regional: Focus on Former East Prussia," *Post-War Soviet Geography and Economics* 38, no. 1, (spring 1997): 54–62.

13. Harris, "Europa Regional," 62.

14. Gennady M. Fyodorov, "The Social and Economic Development of Kaliningrad," in *Kaliningrad: The European Amber Region*, ed. Pertti Joenniemi and Jan Prawitz (Aldershot, England: Ashgate Publishing, 1998), 35.

15. Harris, "Europa Regional," 60.

16. Fyodorov, "The Social," 35.

17. Pacuk and Palmowski, "Changes and Perspectives," 270.

18. Stephen K. Wegren and Vladimir Belensky, "The Political Economic of the Russian Land Market," in *Problems of Post-Communism* 45, no. 4 (July–August 1998): 58.

19. Wegren and Belensky, "The Political Economic," 59.

20. Wegren and Belensky, "The Political Economic," 59.

21. Pacuk and Palmowski, "Changes and Perspectives," 263.

22. Pacuk and Palmowski, "Changes and Perspectives," 271.

23. An *enclave* is part of a country enclosed in a foreign country. An *exclave* is territory of one country that is surrounded by territory of other countries. Pertti Joenniemi argues that because Kaliningrad is not completely surrounded by foreign countries—it borders on the Baltic Sea to its west—it might be called a *semiexclave*. Pertti Joenniemi, "Appendix I: Kaliningrad Enclave or Exclave" in *Kaliningrad: The European Amber Region*, ed. Pertti Joenniemi and Jan Prawitz (Aldershot, England: Ashgate Publishing, 1998), 261–65.

24. Pacuk and Palmowski, "Changes and Perspectives," 273.

25. Ingmar Oldberg, "The Kaliningrad Oblast—A Troublesome Exclave," in

Unity or Separation: Center-Periphery Relations, ed. Daniel R. Kempton and Terry D. Clark (under review for publication), 3.

26. Oldberg, "The Kaliningrad Oblast," 3.

27. Fyodor I. Kushnirsky, "Post-Soviet Attempts to Establish Free Economic Zones," in *Post-Soviet Geography and Economics* 38, no. 3 (fall 1997).

28. Interview with Matochkin, spring 1998.

29. Ingmar Oldberg, "Kaliningrad: Problems and Prospects," in *Kaliningrad: The European Amber Region,* ed. Joenniemi and Prawitz, 27.

30. Lyndelle Fairlie, "Kaliningrad: Visions of the Future," in *Kaliningrad: The European Amber Region,* ed. Joenniemi and Prawitz, 199.

31. Fairlie, "Kaliningrad: Visions," 188.

32. Vera Tolz and Irina Busygina, "Regional Governors and the Kremlin: The Ongoing Battle for Power," in *Communist and Post-Communist Studies* 30, no. 4 (winter 1999): 401.

33. Tolz and Busygina, "Regional Governors," 402.

34. Tolz and Busygina, "Regional Governors," 403.

35. Tolz and Busygina, "Regional Governors," 404.

36. Tolz and Busygina, "Regional Governors," 404.

37. Tolz and Busygina, "Regional Governors," 404.

38. Leonid Smirnyagin, "Putin Brain Trust Seeks to Improve Federal Agencies in Regions," EWI, *Russian Regional Review* 6, no. 11 (22 March 2000): 6.

39. *Biuletyn Kaliningradzki, Warsaw* (February 1997), 10–12.

40. *Biuletyn Kaliningradzki,* 10–12.

41. Solomon Ginzburg, interview, spring 1998.

3

Kaliningrad as a Flash Point of Conflict

F OR MOST OF THE 1990s, foreign-policy scholars and practitioners alike dwelled upon what they deemed the greatest threat to stability in the Baltic Sea region—the massive number of Russian troops that remained there. In 1997, a Polish scholar cited the heavy troop concentrations in Kaliningrad and said it was "one of the most explosive issues in relations between Russia, former Soviet vassals in the region (Poland and Lithuania) and in the Baltic Sea area in the wider meaning of the word."[1] This view was prevalent not only in Warsaw—German, Nordic, and Lithuanian commentators were of the same opinion as well.

Meanwhile, the Lithuanians came under heavy pressure from Moscow to provide a corridor through their country to facilitate military traffic to and from Kaliningrad. Unlike Kaliningrad's other neighbor, Poland, Lithuania was a much smaller country occupying territory close to the Russian Federation while sharing a border with Belarus, also a source of concern to Vilnius because of the unstable situation there. By 1994, the political upheaval and economic chaos in Belarus would thrust into power in Minsk a Soviet-style despot, Aleksandr Lukashenko. Although elected democratically, Lukashenko disbanded the Belarus parliament and forced through a referendum that unconstitutionally extended his rule until 2001. Moreover, Lukashenko's campaign to forge a union with Russia was unsettling, because those in Moscow who favored such a marriage were the same ones who openly proclaimed the Baltic countries were part of Russia's patrimony.

A third source of concern in Warsaw and Vilnius was unrelated to fears about Russia or former Soviet states; instead Poles and Lithuanians were worried that the Germans would return to their former East Prussian lands and once again pose a threat to their smaller neighbors.

Western Concerns

Kaliningrad as an Armed Camp

In the early 1990s, Western defense analysts estimated that 120,000 to 200,000 Russian military personnel remained in the oblast. Most of them belonged to the 11th Guards Army, and the Baltic Sea Fleet; its ships and sailors were located at Kaliningrad City's "inner port" and the "outer port" at Baltijsk, where the fleet was headquartered.

The naval and army formations had their own air wings and all together constituted a military force with significant power projection capability. Writing in February 1993, two U.S. researchers concluded: "These units, if taken together, hold approximately 620 tanks, 940 armored combat vehicles, 695 artillery pieces, 95 rotary-wing aircraft, and 155 fixed-wing combat aircraft."[2] They were a formidable force, even if Russian troops, which had been withdrawn from Poland and Czechoslovakia and were redeployed in Gusev, Chernyakhovsk, and Chernyshevskoye, were excluded from this estimate. If the 200,000 military pensioners living there were summed with the active military personnel in Kaliningrad, an estimated 20 percent to 30 percent of the region's population had military affiliations. It was to the dismay of the oblast's neighbors that more naval units would be relocated there, since St. Petersburg Mayor Anatoly Sobchak refused their redeployment in his city. Here was an early indication that the authorities in both Russian port cities would see the vital interests of their communities in conflict. Later lobbyists from St. Petersburg would support those in Moscow who wanted to discontinue Kaliningrad's free economic zone.

Kaliningrad's neighbors also recalled the missions of the Soviet units in the oblast during the Cold War; to strike targets in Denmark and southern Norway, to land assault troops on the shores of Sweden, and to deny enemy air, ground, and sea assets access to Soviet installations and cities in western Russia. World War II had demonstrated to Soviet defense planners that control of former East Prussia was a critical military asset for the Soviet Union. This was not a new idea since it had its origins in the policies of Peter the Great early in the eighteenth century, but it was in the twentieth century that Russian defense planners would truly recognize this fact. A military bastion in Kaliningrad would deny enemy forces a strategic base from which the Germans launched strikes against Leningrad and Moscow in 1941.

Western commentators saw no justification for the military assets that remained in the oblast and asked, "Now that the Cold War was over why were so many troops needed in Kaliningrad?" For example, in 1993, the former "Polish Defense Minister Parys rhetorically asked why Russia needed such a large concentration of troops in the Kaliningrad Oblast when Poland has only 220,000 troops to defend its entire territory."[3] Lithuania's "president," Vytautas Landsbergis, expressed the same sentiment.

Simultaneously, U.S. defense analysts scoffed at the idea that Kaliningrad had any real military value given the vulnerability of the isolated forces there. It made no sense for Moscow to keep large numbers of troops in an exposed exclave for they would be subject to overwhelming attacks from day one of a war. Russia had other assets to protect its territory such as its awesome nuclear arsenal, which would remain its major deterrent in the post–Cold War era even with dramatic drawdowns dictated by START. Indeed, General Lebed, in a 1997 trip to the United States reminded a U.S. audience: "Our rockets are rusty but they still work!"[4] Of course, any potential aggressor did not need Lebed to remind them of that fact.

It is plausible that some Western defense analysts downgraded the military significance of the Russian forces in Kaliningrad to enhance their case against NATO enlargement. They perceived membership for the Czech Republic, Hungary, and Poland as a threat to the fighting effectiveness of NATO. To acknowledge even in the early 1990s that Russian troops in Kaliningrad conceivably represented a threat to its neighbors would justify Poland and Lithuania's drive to join the alliance, so such an admission could not be made.

The Clinton administration championed enlargement, but some of its officials, like Deputy Secretary of State Richard Holbrooke, dismissed the notion that Kaliningrad represented a threat to the region. In 1994 he said, "The problem of the Kaliningrad district looks complicated only from the geographical point of view, this Russian region will not act independently of Russia, thus the issue of Kaliningrad is an issue of relations with this country in general."[5] He was right to assess the Kaliningrad Question against the backdrop of Russian–Western relations, but many former Soviet republics could not take comfort in this observation; a month later Russian troops attacked Chechnya and flattened the buildings in its capital, Grozny. Many old Russians were entombed in their flats. Unlike their Chechen neighbors they could not seek safe haven with relatives in the nearby mountains.

The presence of large numbers of troops and their heavy weapons, however, was criticized from another perspective that was harder for Moscow to ignore. Foreign business interests proclaimed that demilitarization was a precondition to significant Western economic investment in the region. As long as there was a strong military presence there, much of the territory in

Kaliningrad was off-limits to foreigners. Furthermore, the commercial "inner port" at Kaliningrad City—entered from the Baltic Sea via a long canal—could only handle ships with a displacement of 10,000 tons. The naval base at Baltisjk—the "outer port" on the Baltic Sea—by contrast could service ships with a displacement of 40,000 tons. As long as the Navy restricted non-Russian commercial vessels access to that port, many foreign investors would balk at the idea of using the shallower Kaliningrad City installation.

Western politicians added that Moscow could not expect to achieve warm, cooperative relations with its former Cold War adversaries—an objective the Yeltsin government said it favored—as long as the troops remained there. Consequently, in 1995, New York Republican Congressman Benjamin Gilman introduced an amendment to the "Cox Bill"—Christopher Cox is a Republican congressman from California—calling for the internationalization of Kaliningrad and offered economic assistance to the oblast in return for its demilitarization.

Many Russian defense analysts did not agree with their Western counterparts who said Kaliningrad was valueless as a military base. They argued that, on the contrary, Kaliningrad was even more critical to Russia's security after 1991 than it was during the days of the Soviet Empire. Dmitri Trenin wrote in 1997, "The Russian Federation today controls about one-fifteenth of the Baltic Sea coast, whereas the USSR and its Warsaw Pact allies used to control one-third." Furthermore: "Russia lost approximately 80 percent of its naval bases and basing facilities, a considerable part of airfields, air defense and radar facilities, and 60 percent of its shipbuilding and overhaul factories. Since 1996, the strength of the Baltic fleet has decreased by half, the number of ships and naval aviation aircraft by three times."[6]

Citing such facts, some of Trenin's former colleagues in the Soviet army justified their claim that the naval assets in Kaliningrad were even more critical to Russian naval operations in the Baltic Sea than they were prior to the USSR's demise. After losing naval bases in Estonia, Latvia, and Lithuania, Russia had to rely upon Kaliningrad and St. Petersburg and, of course, naval facilities in the latter instance were of diminished value since the adjacent waters were iced over during the winter.

The utility of those troops aside, Russian authorities reacted in anger to suggestions that the oblast be demilitarized. Since it was sovereign Russian territory, Moscow had the right to station troops there as long as their number was consistent with the Conventional Force in Europe Treaty (CFE). And later in the decade when their number declined, and Western commentators continued to talk about Kaliningrad as a "military enclave," they reminded their tormentors that Russia could deploy even more weapons under CFE than were already deployed there.

Concern about the troops in Kaliningrad did not subside as the years passed; after the demise of the USSR, their numbers actually increased as former Soviet troops left Germany, Eastern Europe, and the Baltic States. Yeltsin argued that Russia did not have housing for the men and their families nor warehouses and space for their weapons and rolling stock, so they had to be temporarily based in Kaliningrad. On this score he was telling the truth. Nonetheless, their presence continued to feed concern among Western observers that Kaliningrad was a serious point of discord between Russia and the West.

Moscow Demands a Corridor through Lithuania

The concerns of Kaliningrad's Baltic Sea neighbors that it was a source of regional instability was advanced by Moscow's demanding that Lithuania grant special transit rights to facilitate the movement of Russian troops and equipment to and from the oblast. Russian authorities reasoned that since Lithuania had been part of the USSR, "special relationship" justified their demands. The Lithuanians stated categorically that to grant Russia such rights was to violate their sovereignty. The inference, which even some liberal-minded Russian commentators endorsed, that Lithuania's former association with the USSR justified this demand sparked the angry retort, "We were forced into the Soviet Empire, we did not join it voluntarily." What galled the Lithuanians even more was that some Western leaders accepted this bizarre rationale for "Russia's special rights" as a legitimate demand. The word *bizarre* is appropriate because the Baltic countries were forced into the USSR in 1940 after phony elections. They were rigged by Moscow as evidenced by the curious fact that the Soviet media announced the results even before the polls were closed in Lithuania. The refusal of the Yeltsin administration and moderates in Moscow to concede that point—even though Yeltsin supported the Baltic's drive for independence in 1990–91—troubled the Lithuanians.

When confronted with Western analysts, who subscribe to the idea that none of the Balts can think rationally about Russians and are inclined to demonize them, Lithuanians recommended the following test. "The next time you talk to a member of the Russian Foreign Ministry ask him a very simple question: 'Were the Baltic states forced into the USSR or did they voluntarily join the Soviet Empire?' " Many Americans who have conducted this simple test in visits to Moscow have been unpleasantly surprised by the results. Granted, many Balts cannot speak about Russians with objectivity, but the same thing holds true for many of their counterparts in Russia including Russians who are supporters of democracy.

Early in 1992, Moscow demanded Lithuania sign a formal agreement to facilitate the transit of Russian troops and equipment to and from Kaliningrad. The Lithuanian government, protective of its sovereignty and wary of foreign troops moving about its territory, refused to sign. It did not help matters, moreover, that Russian military fixed-wing aircraft and helicopters periodically flew over Lithuanian air space without asking permission to do so. And many Lithuanians will never forget that when Russian troops exited their country in the fall of 1993 one army truck carried an ominous sign declaring: "We will be back!"

The Lithuanians reminded their Russian colleagues that in the July 29, 1991, Agreement on Co-operation between Lithuania and Kaliningrad—facilitating the region's social and cultural development—no arrangement was made for military transit. Likewise, earlier the next year, Lithuania rejected a Russian proposal that gave Russia the right to move military assets through Lithuania to Kaliningrad.

"By a special November 18, 1993, agreement, Lithuania began to allow only the transit of Russian armaments and military personnel withdrawing from Germany and coming from Mukran through Klaipeda, then following the railway on to Belarus. Until the beginning of 1994, Russian military transit to and from Kaliningrad, across Lithuanian territory, was carried out only on the basis of ad hoc permission."[7] These regulations soon became known as "the German rules."

Dismissing the Lithuanian government's right to block transit through their own country, a Russian train carrying military cargo crossed into Lithuania the evening of February 19–20, 1994, and was detained by authorities there. The Russians had not first asked permission to enter. When the Russian ambassador was called to the Lithuanian Foreign Ministry to explain his country's illegal entry, the ambassador proposed that both countries sign the treaty the Lithuanians previously rejected. On February 28, 1994, the Lithuanians announced that "Lithuania was going to prepare its rules and procedures for military transit, and that temporarily those regulations would apply that were already in force and applicable to the Russian troops withdrawing from Germany."[8]

The Russian government expressed its displeasure with this pronouncement and the dispute continued until demonstrators took to the streets in Vilnius in the summer proclaiming "No to military transit!" At this point, friendly Western countries got involved; on August 2, 1994, British Prime Minister John Major urged Lithuania to sign a transit agreement with Moscow. Ten days later, Lithuanian Prime Minister Adolfas Slezevicius stated that rules for military transit through Lithuania would apply "to all countries that wished to transport dangerous cargo and military cargo across Lithuanian territory," not only to Russia.[9] The Lithuanians refused to acknowledge that the Russians had a special right to move military assets through their territory.

On October 3, 1994, at the CSCE Review Conference in Budapest, Albinas Januska, the Lithuanian deputy foreign minister, said that Lithuania "had to state very clearly that Lithuania . . . would not be obligated in advance to ensure transit of any type and for any state across Lithuanian territory."[10] During this period when Russia refused to accept the Lithuanian offer, no Russian military transit through Lithuania was impeded. The Lithuanian government stated that by January 1, 1995, all governments would have to abide by Lithuania's rules of military transit. The EU pressed Lithuania to reach an agreement with Russia—clearly dismissing the fact that under the Lithuanian proposal, Russia's military assets could enter and exit Kaliningrad via Lithuania.

Vilnius remained resolute even after Moscow threatened to withhold favorable trade status from Lithuania. The "German rules" remained in force but politicians in both Kaliningrad and Moscow continued to demand a more formal agreement of military transit. Even after Lithuania and Russia signed an October 1997 border treaty, which essentially resolved all outstanding territorial disputes between the two countries, some members of the Kaliningrad Duma urged their counterparts in Moscow not to sign the treaty until the transit-rights issue was resolved. It was clear to everyone concerned that this issue could be resurrected at some future date and serve as a pretext for Moscow to exert pressure on Vilnius the same way that the "Russian citizenship question" was used by the Russian government to press the Estonians and Latvians.

The Return of the Germans

A subtext of fears regarding Kaliningrad in the early post–Cold War years concerned German policy toward its former East Prussian territories.

From 1764 to 1768, under the urgings of Catherine the Great, 30,000 German peasants colonized southern Russia to help fortify the country's agricultural sector. Later in the century, Mennonites from Prussia sought refuge in Russia to escape religious persecution. Stalin helped create a Volga Autonomous republic in 1924, which allowed the Germans there to use their language. But in August 1941, he deported 800,000 Germans from European Russia to Siberia and Kazkhstan because he feared they would be disloyal to a Russia at war with Germany.

During the early years of perestroika, West Germany provided assistance to ethnic Germans in the USSR to allow them to emigrate to the homeland of their ancestors. Few spoke German but 47,000 emigrated in 1987 and 150,000 in 1989. Two years later, however, in a dramatic turnabout, the Bonn government offered financial assistance to ethnic Germans who would remain in Russia. The prospect of absorbing two million of these people as well as the East Germans was deemed daunting.

At one point a German official suggested Gorbachev resurrect the Volga Republic, but faced with rising ethnic discord in the USSR and knowing that the Russians already living there would not take kindly to the idea, Gorbachev rejected it.[11]

In the meantime, albeit *sotto voce,* the Poles remained wary that the Germans would return to the region "big time." (Once the reunified German government relocated in Berlin, Germany's capital city would only be fifty kilometers distant from Poland.) After all, the Russians had gained control of the region as a result of a war they had helped start with Stalin's 1939 Non-Aggression Pact with Hitler. Some commentators might balk at the word *Russians* rather than *Soviets* and remind us that Stalin was a Georgian, but from the perspective of the Poles the words *Russians* and *Germans* reflect the fact that Poland throughout its history has been subjected to mistreatment at the hands of its two largest neighbors. Hitler attacked Poland on September 1, 1939, because Germany knew that it had nothing to fear from Russia; on the contrary, soon after the Polish army was crushed, the Russians moved into large parts of eastern Poland that had been rewarded them under the nonaggression pact.

The German invasion and occupation of Poland killed millions of Poles, mostly civilians. In addition to wartime casualties, more Poles died in Nazi concentration camps and late in the war when the Polish Home Army attacked the Germans while the Red Army advanced toward the German lines and then stopped to allow the Nazis to crush the Poles. Stalin's betrayal was driven by his respect for the Poles' capacity to resist oppression and he wanted the ranks of anti-Soviet Polish resistance fighters to be depleted when he installed a puppet regime in Warsaw after the war.

The number of World War II casualties, of course, increases dramatically when more than three million Polish Jews, murdered in the name of Hitler's "final solution," are added to the list. And it was with the invasion of Poland that the Holocaust was inaugurated in Europe.

The nearly five-year German occupation of their country seared the Poles' collective consciousness. The postwar democratization of Western Germany and Polish independence could not rapidly assuage Polish nightmares about Nazi oppression during World War II or fears of German might in the wake of the Cold War.

During the Cold War, shrill revanchist's voices in Germany demanded

Poland return "lost German lands in the east" to their rightful owners. They were even more insistent after the Soviet Empire collapsed. Most Germans accepted the fact that the territory their country had lost to Poland with the shifting of borders after World War II was permanent. But after the Cold War some "old Prussians" demanded the Poles return the land that they had received with Potsdam, which was twice larger than that placed under Russian control.

The Poles, like the British and French, believed they had cause to be worried about German reunification. Officials in the Bush administration, which encouraged Helmut Kohl in his bold quest to reunify the divided Germany, acknowledged that both Prime Minister Margaret Thatcher and French President Francois Mitterrand opposed the initiative. The British and French leaders had both worked closely with Kohl and knew that democracy was alive and well in West Germany—but how could they forget the aggressive Germany of their youth? It was no wonder then that the Poles, who had suffered even greater destruction at the hands of the Germans, remained wary of their large western neighbor.[12]

During the 1997–98 debates over NATO enlargement, Polish–Russian relations were discussed by U.S. senators on both sides of the question, but little was said about Poland's fears of Germany as an incentive for Warsaw's desire to join NATO. Indeed, it was a former son of Poland, Zbigniew Brzezinski, who reminded his fellow Americans that NATO had played a pivotal role in reconciling former enemies in Europe. "Without NATO, France would not have felt secure enough to reconcile with Germany. . . . Similarly, the ongoing reconciliation between Germany and Poland would not have been possible without the American presence in Germany and the related sense of security that Poland's prospective membership in NATO has fostered in Poland."[13]

The Lithuanians also recalled their experience with Germany during World War II. Hitler through the 1939 pact with Stalin sealed Lithuania's fate via a secret protocol to that pact. (Initially Germany was to get Lithuania but later Hitler acceded to Stalin's demand that it be awarded to him.) When German forces crossed the Nemunas River from East Prussia in June 1941, and soon overran the same Soviet units that occupied Lithuania a year earlier, the Lithuanians had hoped the Germans would allow them to restore an independent Lithuanian state. A provisional Lithuanian government was established even before the Red Army retreated from Lithuania and administrative structures that had existed during Lithuania's period of independence were resurrected. So when German units entered Kaunas, which had been Lithuania's capital during most of the prewar independence years, they found a provisional government in place. Without any real power to influence the

German occupying forces and the Nazi's refusal to tolerate any independent polity, however, it soon disbanded.

Alfred Rosenberg, a Baltic-German, was Hitler's authority on racial matters, and he was appointed Reichminister of the occupied eastern territories. His office planned to deport two-thirds of the existing Lithuanian population and to replace it with German immigrants. The massive deportation of Lithuanians was to be postponed, however, until the Third Reich won its final victory on the battlefield against Bolshevism.

During the German occupation, some 20,000 Lithuanians, who had been compelled to fight with the Red Army but surrendered en masse with the German invasion, were given the option of entering PW camps or fighting with German-led units. Most chose the latter option although Lithuanians refused to organize a Lithuanian Waffen SS unit even though the Nazis pressed them to do so. The Germans allowed the Lithuanians to organize local units to fight Soviet partisans, but the primary rationale for their formation in the minds of Lithuanian nationalists was to have military units in place in the event the Soviets returned to their homeland.[14]

Those Lithuanians who had hoped to receive decent treatment from their German occupiers saw their hopes dashed after 75,000 Lithuanians were sent to Germany to fill compulsory labor drafts. Others deemed anti-Nazi were placed in concentration camps. The father and brother of Lithuania's future president, Vytautas Landsbergis, were among those Lithuanians incarcerated in Germany. The Jewish community in Lithuania suffered an even more comprehensive and deadly fate. With the help of some Lithuanians, the Germans killed an estimated 140,000 Jews who had lived in Lithuania for centuries and had produced some of the most prominent Jewish religious thinkers in Europe.[15] But many Lithuanians would join Lithuanian partisans who took to the forest to resist German occupation of their country.

Given their mistreatment at the hands of the Germans during World War II, it should have surprised no one that although the Lithuanians suffered under Soviet occupation, they displayed grave concerns about the Germans returning to what their ancestors called Lithuania Minor after they regained their independence.

Russian Concerns

After Kaliningrad became an exclave, Moscow demonstrated sensitivity toward the region that was especially acute. While Russian officials stated categorically that a range of postwar agreements justified Moscow's legal claims over the territory, foreign commentators disagreed. Furthermore, since Kaliningrad was the only region outside of Russia and its population was susceptible to foreign ploys "to rip it from the breast of the Russian Federation," Moscow feared that Kaliningrad by design or circumstance might separate from Russia. And in the late 1990s, when NATO began making preparations to enlarge the alliance and include the Czech Republic, Hungary, and Poland, Russia feared this move eastward would jeopardize its security.

Kaliningrad's Legal Status

Once Kaliningrad became an exclave, some Western observers revisited the question of its legal status and raised eyebrows in Moscow. The former contended that with the September 12, 1990, treaty between the Federal Republic of Germany and the German Democratic Republic, Germany surrendered control of the former Konigsberg region, but "it did not transfer its sovereignty over the Kaliningrad Territory to the Soviet Union or to any other country."[16]

At the time of German reunification, the four World War II allies did not settle the issue, so the Soviet Union never enjoyed sovereignty over Kaliningrad. Consequently, after the USSR imploded, Russia could not legally acquire the territory.

The official U.S. government position supports those analysts who question Moscow's claim that Kaliningrad belongs to Russia. It is that Kaliningrad is under Russian administration, but Moscow does not enjoy de jure control of the territory. The fact that the world's only superpower does not acknowledge Russia's de jure control over Kaliningrad partially explains why the authorities in Moscow do not welcome Americans traveling to the region and with an edge of anger reject U.S. offers "to discuss the Kaliningrad Question."

Doubts about Russia's de jure control of Kaliningrad has prompted recommendations that an international body determine the oblast's ultimate fate. Soon after Kaliningrad became an exclave, Marion Grafin Donhoff of Germany's *Die Zeit* proposed it be ruled by a condominium composed of Germany, Lithuania, Poland, Sweden, and Russia.[17]

In 1994, the European Parliament passed a resolution that discussed Kaliningrad in terms of obtaining special international status. This was the thrust of a 1995 resolution proposed by U.S. Congressman Christopher Cox. It was never enacted, but the Russian Foreign Ministry reacted to the resolution with heat, saying in effect, "How would the U.S. Congress like it if some foreign parliament suggested Texas be handed over to an international body to determine its future?"

Some Lithuanian nationalists have argued that Russians never lived in the region but many Lithuanians did live in Lithuania Minor and Lithuania is justified in claiming part of the Kaliningrad territory. With the collapse of the USSR, the status of Kaliningrad became a raw nerve in Lithuanian–Russian relations. In the 1993 presidential campaign, Stasys Lozoraitis—Lithuania's ambassador to the United States—said Kaliningrad belonged to Lithuania. And in the summer of 1997, Vytautas Landsbergis, the conservative Lithuanian Parliamentary chairman and leader of the Lithuanian independence movement, Sajudis, said that the status of Kaliningrad remained to be settled. He remarked afterward that his comments had been taken out of context, but they prompted the oblast's governor, Leonid Gorbenko, to respond that Klaipeda had been unlawfully incorporated into Lithuania. The implication was clear: if Lithuania pressed its case for Kaliningrad there were others who would challenge Lithuania's right to occupy its only port city, Klaipeda.

Within Kaliningrad itself, local scholars have suggested that the region's residents possessed the legal authority to decide its fate. Through a referendum, they could choose the status quo, decide to remain within the federation but with the enhanced powers enjoyed by ethnic republics like Tatarstan, or elect to become an independent fourth Baltic republic.

As long as foreign commentators question the legal status of Kaliningrad, authorities in Moscow will continue to see it largely as a foreign-policy problem, although they refuse to acknowledge it publicly.

Fears about Separatism in Kaliningrad

After Kaliningrad became an exclave, some intellectuals there openly discussed the region separating from Russia. Kaliningrad's legal status, they said, remained to be determined, feeding talk about a "fourth Baltic state." Such rhetoric aside there was no organized grass-roots secessionist movement in the oblast, but officials in Kaliningrad made public statements that abetted fears in Moscow about the centrifugal forces of separatism. Yuri Matochkin, the region's first post-1991 appointed governor, said in 1994 that he favored a special relationship between the EU and Kaliningrad. A year later he warned, "Unless Moscow pays heed to Kaliningrad's resident's views, a referendum on secession from Russia may be held in the oblast." Later his successor, Leonid Gorbenko, remarked, "It makes no sense to go to Moscow. There is no money (there), the goal is therefore to become self-sufficient. We have no other option."[18]

The specter of separatism, of course, was given new resonance with the Chechen uprising, and Moscow's clumsy but deadly attempt to deal with it resulted in the assault on Chechnya in late 1994. The fighting stopped a year-

and-a-half later but not soon enough to spare a significant number of casualties; the low estimate is 40,000 killed—civilians and combatants—and the high one is 100,000 killed. As Anatol Lieven has pointed out in his book on the war, it was waged because of the weakness of the Russian state and the absence of strong leadership in Moscow.[19]

After the USSR's demise, the central government in Russia no longer could dictate to the regions as it could during the Soviet era. Moscow's leverage declined as its revenue transfers to the regions declined and the regions were compelled to generate their own taxes. And the privatization program championed by Yeltsin's young reformers created new sources of regional wealth not under Moscow's control. Nonetheless, Yeltsin complained that the regional authorities failed to pay workers and provide pensioners with their doles. The struggle between authorities in Moscow and those in the regions over taxes, energy, and commerce exemplified the tense relations between the Center and the federation's extremities. But the regional authorities, in turn, groused that Moscow demanded more from them in the way of taxes and other revenues than was justified. Moreover, in regions like Kaliningrad, local authorities and business leaders argued that Moscow had withheld legislation that enabled their economies to function effectively. The absence of enabling legislation to make the special economic zone a viable mechanism for economic development was a subject of complaint by a wide cross-section of elites in the region.

Today, Kaliningrad's exposed geographical location and separatist tendencies elsewhere in Russia explain why Moscow bridles at outsiders referring to Kaliningrad as "a problem." What's more, the fear of losing de facto, if not de jure, control of the region accounts for officials in Moscow having mixed feelings about extensive foreign investment in Kaliningrad.

NATO Encirclement

One of the few issues that has fostered consensus among Russia's squabbling political elite has been NATO enlargement. The idea of providing membership to three former Warsaw Pact states, the Czech Republic, Hungary, and Poland, in particular, caused liberal reformers and hard-liners alike to join in lockstep in opposition to it. Toward this end they make the following arguments:

- Mikhail Gorbachev agreed to a reunified Germany in NATO believing that the alliance would not spread east.
- Boris Yeltsin warned that to move NATO borders to those adjoining Russia was to ring down a new Iron Curtain dividing Europe east and

west once again, and Russia naturally deemed the initiative a threat to
its security.

- Russian military analysts argued that there was no threat to justify
  enlargement.
- Russia could turn a blind eye to three former satellite countries in the
  Soviet Union's "outer empire" entering NATO but it could not accept
  the three Baltic countries gaining membership since they belonged to the
  "inner empire." To include the Baltics was to cross what was to become
  known as the "Red Zone."

Yeltsin said Europe would be forced to endure a "Cold Peace" once Poland
became a member of the alliance. Henceforth, NATO troops would be sharing a common border with Russian units stationed in Kaliningrad. This specter prompted Russian generals and civilian defense analysts alike to fire off
salvo after salvo of criticism against expansion, followed by threatening
counteractions. Included in this menu of threats was one contending that
Russia would have to deploy tactical nuclear weapons in Kaliningrad to protect Russia. Also Russia's strategic nuclear strike doctrine would have to be
recalibrated presumably away from the one of no first use to a more provocative posture.

Here was one of the first examples of how Moscow would subsequently
treat Kaliningrad as a card to be played in achieving Russia's foreign-policy
objectives in Europe. Kaliningrad was deemed a special security problem for
Moscow but it also was a pressure point that could be applied to good effect
against the NATO countries. From this perspective, Kaliningrad was not a
liability but an asset to be used as a pawn in the game between NATO and
Russia over what security architecture should be built in the aftermath of the
Cold War. Some Russian political leaders indicated that perhaps a deal could
be made: if Poland were kept out of NATO, Kaliningrad might be demilitarized.

Even after Moscow's campaign to block Poland's accession to NATO
failed, commentators in Moscow persisted in claiming that enlargement
placed Russia's security at risk. NATO was neither a political club nor a cultural forum, it was a military alliance, so Russia had reason to be concerned
about Poland's membership in it. And as the infrastructure of Poland's
armed forces was upgraded and integrated into NATO's air, ground, and
naval systems, Moscow would have even greater reason to worry about this
"ill-conceived move." Some Western opponents of enlargement warned, "If
the pro-Western regime of Boris Yeltsin got so exercised about NATO
enlargement, just imagine what position a hard-line president replacing him
might take on this matter?"

Notes

1. Jakub Godzimirski, "Soviet Arbitrariness and Baltic Security: The Case of Kaliningrad" (NUPI, Conference on the Long-Term Security Prospects for the Baltic Sea Area, Oslo, May 23–24, 1997).

2. Philip Peterson and Shane Peterson, "The Kaliningrad Garrison State," *Jane's Intelligence Review* 60 (February 1993): 59–62.

3. Peterson and Peterson, "The Kaliningrad Garrison State," 62. For a detailed discussion of Russia's military assets in Kaliningrad and inflated estimates of Russian troops there, as well as a discussion of Kaliningrad and CFE, see Christian Wellmann, "Russia's Kaliningrad Exclave at the Crossroads," *Cooperation and Conflict* 31, no. 2 (summer 1996): 161–83.

4. *Washington Post* (14 January 1997).

5. *Baltic News Service* (25 November 1994).

6. Dmitri Trenin, *Baltic Chance* (Washington, D.C.: Carnegie Endowment for International Peace, 1997), 18.

7. Ceslovas V. Stankevicius, "Enhancing Security of Lithuania and Other Baltic States in 1992–94 and Future Guidelines," NATO Individual Fellowship Program, Vilnius paper 1994–96, 52 (unpublished paper).

8. Stankevicius, "Enhancing Security," 52.

9. Stankevicius, "Enhancing Security," 52.

10. Stankevicius, "Enhancing Security," 52.

11. Angela E. Stent, *Russia and Germany Reborn* (Princeton, N.J.: Princeton University Press, 1999), 165–66.

12. For a discussion of German reunification, see Philip Zelikow and Condoleezza Rice, *Germany Unified and Europe Transformed* (Cambridge, Mass.: Harvard University Press, 1995).

13. Zbigniew Brzezinski, "Living with a New Europe," *The National Interest* (summer 2000), 13.

14. For the German occupation of Lithuania, see Romuald J. Misiunas and Rein Taagerpera, *The Baltic States: Years of Dependence, 1940–1990* (Berkeley: University of California Press, 1993), 47.

15. Daniel Jonah Goldhager, *Hitler's Willing Executioners* (New York: Knopf, 1996), 423.

16. Algimantas P. Gureckas, "Lithuania's Boundaries and Territorial Claims between Lithuania and Neighboring States," *New York Law School Journal of International and Comparative Law* 12, nos. 1 & 2 (1991): 114. See also Raymond A. Smith, "The Status of the Kaliningrad Oblast under International Law," *Lituanus* 38, no. 1, (1992): 7–52.

17. See Marion Grafin Donhoff, "Kaliningrad Region and Its Future," *International Affairs,* no. 8 (1993): 46–49.

18. Matochkin, interview 1998.

19. Anatol Lieven, *Chechnya: Tombstone of Russian Power* (New Haven, Conn.: Yale University Press, 1998).

4

A More Positive Assessment

B Y THE LATE 1990s, there was ample reason to depict the Kaliningrad Question in dark hues, that is, stressing the serious social and economic problems there. But there was a more positive view of Kaliningrad; namely, the latent points of conflict there had not become manifest, as many observers feared they would. The gap between perception and reality had its roots in the fact that aside from a small number of academics, policy makers, and diplomats who closely watched developments in Kaliningrad, the oblast was not the subject of much attention among Western foreign-policy analysts. Scholars and diplomats from neighboring states, who had less trouble visiting the region, had an advantage over their U.S. counterparts; few Americans traveled there and Moscow made it difficult for them to do so.

For the most part, however, Western commentators did not closely watch developments in Kaliningrad so they continued to provide grossly inflated estimates of the troops remaining there—even though their numbers were declining. Therefore, other changes, which justified a more positive assessments of developments in the exclave, went unnoticed.

Russian observers were equally guilty of this practice. No foreign government claimed the region, yet Russian officials continued to cite the outcries of fringe voices in the West and to mischaracterize them as reflecting the true sentiments of Western authorities.

By this time, however, both Western and Russian observers, who took the trouble to assess the Kaliningrad Question, had reason to take some comfort in the fact that latent points of discord had not become manifest. Western officials could take heart in the following developments.

A Marked Decline in Troops

Although many Western observers continued to speak about Kaliningrad as a "military bastion," the number of troops located there had declined dramatically. Yet some foreign-policy analysts persisted in making excessive estimates of how many troops remained in the region. A Polish official told this writer, for example, that half of the oblast was composed of military personnel and retirees and their families. Perhaps that was the case even three years earlier but not in 1998. Meanwhile, U.S. foreign-policy analysts, who were not Kaliningrad experts but well informed about Russian and European affairs, were likewise surprised when they learned about the number of troops remaining in the region. "That's all!"

Analysts who closely monitored the Russian troop deployment in Kaliningrad all agreed that there had been a substantial reduction in their numbers. While U.S. analysts estimated that only 24,000 troops remained in the region, the Polish figure was higher—40,000—while the Lithuanians settled for an estimate of 33,000.[1]

President Yeltsin announced in a 1997 fall visit to Sweden that his government intended to cut the number of troops in the northwest region of Russia by 40 percent. He did not give precise figures about where the reductions would take place, and journalists indicated that at times during his trip he made a number of disjointed pronouncements, so his comments were greeted with skepticism. He also reiterated his offer to sign an agreement with the Baltic countries guaranteeing their security. They politely declined the offer.[2]

Moscow's effort to court the Balts did not last long. In the winter of 1997–98, Russian officials began a blistering campaign against the Baltic countries. The Kremlin complained about the plight of Russians in Estonia and Latvia who had been denied citizenship; but the assault indiscriminately tarnished all three democracies including Lithuania; that was misdirected since Lithuania had adopted a liberal citizenship law in 1989. Under it, all Russians living in the country had little trouble acquiring Lithuanian citizenship, so the accusation was groundless. But the plight of Russians living in the Baltic democracies really was not the motive behind the outcry. The campaign was part of an offensive to block the Balts from being named in the second round of NATO enlargement. NATO had stipulated that it would deny membership to countries that had resolved neither their "minorities problems" nor their "border disputes."

Moscow claimed the governments in Riga and Tallinn were guilty of mistreating their Russians while the government in Vilnius still had not settled its border questions with Russia. Russian officials, however, failed to mention that the OSCE did not find Estonia and Latvia guilty of human-rights violations although prudence suggested that they be more liberal in their citizenship laws. And, of course, the Lithuanian–Russian border agreement remained in question because the Russian Duma refused to sign it.

But Moscow's campaign to prevent the Balts' access to NATO aside, by the mid-1990s a dramatic drawdown in Russian troops stationed in Kaliningrad had taken place. A large inventory of weapons and other military assets—originally located there or redeployed after Soviet-Russian forces left Germany, the Baltics, and Poland—remained in the exclave. But in keeping with the status of military hardware located in other parts of Russia, much of it had not been warehoused or maintained and was inoperative. Still, what remained in working order was not altogether insignificant and this perhaps explained why some Western defense analysts continued to consider Russia's military presence in the oblast excessive. Also, while the Soviet and Russian governments in 1991 and 1992 respectively had indicated that all nuclear weapons formerly deployed in Central and Eastern Europe had been returned to Russia—and Moscow declared the Baltic a nuclear free zone—Western defense analysts expected that some tactical nuclear weapons remained in the oblast. However, it was assumed that they were not linked to operational delivery systems and probably remained there because there was nowhere else to put them or they had been left there inadvertently.

But expressions of concern in the West about Russian military presence in the region were associated with the tough rhetoric that emanated from Moscow, that is, Russian threats to counter NATO efforts to move east. On several occasions, as previously indicated, some generals spoke about responding to NATO enlargement by deploying nuclear weapons in Kaliningrad—although it was not altogether clear that they were speaking in an official capacity. Also, one might recall that several years earlier when the issue of Russian troops in the Baltic states was still the subject of discussion, Moscow responded negatively to demands from Vilnius, Riga, and Tallinn that they be removed while quietly withdrawing them.

Estimates of Russian troops in Kaliningrad originating in Moscow were consistent with those in the West. In 1996, Russian authorities claimed there were 24,560 troops in Kaliningrad with 853 tanks, 930 armored combat vehicles, and 426 artillery pieces. Naval personnel were not included in these estimates but a spokesman for the Russian Baltic Fleet stated in March 1998 that there were about 30,000 military personnel in Kaliningrad altogether and by the year's end the number would dip to 20,000. All the forces in the region were under the Baltic Fleet commander, Admiral Vladimir Yegorov.[3]

Some Russian defense analysts, like Arkady Moshes, believed Kaliningrad was indefensible, so the troop reduction was justified on those grounds alone.

He indicated that this was not necessarily the view of the Russian Ministry of Defense.[4] Officials there faced with a freefall in tax revenues had no other recourse but to accept the attenuation of Russia's military presence in the region. Others, moreover, might not say so publicly but they reasoned that Russia's security problems were not on their borders with the new democracies of Europe but inside of the federation itself and to its south and east.

Whatever the source of the troop reduction, Russian defense analysts argued that since the troops remaining there were not directly linked with supporting units in Russia—and were far from sources of logistical support—they did not represent a threat to their neighbors. They were capable of protecting Kaliningrad from an outside attack if it was a frail one, but they clearly could not launch significant offensive operations on their own.

In 1998, a year after NATO welcomed three new states into the alliance, the troops stationed in Kaliningrad were reduced tenfold from their 1991 strength. For most Western analysts the troop issue was deemed passe. Perhaps it was for Poland. Indeed that year a U.S. defense analyst in Moscow shared with the author a conversation that he had with a visiting official from Washington. The latter asked: "What would happen if the Russian Army attacked Poland?" The Moscow-based defense analyst responded: "The Poles would win! Assuming Moscow did not use its nuclear weapons." In light of the Russian Army's performance in Chechnya, this observation could not be deemed a witticism.

Publicly Lithuanian officials responded favorably to the troop drawdown but in private they continued to voice concerns about Russian units stationed on their border. After the first round of enlargement became a reality, Lithuania occupied a gray area between NATO and Russia. Today the government in Vilnius has about 20,000 troops under arms in an active or reserve capacity, with no heavy weapons at their disposal; even a small tank-led strike against them could be lethal.[5]

The fact that the Russian army did not fight well in the 1994–96 Chechen war (and in the 1999–2000 fighting) was not a source of comfort to the Baltic countries and other former Soviet republics either. In the aftermath of the USSR's collapse, Lithuania had worked closely with Russian military authorities in Kaliningrad. Lithuanian construction firms had built housing for Russian officers and their families and the authorities in Vilnius knew that thousands of Russian military families had been forced to live on naval cargo ships in Kaliningrad's ports.

Russian military personnel and their families were destined to live in squalid conditions throughout the Russian Federation for years; they were not adequately housed or fed, and their health needs were neglected—most officers and soldiers alike were demoralized, angry, and despondent. The

Russian military's plight spawned fears in many former Soviet republics that as Russia continued to be wracked by revolutionary upheaval, rogue elements in the military would engage in provocative and unauthorized actions. They clearly had done so in Moldova and Azerbaijan and Georgia. In the face of such uncertainty concerning the fate of Russia's military, was it any wonder that the Lithuanians sought a safe harbor in NATO?

But the fears of some Lithuanian elites aside, the profound drawdown in Russian troops in Kaliningrad clearly indicated a diminishing military capability in the oblast.

The Transit Question

The Russian Foreign Ministry's Vladimir Pozdorovkin, responsible for the regions, informed the author in the summer of 1998 that "We are happy with our transit agreement with Lithuania." The "German rules" continued to govern the transit of Russian troops through Lithuania to and from Kaliningrad. Lithuanian authorities noted that most Russian heavy equipment no longer moved over land but via the Baltic Sea. With the diminution of forces in the oblast, and the use of seaborne transit, the number of soldiers and material moving through Lithuania had declined. Both Lithuanian and Russian authorities claimed to be happy with the status quo. Yet on occasion, Russian politicians such as the speaker of the Russian Duma, Gennady Seleznev, continued to ask for a formal transit agreement. He did so as late as the summer of 1998.

Lithuania's President Algirdas Brazauskas and his Russian counterpart, Boris Yeltsin, signed a treaty in 1997 that settled border issues not covered by the 1991 Lithuanian–Soviet Russian Treaty. But the Russian Duma, dominated by Communist and ultranationalist deputies, refused to ratify it. It was not a figment of the Balts' imagination that many Russian politicians coveted the Baltic countries and had used "unresolved" border agreements with Estonia, Latvia, and Lithuania to destabilize the three democracies. As noted earlier, when Moscow began to blister the governments in Riga and Tallinn in the winter of 1997–98 for not awarding citizenship to Russian speakers in Latvia and Estonia, it was difficult to include Lithuania in the indictment, but Moscow did so all the same. Consequently, outstanding border questions between Moscow and Vilnius—albeit relatively minor in substance—were being exploited by members of the Russian elite who still deemed the Baltics part of Russia's patrimony. Hard-liners in Kaliningrad driven by like-minded ambitions encouraged the Russian Duma not to ratify the treaty either.

But cooler heads in the Kremlin realized that it was counterproductive to threaten the Baltic democracies. The support for them in the United States exceeded the number of Baltic–Americans that live there, and the Balts could cite Russian threats as a rationale for their gaining entrance into NATO. The Lithuanian Foreign Ministry, with the support of Brazauskas and his successor in early 1998, Adamkus, had made good relations with Russia a priority of Lithuanian foreign policy. Even conservatives in the Lithuanian Seimas realized the wisdom behind such initiatives. Following the advice of Mechys Laurinkus, a conservative deputy and close associate of the Seimas chairman Vytautas Landsbergis, Lithuanian deputies began conducting tête-à-têtes with their counterparts in the Russian Duma. Witnesses of these amazing discussions alleged that even Landsbergis had fruitful talks with Russian hard-liners, which in the fateful years of 1990 and 1991 had sought his arrest for leading the Lithuanian rebellion.

Meanwhile, Lithuanian diplomats in Kaliningrad made a special effort to achieve close relations with leaders there, including the governor, Leonid Gorbenko. Such efforts paid off, as will be discussed below, in relations with authorities in Kaliningrad but in Moscow as well. In June 1998, on his way back from a Western visit, Russia's Foreign Minister Yevgeni Primakov—soon to become prime minister—stopped in Vilnius and met with Lithuania's major leaders. He stated publicly that relations between Lithuania and Russia were excellent. In particular, he praised the Lithuanian government for its close cooperation with Kaliningrad.

One could interpret Primakov's visit as a ploy to underscore the fact that while Lithuania had liberal citizenship requirements, making it possible for all Russians there to become citizens, the same was not true of the Russians living in neighboring Estonia and Latvia. It was also likely that he was sending a message to Lithuania's supporters in the United States: given the warm relations that existed between Moscow and Vilnius there was no reason for Lithuania to seek membership in NATO.

Even granting these motives for Primakov's visit, there were good reasons that Russian authorities could be pleased with Lithuania's efforts to demonstrate that Vilnius desired to work in harmony with Russia. Lithuania's warm relations with Kaliningrad in particular had won them plaudits from discerning Russian commentators.

By 1998 the issue of a Lithuanian corridor to Kaliningrad was no longer a source of discord between the Lithuanians and Russians as it had been several years earlier. Efforts made by various Lithuanian governments to placate the Russians had not gone unappreciated by moderates in Moscow.

The Germans Never Arrived

By the late 1990s, the prospect that ethnic Germans would move from other areas of the former Soviet Union to Kaliningrad—an event which some people in Kaliningrad and Moscow welcomed and others feared—had not materialized.

Bonn offered the ethnic Germans economic aid if they remained in Russia but they had good reason to emigrate to Germany instead. "In addition to their past sufferings, the Germans in Kazakhstan, who had meanwhile grown to a million people, faced Kazakh nationalism and assertive Islam, and those leaving for Russia had to confront the suspicions and prejudices of Russians and other ethnic groups."[6] Germans returning to the homeland of their ancestors did not have to endure such problems. Besides, Germany was a rich country while alternative relocation sites for the Germans in Russia were suffering from the same economic crisis that plagued the rest of the country. Prior to the USSR's demise, it was rumored that Chancellor Helmut Kohl and President Mikhail Gorbachev thought about creating an "autonomous German" republic in Kaliningrad, but nothing came of the idea.[7]

After Yeltsin emerged as the dominant leader in Russia, he estimated that as many as 200,000 ethnic Germans might relocate in Kaliningrad, but less than 10 percent of that number actually did so. According to Angela Stent, "Officially, there are 5,000 ethnic Germans there, but the actual total might be as high as 15,000—as against 200 in 1989—out of a population of 500,000 in the city of Kaliningrad."[8] Poverty, a predominant Slavic population, and the pull of more congenial prospects in Germany, explain why ethnic Germans from elsewhere in Russia have not relocated in the oblast.

Today German investors and the German government alike have adopted a low profile in Kaliningrad in recognition that after USSR's implosion, authorities in Vilnius and Warsaw, not just in Moscow, harbored fears that Germany would once again become a dominant political and economic force in the area. The Lithuanians and Poles have taken advantage of the Germans not making their presence felt in former East Prussia in a big way as most observers had assumed they would.

Both Poland and Lithuania are vital to the daily lives of Kaliningraders. Products from both countries—foodstuffs but also textiles and furniture—are prominent in the oblast's stores and kiosks. Daily, at all of Kaliningrad's border points with Lithuania, shuttle traders buy and sell their goods. The Lithuanians have food products the Kaliningraders need and, given the exclave's special economic status, its entrepreneurs, in turn, can sell the Lithuanians imported products at reduced prices. The same kind of commercial relationship with Poland persisted until early 1998 when Warsaw adopted stricter border crossing rules consistent with EU visa practices. By that time, Lithuanian and Polish investors had become increasingly important to Kaliningrad. Together they constitute the heaviest foreign investors in the oblast.

For example, a Lithuanian meat processor, Klaipedos Maistas, has invested what will eventually amount to $5 million in a meat processing plant there.

By the end of 1999 it was anticipated that the operation would provide 120 jobs for local workers. The Russian partner in the joint venture indicated that he expected to sell most of the meat produced in Kaliningrad to customers in the Russian Federation.[9]

As was the case during the Soviet era, Lithuania continues to play an important part in Kaliningrad's day-to-day functioning as it still gets 80 percent of its electricity from Lithuania. Also Vilnius, in addition to administering air traffic to and from Kaliningrad over land, now handles the air traffic control via the Baltic Sea to and from the oblast. And Moscow has sought Vilnius's cooperation in running a gas pipeline through Lithuania to service Kaliningrad underscoring how important Lithuania is to the exclave's welfare.

In comparing Lithuanian and Polish day-to-day relations with Kaliningraders, one is struck by the conclusion that having lived and worked in the Soviet system for a half-century, and having internalized Soviet behavioral traits, the Lithuanians work more effectively with the Kaliningraders than do the Poles. Indeed, Lithuanian officials claim that their Polish counterparts seek advice from them about how to cooperate effectively with the Kaliningraders.

Residents of Kaliningrad and their leaders have openly expressed their disappointment that more Germans have not come as tourists and investors in the oblast. After the Soviet Union's collapse, some German businessmen built hotels in joint ventures with local entrepreneurs to attract German tourists to the area. The results of "nostalgia tourism," however, have been disappointing; frequently the first visit German tourists make to the region is their last one. Also, while there is a German-language weekly published in Kaliningrad and it carries pictures of homes that presumably are available to Germans seeking summer or year-round homes in the oblast, not many Germans who have visited their old homeland have chosen to stay there.

Those who once lived there cannot find many buildings or other structures that existed in East Prussia when they were young. And their offspring cannot understand why anyone would speak nostalgically about the area in the first place. The city of Kaliningrad is dismal and unkempt; its cityscape is characterized by ghastly Soviet-style buildings in advanced stages of decay. Potholes often pockmark even midtown streets and there are few Western-quality hotels or restaurants in the city. The only Western style hotel is Lukoil's Commodore. The walled compound is located on Kaliningrad's fringes not far from a forlorn prison still in operation, and adjacent to a small village where cows are tended by Babushkas. Most of its patrons are young men with thick necks who hardly look and dress like representatives from Western firms anxious to make Kaliningrad another Hong Kong.

The countryside is pretty but the small towns are stricken by poverty and ill-kept—even though on occasion one might discover new housing being constructed by one of the small number of people who have done well in the new economy. Indeed the gross disparities of wealth that are clear to anyone visiting the area are an added incentive for avoiding the place. Foreign visitors, who exit the oblast through Lithuania, often comment upon crossing the Nemunas River that they feel as if they "have returned to the West."

There is little reason to expect German investors to significantly increase their exposure in the region under existing circumstances. Germany's politicians are not eager to get entangled with Kaliningrad either and this was the case even prior to the 1998 economic crisis. West Germany has invested close to $1 trillion (U.S.) in East Germany, and Germans both east and west have not been happy with the results. Helmut Kohl lost his bid for reelection as German chancellor in 1998 in part because "westies" and "easties" alike have complained about the high price both have paid for reunification. The former are angry about the awesome tax burden they have had to endure; while the latter are despondent that in spite of substantial investments made by West German entrepreneurs, the economy in their part of the country continues to suffer. Millions of people in the former GDR are angry because western German business interests bought factories in the East but then vacated them, claiming they were "uneconomical." Unemployment is about twice as high in the eastern as in the western sector of Germany and journalists report growing alienation in the east and the penchant for young people to fancy neofascist ideas and movements.

Given the environment, German politicians of all persuasions have little reason to adopt more comprehensive policies toward Kaliningrad. Indeed, it is safe to assume that German colonization of the area, which began more than six hundred years ago, has ended. And it is noteworthy that German democracy has helped assuage the fears that Germany's neighbors have harbored toward it for centuries. For example, on the eve of the twenty-first century, "when Poles were asked whom they most liked to work with in business and in politics: Germans ranked 77 percent and 74 percent respectively, Americans 58 percent and 67 percent."[10]

By 1998, Kaliningrad's neighbors had less cause to see it as a flash point for conflict, but what about Russian assessment of developments there? While the oblast faced many internal problems, neither authorities in Kaliningrad nor those in Moscow had reason to speak about "foreign provocateurs" who wished to wrest control of the territory from them.

No Foreign Government Claims Kaliningrad

For several years after Kaliningrad became an exclave, former residents of East Prussia, through a host of émigré organizations, demanded the territory be returned to Germany. On June 17, 1995, a "Free State of Prussia (Freistaat Preuzan) was formed in Berlin, and a physician, Dr. Rigolf Hennig, was selected president. In a letter to the U.S. House of Representatives, Dr. Hennig wrote: "Under valid national and international law the free state of Prussia, as a constituent part of the German Empire, has never been extinguished." Hennig asked the U.S. Congress to help create a free and independent "fourth Baltic republic."[11]

Ultranationalists in Germany, seeking support for their revanchist policies, have endorsed such claims. But neither the Prussian émigrés nor the far-right parties in Germany constitute a significant political force, and they are incapable of successfully pressing their case in Bonn even though they employ heated rhetoric and make exalted demands.

The Kaliningrad Question was settled with the signing of the 1990 treaty of German reunification, and the oblast belongs to Russia; that is the official position of the German government. Henceforth, any governmental initiatives that Germany undertakes concerning Kaliningrad is to be processed through federation authorities in Moscow or the European Union. Consequently while some elderly folk in Germany persist in claiming that East Prussia should be returned to Germany, no one takes their claims seriously. As each year passes, the ranks of these people shrink as nature takes its course.

Poland has made no claim on Kaliningrad-Krolewiec. It signed treaties with both Germany and Russia indicating it had no territorial claims on either country. Poland was beneficiary of the Potsdam agreement—since it was awarded two-thirds of East Prussia—and any changes in territorial boundaries that Warsaw might consider could spawn similar claims from the German side for German territory that was awarded to Poland after World War II.

In Lithuania, some conservative politicians continue to assert that parts of Kaliningrad—what was once Lithuania Minor—belong to Lithuania, roughly the territory located between the Pregel and Nemunas Rivers. But they wield little political influence. Lithuanians, who once lived in East Prussia, and their supporters, continue to press their case through the Lithuanian Minor (Mazoji Lietuva) community. At the organization's 1995 7th Congress held in Klaipeda, representatives from the organization demanded "the summoning of an international conference on the future of Prussia as it was also envisaged in the (Postdam) forum." In addition, they passed a number of resolutions, one of which included the rights of former residents to return to their old homeland, another that demanded "the demilitarization" of Kaliningrad, and a third, which recognized that parts of Kaliningrad belong to Lithuania.[12]

The most prominent Lithuanian politician who has expressed interest in Kaliningrad, has been Vytautas Landsbergis. He has demanded that the authorities in Kaliningrad respect the rights of Lithuanians living in the oblast but has stopped short of claiming the area for Lithuania. Nonetheless, he contends that with the disintegration of the USSR, the legal status of Kaliningrad remains unresolved and, "The new residents of the Kaliningrad region sooner or later will want more autonomy because such is the natural and unavoidable path of every colony."[13]

Russian analysts have frequently cited Landsbergis's comments to justify their contention that "foreign politicians" want to wrest the oblast from Russia, but such claims are groundless. First, there is no government in all of Europe that has claims on Kaliningrad. The Germans are categorical in stating that they have no such claims; neither do the Poles have a claim. And it is noteworthy that Algirdas Brazauskas when he was president and his successor, Valdas Adamkus, have indicated that Lithuania has no claim to Kaliningrad. In 1991 and 1997, Lithuania signed border treaties—and in a 1999 agreement of cooperation in Moscow as well—with Russia that support this conclusion.

As noted earlier, it is also disingenuous for Russian leaders to cite claims of old residents of East Prussia in Germany to sustain their "fears" that "foreign provocateurs" have designs on the region. The political powerlessness of these organizations aside, former old Prussian residents are not only small in number but they are advanced in age and clearly too frail to relocate in Kaliningrad and run their former farms or business enterprises, even if they were invited by Moscow to do so.

The same holds true for those Lithuanians who assert that those parts of the oblast belong to them. Lithuanians who once lived there also are small in number and advanced in age. Even if they were welcomed back by the authorities in Kaliningrad, how many would come? Furthermore, the small number of Lithuanians who reside in the region today are not long-time residents, but arrived after World War II and they have neither the influence nor the desire to claim the area for Lithuania.

It is noteworthy as well that there are few non-Lithuanian scholars or policy makers who believe the Lithuanians have much evidence to support their claims to the territory. Indeed, according to Lithuanian sources, before World War II there were 61,000 residents of East Prussia who spoke Lithuanian out of an estimated population of 1.5 million, about 5 percent of the population.[14]

Here again it is not clear whether the territory in question is all of East Prussia or part of that territory when it was under German control since German population figures for prewar East Prussia is more than three million.

That estimate, in turn, probably includes the Polish territory that was annexed by East Prussia after Germany overran Poland in 1939. Perhaps the figures above refer to what the Lithuanians call Lithuania Minor (including what the Germans call Memelland). Perhaps their numbers were far higher before that time and one might argue that Baltic peoples lived in the area when the Germans first colonized it in the thirteenth century, but this hardly represents a strong case for Lithuanian claims to the territory today.

The Lithuanians, moreover, cannot be unmindful of the fact that they acquired a significant part of East Prussia after World War II—the former Memelland. Prior to the war, Lithuanians represented a majority of the population outside of the city of Memel, but ethnic Germans represented a majority within its municipal boundaries. And that city today, Klaipeda, which is one of the largest in Lithuania, was populated by ethnic Germans for centuries.[15]

For all these reasons, the Lithuanian government has not made claims on Kaliningrad. And in private, Lithuanian officials assert "what would we do with close to one million Russian speakers?" Recall that during the Soviet Era, Lithuanian Communists loyal to Moscow rejected Khrushchev's offer to place Kaliningrad under Lithuanian authority for the same reason. Finally, none of the Western organizations that Lithuania wishes to join, most particularly the EU and NATO, would condone a Lithuanian campaign to reclaim lost territories in the former East Prussia. Such claims would provoke counterclaims from Russia and Belarus regarding Lithuania's de jure rights in Klaipeda and large parts of eastern Lithuania bordering on Belarus that include the city of Vilnius.

Nonetheless, the U.S. government continues to hold that the oblast is under Russian administration and does not grant Moscow de jure control of Kaliningrad. Russian legal scholars and some of their Western colleagues deem this position unjustified.

Valentin Romanov makes the following arguments in support of his claim that Russia enjoys de jure control over Kaliningrad: "On June 5, 1945, the allied governments signed the Declaration of Germany and the Assumption of Supreme Authority over Germany. It stipulated that the four powers would determine the 'boundaries of Germany or any part thereof and the status of Germany or any area at present being part of Germany.' "[16]

Stalin raised the question of Konigsberg at Tehran when he said that the USSR needed an ice-free port on the Baltic. "The British Prime Minister reacted at once by saying that it was a very interesting proposal and he would study it by all means. Roosevelt, who was concerned about how Polish Americans were going to vote in the U.S. presidential elections due in 1944, took a cautious stand on issues concerning Poland. Nor did he comment on

Stalin's utterances about Konigsberg, but his silence suggested acceptance of the idea of transferring Konigsberg to the Soviet Union."[17]

At Potsdam it was agreed in principle by both Churchill and Truman that part of Konigsberg would be transferred to the USSR. Stalin said, "If the U.S. and British governments approve in principle of this proposal, that is enough for us." Upon concluding discussion of the matter Churchill said, "I agree." Truman also said, "I agree."[18]

Romanov reminds Western commentators that Poland's de jure control over the portions of Germany has not been challenged: "The Potsdam accord on Konigsberg was as fundamental and irreversible as the Potsdam decisions on Poland's frontier along the Oder and Neisse."[19] Furthermore, facts on the ground have provided further support for the Russian case. Romanov cites elections that were held in February 1946 according to Soviet law, the out-migration of Germans from East Prussia, and the resettlement of citizens from the USSR in their place.

Finally, the question of Kaliningrad's legal status was settled with the German reunification treaty signed "by the Soviet Union, the United States, Great Britain, and France in Moscow on September 12, 1990, with the GDR and the FRG signing it on the German side." Romanov concludes, "Thus the German settlement has drawn the line once and for all at the problem of the status of Konigsberg and the adjoining area as an inseparable integral part of the territory of our country to which Russia has legal title as indisputable from the point of view of international law and from any other, as the sovereign title of any other state of its territory."[20]

British legal scholar C. A. Whormersley supports this conclusion. He has written the following:

> The Treaty on the Final Settlement with respect to Germany provides that "the united Germany has no territorial claims whatsoever against other States," and from this it must follow that it has renounced any claim to this part of East Prussia. Likewise, as a matter of law, the United Kingdom, the United States, and France must be taken to have waived their right to require the Soviet Union (of which the Russian Federation is accepted as the continuation) to secure some appropriate provision in the peace settlement and thus to have acquiesced in the Soviet Union perfecting its title to the territory in 1990.[21]

The foregoing legal opinions support the Russian case for de jure control of the oblast but perhaps of larger consequence, there is no reason for Russian authorities to express concern that "foreign provocateurs" seek to wrest it from Moscow's control since no foreign government claims the region.

The Question of Separatism

There is no mass movement in Kaliningrad seeking to break loose from Russia. Statements from the oblast's first governor, Matochkin, and his successor, Gorbenko, concerning Moscow's inability to address Kaliningrad's problems, are declarations of fact. But both men, and their political allies, have taken no concrete steps to bolt from the Russian Federation.

Of course, fears along these lines are compounded by Kaliningrad's location; it is the only region that exists outside of Russia and therefore is singularly susceptible to foreign influence. Furthermore, the central government in Russia has been weak in the post-Soviet period and the authorities in Moscow have experienced great difficulty in efforts to secure cooperation from the regions. For years now, the struggle between authorities in Moscow, and those in Russia's Far East and republics like Tatarstan, over taxes, energy, and commerce exemplify tense relations between the Center and the regions. When he was president, Yeltsin blamed regional authorities for not working with Moscow in promoting economic reforms and chided them for not providing back pay to workers in their jurisdictions.

Regional leaders, in turn, have complained that neither the Russian president nor the Duma has provided them the help they need. And money is not the only issue. As authorities in Kaliningrad—and other regions—have observed, by refusing to pass enabling legislation, the oblast's campaign to attract foreign investment has been obstructed.

Even though no foreign government challenges Russia's control of the region, Kaliningrad's exposed geographical location, Moscow's weak control of the federation's regions, and separatist tendencies elsewhere in Russia explain why Moscow has bridled at outsiders referring to Kaliningrad as "a problem." What's more, the fear of losing de facto if not de jure control of the region explains, in part, why Moscow has had mixed feelings about extensive foreign investment in Kaliningrad.

But as Solomon Ginzburg, a close associate of Matochkin, has observed: "Poverty will promote separatism here!" He made this observation in complaining about the failure of Moscow to address Kaliningrad's problems. He also interjected an observation that was not pleasing to officials in Moscow, namely, that Kaliningrad's problems cannot be resolved without "outside help." To support this claim that poverty and separatist sentiments are linked, he said that sociologists in Kaliningrad have conducted surveys indicating that whereas less than 2 percent of the population had expressed such tendencies earlier, by 1998 the percentages reached as high as 10 percent. He attributed this increase to the growing economic plight of the population and the failure of his political enemy, Gorbenko, to do anything about it.[22]

Whatever fears Moscow may have about separatist sentiments in Kaliningrad, they are not a product of foreign provocation but rather are linked to domestic circumstances and the federation's neglect of the oblast. Moreover, there is no meaningful grass-roots movement in Kaliningrad that is seeking to bolt from the Russian Federation.

The Threat of NATO

Complaints about the first round of NATO enlargement continue to emanate from Moscow and they have gained stridency since the crisis in Serbia. But the reasons for it have little to do with fears that NATO represents a threat to Russia. Rather it is a ploy on the part of Russian authorities to prevent any former Soviet republic from gaining membership in it with a second round of enlargement scheduled for 2002. Uppermost in the minds of Kremlin officials is the prospect that Lithuania has been identified by U.S. analysts to be best prepared to join the alliance.[23]

Western proponents of enlargement, however, respond to Russia's concerns as follows:

- First, regarding the claim that Gorbachev would not have permitted a reunified Germany to enter NATO if he had known about expansion: the Soviet Union no longer exists, and besides, Soviet Russia in 1991 signed an agreement with Lithuania that allows it to join any defensive alliance it chooses. This, of course, holds true for Estonia and Latvia as well, which as sovereign states can make the same choice.
- Second, Yeltsin's claim that Russia deems enlargement a threat against its security is groundless. It is in Russia's vital interest to have stable democratic NATO member states on its Western borders. A stable Western flank is in its vital interest because whatever combat-ready troops Moscow possesses must be deployed in the Caucasus, where many Russians have been killed—as combatant or civilian casualties. Others have lost their lives in the former Soviet Central Asian republics, where a real threat to Russia's southern underbelly exists. And in the long term, the specter that must haunt Russian defense planners is China, not NATO, as more than one billion people live below a vast reservoir of wealth in Siberia, which by contrast is scarcely inhabited.
- Third, the major threat which concerns the Balts and other former Communist states in Central Europe, is not a reconstituted Russian army that will invade them any time soon. Rather it is the upheaval to their east that is associated with the daunting transition from a closed to an open

society. Russia is such a large country that turmoil there is likely to spill across its borders and do harm to the economies of smaller neighbors or exacerbate existing political problems within these societies, which also are in transition. Of course, revolutionary upheaval in Russia may be exploited by neo-Stalinists and ultranationalists to gain power there. And these people, let us not forget, continue to proclaim that the Baltic countries are part of Russia's patrimony. The neo-Stalinist regime in Minsk and the dismal prospects for democracy in Kiev are further cause for the Balts to seek shelter in NATO.

- Finally, the Baltic states were forced into the Soviet Union and did not join the USSR voluntarily. To cite their previous status as Soviet states to justify their being prohibited from joining NATO not only ignores history but disregards the fact that it is in the interest of the Euro-Atlantic democracies to empower peoples who embrace Western values. One lesson of Serbia is that today any European government that attempts to rule through political power (force) and not political authority (popular rule) is inherently unstable. It is a source of instability to its neighbors as well.

Moscow tacitly accepted the first round of enlargement after it was given military and political concessions. First, NATO had pledged that it had no intention of either deploying nuclear weapons or nonindigenous combat troops in the Czech Republic, Hungary, and Poland. Further, most of Poland's forces will remain in the western part of Poland—just as they were deployed when Poland belonged to the Warsaw Pact—or be dispersed throughout the country and not concentrated on the border with Kaliningrad. At that point when Poland's air, sea, and land units are linked to Western contingents, their mission will be defensive in nature. Finally, under the Conventional Forces in Europe (CFE) Treaty's inspection regime, Russian inspectors will be permitted to assess NATO's assets in the three new member states. Additional arms control inspections are provided under the OSCE agreements.

Second, the NATO–Russian Council was formed in May 1997 under Russian pressure. While membership in the council does not allow Moscow to veto NATO decisions, it clearly provides Russia with a forum to discuss security issues that are pertinent to all parts of Europe.

One cannot make any definitive statement about Russian reaction to Poland's becoming an active member of NATO in the future. Russia and NATO are likely to argue over the small number of non-Polish troops that will be required to link Poland's security infrastructure with installations to its west. NATO will interpret their presence as benign while Moscow may cite them as evidence that the West is acting in bad faith. A heavy redeployment of Russian troops in Kaliningrad is unlikely but Moscow may demand that the CFE treaty be renegotiated.

Currently, relations between Poland and Russia are good in spite of some occasional spats. Like Russia, the Poles at Potsdam were awarded a southern part of Prussia—two thirds of the former German territory. The USSR and Poland signed a border agreement in 1945 that was renewed in 1990. And currently there are no outstanding territorial disputes between Poland and Russia. Any concerns Moscow might have had about the Poles reacting with hostility toward Russia after close to fifty years of occupation have not materialized. All post–Cold War Polish governments have made it clear that they welcome close and harmonious relations with Russia. Polish commercial activities and investments in Kaliningrad are especially critical to the oblast's residents. Poland's northeastern provinces have developed close relations with neighboring jurisdictions in Kaliningrad and shuttle trading across their common border has been brisk. Also, cultural and educational exchanges between them have been extensive.

Russian authorities, moreover, have reason to believe that once Poland enters the EU, that organization is likely to adopt special measures to facilitate commercial relations between the EU and Russia's westernmost region. The government in Warsaw—like its counterpart in Vilnius—has lobbied the EU to adopt such special policies toward Kaliningrad. Helping the oblast represents a small, concrete step toward eventual Russian integration into Europe, but it should be exploited to provide insight into the problems and prospects of greater EU–Russian economic cooperation.

As regards future NATO enlargement and the prospects that the Baltics may become members, the arguments cited here suggest that Russia has no cause to fear for its security. On the contrary, the existence of stable democratic states on its Western borders, which enjoy the security of NATO membership, will enhance Moscow's prospects of dealing with serious upheaval within Russia and to its south and east.

The benefits, which Russia acquires with NATO expansion eastward, are not restricted to security gains alone. Mikhail Alexseev and Vladimir Vagin, in their study of Pskov, have observed. "With NATO enlargement to include Poland, the Czech Republic, and Hungary, and a possibility that the Baltic states may be considered for membership in the 'second wave' of enlargement, Pskov has already enjoyed some tangible benefits from Eastern Europe's race to the West." Under pressure from the West, Estonia adopted "a pacification with the East" strategy and dropped territorial claims that it had on the Pskov region. "In a similar manner, Latvia dropped its territorial claims to Russia in the south of Pskov."[24]

The leadership in the Pskov region, meanwhile, understands that the growth, which is taken place in neighboring Baltic states, is fostering an economic environment that will enhance Pskov's economic prospects as well. "In this sense, while presenting a conundrum for the Kremlin strategists, the Baltic movement toward NATO has already improved prospects for trade and family contacts across the Pskov–Baltic border—and the economic prospects of the Pskov region's nearly one million people."[25]

Notes

1. These estimates were provided by U.S., Polish, and Lithuanian diplomats in private consultations with the author.

2. At that time, a prominent group of Russian foreign-policy analysts led by Sergei Karaghanov had conducted a study of Russia and the Baltics and urged Moscow to seek accommodation and not confrontation with the governments in Riga, Tallinn, and Vilnius.

3. These estimates come from Steven Woehrel, "The Baltic States: U.S. Policy Concerns" (Washington, D.C.: Congressional Research Service Report For Congress, updated 12 June 1998), 19. See also Arkady Moshes, "Changing Security Environment in the Baltic Sea Region and Russia," in *Baltic Security*, ed. Gunnar Arteus and Atis Lejins (Riga: Latvian Institute of International Affairs, 1997), 140–41.

4. Interview, spring 1998.

5. For a discussion of the Lithuanian defense forces, see *White Paper 99* (Vilnius: Ministry of National Defense of the Republic of Lithuania, 1999).

6. Angela E. Stent, *Russia and Germany Reborn* (Princeton, N.J.: Princeton University Press, 1999), 166.

7. Some German scholars, such as Christian Wellmann, assert that no such idea had ever been considered by the two leaders (personal correspondence).

8. Stent, *Russia and Germany*, 169. For a discussion of German migration to Kaliningrad see Christian Wellmann, "Russia's Kaliningrad Exclave at the Crossroads," *Cooperation and Conflict* 31, no. 2 (summer 1996): 161–83.

9. Spring 1998 interview with David Eppelfeld, the Russian partner in the joint Lithuanian–Russian meat processing venture.

10. Elizabeth Pond, *The Rebirth of Europe* (Washington, D.C.: The Brookings Institution Press, 1999), 236.

11. Reprint of letter from Dr. Rigolf Hennig to the U.S. Congress (14 June 1995).

12. Deliberations of 7th Congress of Lithuania Minor, Klaipeda, 1995, 181.

13. Deliberations, 181.

14. Bronius Kviklys, *Musų Lietuva (Our Lithuania)* (Boston: 1968), 623.

15. Anatol Lieven, *The Baltic Revolution* (New Haven, Conn.: Yale University Press, 1993), 60.

16. Valentin Romanov, "Kaliningrad as an Integral Part of Russia," *International Affair* 6 (1995): 43–44. See also Raymond A. Smith, "The Status of the Kaliningrad Oblast under International Law," *Lituanus* 38, no. 1, (1992): 7–52.

17. Romanov, "Kaliningrad," 45.

18. Romanov, "Kaliningrad," 47.

19. Romanov, "Kaliningrad," 47.

20. Romanov, "Kaliningrad," 48–49.

21. C. A. Whormersley, "The International Legal Status of Gdansk, Klaipeda and the Former East Prussia," *International and Comparative Law Quarterly* 42 (October 1993): 919–27. It is noteworthy that European students of Kaliningrad have expressed disbelief when confronted with the U.S. position; for example, in private correspondence, both Ingmar Oldberg and Christian Wellmann indicated that they assumed that Washington had conceded Russia's de jure control of Kaliningrad. Note further in the conclusion to this book that the Clinton administration's point man on Russia, Deputy Secretary of State Strobe Talbott, was of the same opinion until early 2000.

22. Interview, spring 1998. For a discussion of separatism in Russia see Gail W. Lapidus, "Asymmetrical Federalism and State Building in Russia," *Post-Soviet Affairs* 15, no. 1 (winter 1999): 87–106.

23. See the Council of Foreign Relations, *Task Force Report: U.S. Policy toward Northeastern Europe* (New York: Council on Foreign Relations, 1999).

24. Mikhail A. Alexseev and Vladimir Vagin, "Fortress Russia or Gateway to Europe? The Pskov Connection," in *Center Periphery Conflict in Post-Soviet Russia,* ed. Mikhail Alexseev (New York: St. Martin's Press, 1999), 184.

25. Alexseev and Vagin, "Fortress Russia," 185.

5

From a "Gateway" to a
"Black Hole" in Europe

Kaliningrad's Economic Plight

A T THE SAME TIME that foreign-policy analysts took comfort in Kaliningrad not becoming a flash point for conflict in the Baltic Sea region, the
domestic situation there was a cause for concern. Among other things, the
expectation of some that the oblast would develop a solid economy did not
materialize. For years after it became an exclave, some officials there, like
Matochkin, spoke of it as a potential Hong Kong, a gateway allowing foreign
investors access to the huge Russian market. He argued simultaneously in
Moscow that it worked the other way around, too, for Russia could use Kaliningrad as a pathway to the vast wealth of the West European market.

As previously indicated, however, Kaliningrad has not actualized its economic potential. One important reason for its stagnation has been the failure
of FEZ and SEZ to attract new investment into the region. A closer look at
why they failed is required if we are to address the ultimate question: What
can be done to revitalize Kaliningrad's economy in the twenty-first century?
This question is being asked by Kaliningrad's neighbors with a sense of
urgency because they fear that as the economies around the exclave prosper,
while its own remains in the doldrums, the oblast will become a black hole
in the Baltic Sea region.

Ingmar Oldberg and other observers have indicated the FEZ had little
prospect of becoming a success because of a wide range of problems. Today
they all remain as barriers to Kaliningrad's economic revitalization.[1]

1. The legacy of the Soviet command economy continues to influence the thinking and policies of Kaliningrad's authorities.
2. The region's infrastructure is underdeveloped; for example, the commercial port in Kaliningrad City is reached via a thirty-kilometer canal from the Gulf of Gdansk through the Straits of Baltisjk, and at some point the channel is so narrow only one-way traffic can traverse it. Furthermore, the port's depth is only seven meters and large ships cannot use it.
3. Kaliningrad relies on outside sources for most of its energy and cannot refine the oil pumped from its own wells.
4. Moscow has reduced subsidies to an area which has always been heavily dependent on them, and has insufficient revenue of its own to compensate for the federation's curtailing grants in aid to the region.
5. Federal authorities have not enacted legislation making either economic zone fully operational and attractive to foreign investors.
6. In March 1995, Yeltsin abolished exemptions on imports thereby eliminating one of the most important incentives for foreign investors.
7. Foreign investors have been denied the opportunity to own the land on which their enterprises are located.
8. Domestic and foreign firms must wrestle with red tape and arbitrary economic policies which, in turn, provide wide latitude for corruption.
9. Kaliningrad's economic prospects have suffered from constant policy reversals. According to Matochkin, "In these past years . . . we have seen Moscow time and again present us with a decree with one hand and take it back with the other almost the following day."[2]

To complicate matters even further for Kaliningrad, ports in Poland, Estonia, Latvia, and Lithuania are technologically more advanced than those in Kaliningrad and are all linked to extensive road and rail transport systems unavailable to the exclave. Meanwhile, the ports in St. Petersburg have been modernized and they offer additional competition to those in Kaliningrad.

From the outset, discontent with the FEZ was not only restricted to Moscow. Support for it declined rapidly in Kaliningrad as well; for example, one poll indicated growing disenchantment with the FEZ as early as 1993. It is noteworthy that nationalistic sentiment among ordinary folk in Kaliningrad contributed to this negative assessment. Today, for example, 70 percent of the region's population oppose foreigners owning land in Kaliningrad, so barriers to free-market practices are not only associated with neo-Soviet elites in the exclave or Moscow. In face of such nationalist sentiment in the oblast and similar pressure from Moscow, Matochkin was compelled to disavow an earlier agreement with German investors to develop joint ventures on the Vistula Spit.

High-level officials have been wary of extensive foreign involvement in Kaliningrad even while some of their cohorts have lobbied for it. The Russian deputy prime minister, Sergei Shakhrai, wrote two articles in 1994 attacking "local separatism" in Kaliningrad and "creeping (Western) expansion" there.[3] The following year he presented his "Baltic Strategic Initiative." It did not serve as a source of encouragement to investment in the oblast. Shakhrai said: "I have always been in favor of balancing Russia's economic and military strategic interests in this region; . . . therefore, I shall do everything to ensure that the economic development of the Kaliningrad region strengthens and not weakens Russia's military potential in the Kaliningrad region."[4]

In his 1996 presidential campaign visit to Kaliningrad, Boris Yeltsin promised greater economic assistance for the oblast. It was hardly surprising that he dangled the prospect of economic help to potential voters but he courted the nationalist vote there when he stressed the obvious—Kaliningrad belonged to Russia.

Residents there feared foreign economic domination while they also coveted economic privileges associated with the FEZ. Whatever they told pollsters, one positive feature of the zone was that it dramatically reduced prices for Kaliningrad's consumers; after it was scrapped, for example, prices soared by 20 percent to 30 percent.[5] No doubt as they saw a correlation between the two events, many Kaliningraders adopted a more friendly attitude toward the zone.

In contrast to FEZ, the SEZ had a more restrictive agenda and was portrayed by Moscow as serving all of Russia. For example, the new zone was seen by federal officials as an instrument to deal with the plight of Russians in the "near abroad." In Article 22 of Chapter VIII of the SEZ charter, Moscow inserted a provision that gave preferences to native Russian-speakers who wished to migrate from the three Baltic States. "The bodies of state authority of the Kaliningrad Region shall provide preferential conditions for migration to the territory of the Kaliningrad Region and settlement on this territory of persons currently residing or staying on the territory of Lithuania, Latvia, or Estonia who were heretofore citizens of the Union of Soviet Socialist Republics and whose native language is Russian."[6]

Under SEZ, foreign investors were to receive tax breaks and other advantages to attract them to the oblast: for example, there was no duty on materials imported into Kaliningrad if their value increased by 30 percent because of add-on measures adopted while there—even if the goods were then re-exported. The initial reports were that this new effort had helped resurrect the economy. According to one account, by the end of 1996, more than 1,000 joint ventures had been created, about one-third of them fully owned by foreigners. "Free trade status led to a sevenfold increase in the Kaliningrad region's foreign trade since 1992, reaching a total of $1.3 billion in 1996."[7]

In July 1996, officials in Kaliningrad trumpeted their biggest investment catch of all. They announced that the Korean auto manufacturer, KIA Motors, had planned to invest as much at $1 billion to transform the old Yantar Ship Yards into an auto manufacturing plant. It eventually would produce 50,000 to 55,000 cars annually. In contrast to incomes earned via the sale of imported goods in or outside the region, the KIA operation provided manufacturing jobs and tax revenues in the open, and not through the surreptitious underground, economy.

The new zone however was hampered by the same impediments that detracted from the FEZ: the persistence of Soviet-era practices—and even new sources of corruption—and the Russian Duma's failure to pass enabling legislation that met concerns of foreign investors about the safety of their ventures. All of these concerns were given impetus by the failure of the Russian government to honor the pledges it had already made. Foreign entrepreneurs were not the only ones who had lost faith in the zone. By the October 1996 elections, it was clear that most Kaliningraders did not believe SEZ would help reverse the decline in the region's economic fortunes and they chose Gorbenko, a SEZ critic, over Matochkin who had championed it.

Gorbenko entered office claiming that Kaliningrad should rely upon its own resources and reenergize the economy through a strategy of self-sufficiency. At the same time, during the campaign, Gorbenko promised workers in the oblast that he would protect them against unfair foreign competition.[8] His critics said both measures were merely a pretext to give him and his friends license to use political authority to enrich themselves. They were labeled Gorbenko's "Mafia laws." For example, he came up with the idea of giving local officials the power to impose quotas on imported goods. It was designed, he said, to help protect local business, but Gorbenko's opponents claimed it was devised to enrich himself and his friends.

Meanwhile, the TACIS-based economic experts and consultants in Kaliningrad received a cold shoulder from the governor; among other things, he did not cooperate with the TACIS program that was designed to make SEZ a viable economic tool. The director of that program also informed visitors that they should be careful what they said in his office, since there was a good chance that it was bugged. Russian members of the TACIS team did not see such warnings as displays of humor or exaggeration.

Critics contended that Gorbenko's policies also discouraged foreign investment, which declined 20 percent from 1997 to 1998, when his office refused to provide KIA with duty reductions that had been promised to the

Koreans for investing in the region. The KIA project ground to a halt and as a consequence, Volkswagen officials decided against making a major investment in Kaliningrad. The German automobile company had been considering the project for one-and-a-half years.

It is unfair to blame Gorbenko's policies alone for alienating foreign investors and inducing them to back out of deals in Kaliningrad; but whereas the region in 1996–97 was ranked fifteenth in Russian regions receiving foreign investment, by 1998 it had dropped to thirty-second position.

In the summer of 1998, *Izvestia* sent a reporter, Igor Korolkov, to Kaliningrad to take stock of conditions there. The piece he subsequently wrote, "The Kaliningrad District Has Become a Zone of Fear," provided fuel to Gorbenko's enemies in the oblast and in Moscow. Many officials and business people Korolkov wished to interview were afraid to talk to him.[9] Few would speak on the record, and those who did spoke about the most mundane issues in hushed tones as if they were revealing "state secrets." Korolkov alleged that many of Gorbenko's opponents, who had the temerity to speak openly against him, were subject to death threats and some had been beaten. For example, Alexei Rudnikov, the editor of the independent opposition newspaper, *Novyje Koliosa,* was brutally beaten after he was warned twice about running articles critical of the governor, and at one point a bomb exploded near Rudnikov's office. Also, the Duma's press secretary, Mikhail Kucheriavenka, was assaulted with a lead pipe allegedly for his opposition to Gorbenko.

Meanwhile, Gorbenko was said to have surrounded himself with advisers and aides with shady backgrounds. For example, Korolkov indicated that Gorbenko's former vice governor, Georgi Topazly, was arrested at the Polish border in 1992 with $12,000 on his person allegedly as partial payment for ammunition that he had sold. Officers from the Baltic Fleet were also involved in the operation but Topazly was released for lack of evidence against him. Later Gorbenko fired him when the two had a falling out.

The article went into detail about how Gorbenko, and certain economic oligarchs in Kaliningrad, were bent on privatizing the commercial port—and other state property—to enrich themselves. The exposé also characterized in a darker hue what some foreign commentators might have cited as a positive development in Kaliningrad. After Gorbenko became governor, it was announced that his administration had arranged with the German Dresdner Bank to provide borrowers with a $30 million fund. This development could be interpreted as evidence that overseas lenders were interested in the region and saw it as a place to make money.

The *Izvestia* journalist however provided his readers with a different spin on the deal. Borrowers would receive a loan through the Baltika Bank in Kaliningrad at a rate of 13.75 percent and additional interest would be added by other local lending institutions. This meant that the total amount a potential borrower had to pay was 20 percent. Since Russian banks at that time provided loans for 12 percent, why would anyone participate in the Dresdner program? The answer presumably was that firms or individuals inclined to accept the usurious interest rates did so because they wished to launder money they had earned illegally.

Since many other regions of Russia could be subjected to the same scrutiny as Gorbenko's Kaliningrad and with the same conclusions—that corruption was rife and honest officials and business people were victims of violence and extortion—one might ask, Why the spotlight on Kaliningrad?

Perhaps the answer is that people in high places in Moscow were out to get Gorbenko. Some Lithuanian commentators indicated it was rumored that Yeltsin's office had decided to move against him for corrupt practices, but Yeltsin's poor health and then later the August 17, 1998, economic meltdown prevented Moscow from carrying out that campaign. The *Izvestia* piece, one could safely surmise, was part of the campaign to oust Gorbenko from office.[10]

Social and Ecological Problems

While economic problems have been cited as the basis for Kaliningrad's plight—a condition further exacerbated by the August 17 economic crisis—the oblast also has suffered from widespread social problems associated with its economic difficulties. It has the highest incidence of AIDS in Russia, the second highest rate of drug-related crimes, and it is first in Europe in confiscated drugs. Death by alcohol poisoning is an unbelievable 70 percent higher than the Russian average.[11]

Because Kaliningraders can enter Lithuania without a visa, Lithuanian authorities have complained about the heavy flow of prostitutes from Kaliningrad to Lithuanian territory, especially the port city of Klaipeda, which has the highest incidence of AIDS in Lithuania. They also cite Kaliningrad as the source of many of the illegal drugs that have crossed into Lithuania and are used locally, shipped elsewhere in the region, or shipped out of it altogether. The same holds true for weapons that make their way from Kaliningrad to and through Lithuania.

The criminal gangs in Kaliningrad enjoy close ties to political authorities and the business elite. And in many instances, it is an error to distinguish among the three groups, for they are often one and the same. Organized crime cannot operate as openly and as extensively as it does in Kaliningrad without the consent of public authorities, police, and court personnel, and without the cooperation of business oligarchs. And as is the case where there are large numbers of military installations, members of the armed force, officers in particular, have engaged in widespread corrupt and criminal behavior.[12]

Crime, of course, has its roots in the legal nihilism that was endemic to Soviet society and today that affliction has been compounded by economic destitution. Many otherwise honest Russians have resorted to criminal behavior—or have abetted it—because they have no alternative means to care for themselves and their families and they are desperate. Looking at the wealth that a small group of their countrymen have acquired by violating or bending the law via privatization, they believe that they have the right to extract their fair share of the loot from the carcass of the old Soviet system. In every society and at any point in history, otherwise honest people have sought to meet their most basic needs outside the system when existing, legitimate institutions prevent them from doing so. The nineteenth century urban political machines that thrived in many U.S. cities testify to the universality of the truism: "When people cannot meet their needs by working within the system, they work outside of it."[13]

As elsewhere in Russia, a poor diet and inadequate medical care along with heavy drinking has had a deleterious impact upon Kaliningraders' health and longevity. From 1991 until 1995, there was a five-year drop in life expectancy for men and a two-year drop for women. In the 1990s more people died in Kaliningrad than have been born there. By 1997, the population was about 938,000—about 80 percent Russians and most of rest Ukrainians, Belarussians, and some Germans and Lithuanians. It has grown slowly, however, because of immigration.[14] Presumably many Russians living elsewhere in the old Soviet Union continued to be attracted to this "westernmost" area of the federation.

Ironically, Kaliningrad's economic plight has helped reduce its dire ecological problems. Kaliningrad is composed of 15.1 thousand square kilometers and has a population density of 65 persons per square kilometer—that is, some eight times greater than the average in Russia as a whole. But the oblast's population density is variable, with most of it clustered toward the Baltic coast which runs 140 kilometers; its two lagoons add another 280 kilometers to the coastline. Both are ecologically stricken. "The Kuronian and Vistula lagoons stand out as water areas subject to pollution, not only from the Kaliningrad region, but also the Polish and the Lithuanian border regions. The Vistula lagoon has lost its capacity of natural purification because of a combination of factors; its small size, shallowness (less than three meters in depth), and unrestricted flow of polluted waters from the river Pregel."[15] Consequently, Kaliningraders suffer from a high incidence of gastro-intestinal diseases such as dysentery, hepatitis, and stomach ulcers.

About 40 percent of Kaliningrad's contaminated water comes from municipal water companies. There is a real danger of a breakdown in water supplies because most municipal water facilities were constructed prior to World War II and repair of them has been rare. Atmospheric pollution produced by cars amounted to 50 percent in 1990 and soared to 73 percent in 1994. From 1989 to 1995 the number of cars in the region doubled and tripled in the city of Kaliningrad.[16]

Industrial pollution, however, has dropped from 97,200 tons in 1990 to 42,000 tons in 1995 because of the recession and plant closings. Kaliningrad's agricultural region—that comprises 55 percent of the land there and is one-half the average of agricultural land in Russia—uses mineral fertilizers and pesticides, which contribute to area soil pollution.

The August 1998 Economic Crisis

Since the August 17, 1998, economic meltdown in Russia—when Prime Minister Sergei Kiryenko devalued the ruble and Russia defaulted on its debt—all of Kaliningrad's problems have gotten significantly worse.

Devaluation of the ruble drove up the prices of consumer goods for all Russians and swept imported commodities from store shelves when merchants no longer could produce the hard currency to purchase them. Consumers in Kaliningrad were hit even harder than residents elsewhere in Russia because the region relies so heavily on imported food products and consumer goods. Estimates range from 75 percent to 90 percent while inexpensive local equivalents are unavailable. A photo published in *The Baltic Times* (an English-language newspaper published in Riga) spoke volumes about conditions there when it depicted bare shelves in the city's main supermarket in downtown Kaliningrad. As I observed in a visit several months earlier, the supermarket's shelves were full of meat, fish, cheese, and diary products imported primarily from Lithuania and Poland.

Hospitals and institutions serving the elderly and children soon ran out of medicines, and equipment that had been shipped in from overseas could not be replaced. Workers and pensioners, who had endured late pay and pension payments for years, faced an even grimmer future, perhaps no payments at all. Meanwhile fuel supplies were deemed inadequate to meet Kaliningrad's requirements to power cars and heat homes and factories. Even the navy was said to be short of fuel and its food supply was only enough to meet its requirements for thirty-three days. At one point it ran out of bread. Salaries for the military, of course, were also delayed and there was little hope that the problem of insufficient housing for military families would improve; it would only get worse. Under these circumstances, it is no surprise that a Russian survey found afterward that Kaliningrad's residents had the fourth lowest living standard of all of Russia's regions.[17]

In the wake of the crisis, foreign investors followed the lead of their counterparts in other areas of Russia and froze their operations and sought ways to extract as much hard cash and product as they could from Kaliningrad's market. Local enterprises responded to the downturn by culling their labor forces of workers and unemployment in Kaliningrad City reached 10 percent.

Gorbenko panicked and declared a state of emergency but then retracted that proclamation when he received a withering blast of protest from officials in Moscow. Igor Shebdurasulov, a Yeltsin staffer, phoned Gorbenko and reminded him that only the president of Russia had such power. Gorbenko then earned the ire of Boris Fyodorov, Moscow's chief tax collector, when he said that he had decided temporarily to stop sending tax revenues to Moscow. Fyodorov said he had no authority to do so.[18]

Afterward, however, Gorbenko stated that the crisis justified the argument that he had been making for some time that Moscow had to give Kaliningrad greater control over its own affairs. The former governor, Matochkin, used the crisis to punctuate the case he had been making for some time too that the oblast's only salvation was to achieve a special arrangement with the EU, since Moscow was incapable of providing any significant assistance to Kaliningrad. The radical wing of the small Baltic Republican Party even suggested that the time had come perhaps to seek a foreign savior for the area's tribulations.[19]

On September 28, the Kaliningrad Duma chairman, Valery Ustyugov, sent a letter to Prime Minister Primakov warning that "ambiguity in Moscow's position regarding the Kaliningrad Region is currently stimulating increased activity on the part of certain European countries and, at the same time, is heightening the uncertainty among the population about the future." The only activities Ustyugov could be referring to however, were efforts to help the oblast, but he clearly hoped to attract attention in Moscow by exploiting nationalist sentiment there. He added, "The complex geopolitical position of the region makes our land less safe from financial crises than other regions of Russia. The complete dependence of the region on imported goods and food products, the weak financial support from the federal center, and the chronic underfinancing support from the center, and the chronic underfinancing of the Baltic Fleet, border guards, and other structures subordinate to the federation create an insufferable burden for the region and local budgets today." All of these points, of course, were grounded in fact.

And then he added ominously, "All this is creating serious social tensions in society and generating distrust on the part of the population towards the center, thereby weakening bonds" and "all of this is being skillfully used by our closest European neighbors, who are intensifying their economic and political influence on the region."[20] In feeding Moscow's paranoia, Ustyugov followed a common practice of politicians in Kaliningrad whatever their political tendencies.

There were signs of growing disenchantment among the population at the grass roots but they were no different in nature nor magnitude than popular unrest in other areas of Russia and they were benign and restricted to rhetoric. Nonetheless, on September 7, trade union leaders wrote letters to both President Yeltsin and Governor Gorbenko demanding that they resign from office and Kaliningrad given a new change in status.[21] The latter reference was in keeping with demands from officials in the region that it be granted control over its own affairs.[22] On September 28, the Duma approved of an anticrisis program that included demands that Moscow reduces transit tariffs on foodstuffs and fuel. Meanwhile the Pensioner's Party that had been formed on August 3, 1998, reported that the crisis had contributed to a rapid increase in its membership reaching 3,482 members by late September.[23]

Letters of protests and proclamations aside, the plight of the region's residents was grave. It was estimated that 40 percent of its population was living below the poverty line and the October candidates for mayor to Kaliningrad City were told that they would have to provide the money to conduct the election since the city did not have the funds to do so. Doctors treating AIDS patients in the region—estimated at close to three thousand—indicated that they were running out of medicine to care for them. The medicine crisis in Kaliningrad created new concern on the part of Lithuanians living along areas bordering it about the spread of AIDS to their communities. Diana Visockiene, a doctor associated with the Lithuanian AIDS Center in Vilnius, said that researchers in Lithuania estimated that 50 percent of the prostitutes in Kaliningrad were HIV-positive and large numbers of them favored the port city of Klaipeda where they could find sailors and drugs. Both phenomena helped account for the fact that Klaipeda has the highest incidence of HIV-infection in Lithuania.

According to the Lithuanian AIDS researchers, differentials in income explained why women in Kaliningrad wishing to sell their bodies would travel to Lithuania to do so. The monthly income in Lithuania is $200 compared with $38 in Kaliningrad.[24]

It was against the backdrop of rising poverty and social disruption in Kaliningrad that Lithuania, a poor country itself, pledged to provide $1.2 million in food, medicines, and fuel for Kaliningrad and urged other countries in the region to follow its example. Aid soon was forthcoming from Poland, Germany, and the Scandinavian countries, and through regional and international organizations to which it belonged, Kaliningrad received help from countries and cities outside of the region as well.

But as evidence that old practices die hard in Russia, humanitarian assistance was delayed for a while because donors balked at demands from Kaliningrad officials that they had to pay duties on their contributions. As is evident throughout Russia, economic data that can be used with confidence is hard to come by since economic transparency is not a hallmark of Russian economic life and besides, as Richard Rose has indicated, there is more than a single economy operating throughout the former Soviet countries.[25] But one can safely assume that given the range of economic, social, and ecological problems that plagued the oblast prior to the August 17 event, all of them had been exacerbated by declining economic activity in the region and the curse of inflation that it had spawned.

Those who hoped the crisis would facilitate a reconciliation between the Duma and Gorbenko had little cause for optimism. Under the best of circumstances, they lamented, Gorbenko's response to the crisis was bizarre. This was in keeping with accounts from foreign diplomats and analysts who have met the man. Words like *strange* and *unbalanced* are often used in describing him. One thing is clear, after August 17, he made some strange remarks. According to *Moscow News*, he announced that he would not be surprised were Moscow to sell the Kaliningrad region to Germany to cover the Russian Federation's debts.

When members of the Kaliningrad Duma said that the newly appointed prime minister, Yevgeni Primakov, would never let that happen, Gorbenko responded: "Primakov is a good man. I know him, but he's a sick man. He's 70. What can he do? And don't get your hopes up about the Duma either. The price of a vote there has gone up from $18,000 to $30,000."[26]

Gorbenko traveled to Vilnius in September 1998 and met with high-level Lithuanian officials, including President Adamkus, and thanked them for their help. He also stated publicly that he appreciated the assistance that Lithuania was providing, but at the same time he refused to send representatives from his administration to Vilnius in January 1999 to attend a roundtable on Kaliningrad that the Lithuanian Foreign Ministry had arranged.

Like an earlier roundtable held in the Lithuanian village of Nida—situated on the Curonian Spit—the Vilnius Roundtable was designed to provide diplomats and experts from Russia, Finland, Sweden, Denmark, Poland, and Germany with the opportunity to exchange views about how their countries could work with Russia and address Kaliningrad's problems. But Gorbenko refused to send representatives from his administration to participate in the roundtable because his bitterest political rivals, Matochkin and Ginzburg, would be in attendance.

Two days before the January 14 roundtable, which was designed to discuss Kaliningrad in relationship to EU integration, Gorbenko said it was being conducted "behind the backs of the Ministry of Foreign Affairs of the Russian Federation and the Embassy of the Russian Federation in Vilnius. According to the information we possess, entirely different issues will be discussed," Gorbenko alleged. "I am ashamed for some of my compatriots, fellow citizens for their attending the seminar." In a subsequent statement, however, Gorbenko indicated that he did not mean to disparage the Lithuanian Foreign Ministry; on the contrary, he applauded it for its positive work with Kaliningrad.[27]

The West has pressed the Lithuanians to develop harmonious relations with Russia, but Lithuania has not needed it, because it recognizes the following facts:

- Russia is Lithuania's natural trading partner.
- An angry Russia can cause many problems for small neighbors by denying them access to the Russian market, particularly energy and gas imports on the one hand, and food exports to Russian consumers on the other hand.
- Good relations with Russia will help facilitate Lithuanian membership acceptance into NATO.
- Russian cooperation is essential if Lithuania is to address border control problems.

Gorbenko's unhappiness with the roundtable, which the Lithuanians were conducting in Vilnius, was not the first time that he had refused his administration's participation in an international gathering. In May 1998, for example, Gorbenko canceled a seminar on Kaliningrad, which was sponsored by the New York-based East-West Institute, because the organizers had not given appropriate prenotification that they welcomed his appearance at the event. He could have given a "previous engagement" as a reason not to participate himself but he canceled the seminar altogether.

It was clear that as long as Gorbenko was governor, little could be done to address Kaliningrad's problems. But Western analysts familiar with Kaliningrad observed that the specter of a black hole was real, not a product of irresponsible speculation or driven by those who have a passion for hyperbole.

Researchers at Warsaw's Centre for Eastern Studies fear that the crisis of the Russian state will have grave consequences for Poland. They cite, among other things, the collapse of the tax system and the state's inability to provide the rule of law throughout the territory of the Russian federation.[28]

Indeed, Kaliningrad's neighbors have reason to be concerned about how a black hole there will affect them. Criminal gangs in concert with corrupt politicians may run the oblast as the drug cartels do in Latin America—that is, as a virtual government within a government. The Polish analysts at the Centre for Eastern Studies write in this connection about the "emergence and persistence of enclaves in Russia that are beyond control of any central authorities, and in which often all forms of statehood have disappeared."[29]

Officials in Berlin, London, Paris, and Stockholm, just like officials in the United States, may have to spend awesome sums of money and time to fight drug imports from Kaliningrad. Of course, they cannot be indifferent to the fact that even more dangerous contraband—such as weapons and weapons-grade nuclear materials—may transit through the oblast. Some observers of the military in Kaliningrad report that out of desperation they have sold weapons and ammunition to meet their neglected economic needs and that "Kaliningrad is one of the biggest arms bazaars in Russia."[30]

Money laundering, similar to the profitable operations functioning in the Caribbean, is another problem that the governments of Europe cannot ignore. Nor can they be indifferent to the fact that Kaliningrad can become a safe haven from which their own criminals can escape prosecution.

And even though Lithuania and Poland may be the first places where illegal immigrants from Kaliningrad go to escape untenable conditions at home, their final destinations will be farther to the West, where jobs and opportunities are deemed in abundance. European policy makers who think that strict visa regimes will stem the tide of desperate people need only witness the massive flood of Mexicans to the United States, a migration that has been occurring for decades in spite of the vast resources that Washington has allocated to curb it.

The handsome profits that can be gleaned from criminal activities of course will be used to spread corruption to states throughout the Baltic Sea region. Also, indigenous criminal organizations will forge links with the gangs in Kaliningrad giving the latter access to cities throughout Western Europe. There are already signs of such linkages between the Russian Mafia and organized gangs in Europe and in the United States as well.

Finally, one thing is clear. As long as Kaliningrad's economic troubles persist, authorities there will have neither the time, money, nor inclination to address their profound ecological problems. Efforts to cleanse the air, land, and waters of the oblast and adjacent areas will be compromised as a consequence. As indicated earlier, one of the only positive features of declining economic activity in Kaliningrad is that it has reduced the discharge of pollutants such as those produced by fossil powered engines that supply cars, homes, and factories. But even under existing circumstances, the ecological damage that can be traced to Kaliningrad in the Baltic Sea region is considerable and nullifies efforts adopted by other states to safeguard the region's ecology.

Belarus

In assessing the prospects that Kaliningrad will become a black hole, there is another aspect of the Kaliningrad Question that cannot be neglected—and that involves Belarus. A pivotal question here is: What are the consequences for the oblast and its neighbors should Belarus and Russia join in a true union or some other political arrangement?

In April 1996, Boris Yeltsin and Belarus President Aleksandr Lukashenko signed an agreement forming the Russia–Belarus Community. Some commentators interpreted the agreement as a ploy on Yeltsin's part to win the votes of Russian nationalists in his reelection bid that year. Indeed, Lukashenko later complained that Moscow did not live up to the agreement, that is, take actions that brought the two countries closer to a real union. But in the fall of 1999, the two leaders once again signed a union agreement—and the idea was popular with the Reds and Browns in the Russian Duma and apparently with potential Russian presidents such as Moscow Mayor Yuri Luzhkov.

Perhaps after Vladimir Putin was elected president in the spring of 2000, Lukashenko had reason to conclude that the drive toward Belarus–Russian union would be accelerated. After all, Putin was a former member of the KGB and, like most of his former colleagues, looked favorably upon Russia resuming control over areas that previously belonged to the USSR. But when Putin visited Belarus in the summer of 2000, he snubbed Lukashenko, reinforcing the opinions of observers who believe that under Putin a Belarus–Russian union is unlikely; instead, they foresee Putin taking actions that result in Belarus being reabsorbed into Russia.[31]

Lukashenko has been called a Soviet-style leader with good reason because he has employed police-state policies in oppressing his opponents. The Belarus KGB is alive and well in Minsk, and journalists as well as opposition politicians have been faced with beatings and arrests when they question Lukashenko's dictatorial policies. In 1999, several opposition leaders in Belarus disappeared. Unfortunately for democrats there and Belarus's neighbors, Lukashenko enjoys popular support among his people even though the country is in terrible economic shape.

The popularity of the man many people in Belarus call "Batka" (or father) rests upon the fact that the state in this country of about ten million people continues to function as it did during Soviet times. Most people in Belarus continue to work for state-owned enterprises and receive government subsidies and pensions. Lukashenko is especially popular among pensioners who account for 40 percent of the electorate but only 26 percent of the population. Clearly, the younger people in Belarus have remained estranged from the political system and are not active voters.[32]

But it is precisely those elements of the population hit hardest by the country's economic difficulties—the elderly, the urban poor, and those living in the countryside—who have displayed fond, nostalgic memories of the old system, much like their counterparts do in Russia. For them, Lukashenko's neo-Soviet policies are a breath of fresh air.

And sadly, Lukashenko's initial rise to power was accomplished through free elections. After being elected president in a popular election in 1994, Lukashenko disbanded the parliament and, through a referendum, extended his presidential term until 2001; a move that monitors from the Organization for Security and Cooperation (OSCE) have deemed illegal. More recently he has jailed political opponents and courageous journalists who question his dictatorial rule, or has forced them into exile. And to add to the international community's derisive assessment of his rule, in 1998 he ordered the water supply to Western diplomatic missions in Minsk be cut off.

Lukashenko has indicated that above and beyond his hostility to democratic liberties at home, he also favors strong centralized power in Russia. He stated in 1999, for example, that like Prime Minister Primakov he too believed that Russia's governors should be appointed by Russia's president and not selected by the people through popular elections. Lukashenko has attacked the West for adopting policies that he asserts are designed to destroy and not help Russia and other former Soviet republics.

Lukashenko's oppressive policies within Belarus aside, another source of concern to Minsk's neighbors is that Belarus enjoys high ceilings for Treaty Limited Equipment (TLEs) and has maintained a very high percentage of the weapons that it is allowed under the CFE agreement. For example, the CFE tank ceiling for Belarus is 1,800, whereas the tank ceiling for Poland, a country almost four times the size of Belarus, is 1,730. And whereas Belarus has an ACV ceiling of 2,600, it has maintained 2,518 ACVs in its arsenal; the same ACV figures for Poland are 2,150 and 1,442 respectively. Meanwhile, some military sources believe that Belarus has taken better care of its equipment than the Russians have in Kaliningrad.[33]

Lithuania has developed good relations with Belarus, and there are no outstanding border issues separating the two countries, which have signed a treaty of friendship. But in light of Lukashenko's antidemocratic proclivities, his reactionary friends in Moscow, and given the considerable military power under his command, officials in Vilnius and Warsaw have reason to cast a wary eye in his direction. In the fall of 1999, Lukashenko responded with anger to the news that the governments in Warsaw and Vilnius have supported accusations from Western bodies that Lukashenko had committed human rights violations in his country.

The people in Russia who respond most favorably to his appeals for "Slavic unity" are the same people who have complained about the plight of Russians in the Baltic states and overlook the trenchant fact that all Russians in Lithuania who desire citizenship have received it.

A true union between Russia and Belarus may ultimately flounder should Lukashenko conclude that he would not wield as much influence in Moscow as he hopes a union might delegate to him. Or Russian authorities may balk at the prospect of aligning with an economic basket case when their own economy remains problematic. But at some point Putin may seek to reabsorb Belarus into Russia, and if this occurs there will be consequences for Kaliningrad.

As one close student of Kaliningrad has observed: "From the Kaliningrad perspective, if Russia and Belarus become united on major political and economic policies, it would mean in part that Kaliningrad is not hundreds of kilometers from 'mainland' Russia but is only approximately one hundred kilometers from the Russia/Belarus Community."[34]

As long as the government in Moscow seeks close relations with the West, that may not mean very much. But should those who continue to harbor great power ambitions gain ascendancy, they will vent their hostility toward the West and Kaliningrad's neighbors. Therefore, NATO enlargement may be revisited by them and new demands upon Lithuania for a corridor to Kaliningrad may once again resurface.

Notes

1. Ingmar Oldberg, "Kaliningrad: Problems and Prospects" in *Kaliningrad: The European Amber Region,* ed. Pertti Joenniemi and Jan Prawitz (Aldershot: Ashgate, 1998), 1–31.

2. Lyndelle Fairlie, "Kaliningrad: Visions of the Future," in *Kaliningrad: The Amber Region,* ed. Joenniemi and Prawitz, 198.

3. Oldberg, "Kaliningrad: Problems and Prospects," 15.

4. Algirdas Gricius, "Russia's Exclave in the Baltic Region," in *Kaliningrad: The European Amber Region,* ed. Joenniemi and Prawitz, 157.

5. Steven Main, "The Prospects Posed by the Kaliningrad Oblast and Possible Solutions for the Future," paper, June 1997, 6.

6. Fairlie, "Kaliningrad: Visions," 219.

7. Fyodor I. Kushnirsky, "Post-Soviet Attempts to Establish Free Economic Zones," *Post-Soviet Geography and Economics* 38, no. 3 (summer 1997): 147.

8. Fairlie, "Kaliningrad: Visions," 199.

9. Interview, TACIS Staff, spring 1998.

10. Igor Korolkov, "The Kaliningrad District Has Become a Zone of Fear," *Izvestia*, 17 July 1999.

11. "The Social and Economic Situation in Kaliningrad," *Biuletyn Kaliningradzki* 43, no. 2 (Warsaw: February 1997): 11.

12. John Kramer, "The Politics of Corruption," *Current History* (October 1998), 329–34.

13. See, for example, Robert K. Merton, *On Theoretical Sociology* (New York: A Free Press, 1967), 125–36.

14. "The Social and Economic Situation," *Biuletyn Kaliningradzki*, February 1997, 10.

15. Helena Kropinova, "Environmental Issues of the Kaliningrad Region," in *Kaliningrad: The European Amber Region*, ed. Joenniemi and Prawitz, 103.

16. Kropinova, "Environmental Issues," 103.

17. Raimundas Lopata and Vladas Sirutavicius, "Lithuania and the Kaliningrad Oblast: A Clearer Frame for Cooperation," in *Lithuanian Foreign Policy Review*, no. 3 (summer 1999): 57. In discussion with U.S. and Lithuanian diplomats who have observed conditions in Kaliningrad and other parts of Russia closely, the author of this book learned that most seem to think that conditions in Kaliningrad compare favorably with those found in most parts of the federation.

18. *Moscow Times,* 24–30 September 1998, 4.

19. *Moscow Times,* 24–30 September 1998, 4.

20. Kaliningrad Duma Press Service, 28 September 1998.

21. *Jantar TV,* 28 September 1998.

22. *Kaliningradskya Pravda,* 24 September 1998, 6.

23. *Kaskad TV,* 29 September 1998.

24. *Baltic Times,* 11–17 February 1999, 6.

25. Richard Rose, "Similarities and Differences in Micro-Economic Conditions of Nationalities in Baltic States," paper presented at Stockholm School of Economics Conference, Riga, Latvia, 17–18 August 1995, 4.

26. *Moscow News,* 24–30 September 1998.

27. An undated statement from Lithuanian Foreign Ministry.

28. "The Year 1998," report from Centre for Eastern Studies, Warsaw, March 1999, 1.

29. "The Year 1988," 2.

30. Fairlie, "Kaliningrad: Visions," 204.

31. This observation was revealed in private discussions with Russian diplomats in Brussels in June 2000.

32. For a recent and incisive critique of development in Belarus, see Sherman W. Garnett and Robert Legvold, eds., *Belarus at the Crossroads* (Washington, D.C.: Carnegie Endowment for International Peace, 1999).

33. *Swedish Peace Research Institute Yearbook,* 1997, 470.

34. Fairlie, "Kaliningrad: Visions," 183.

Russian woman. *Photo courtesy of Leonardas Surgaila.*

Zheleznodorozhny. *Photo courtesy of Leonardas Surgaila.*

Amber pit mine, Palmnicken. The western Samland coast, and Palmnicken/Yantarny in particular, is the source of more than 90 percent of European amber. *Photo courtesy of Joost Lemmens.*

The House of Soviets, Kaliningrad, was built by Leonid Brezhnev on the site of a ruined Prussian castle. The structure has never been occupied. *Photo courtesy of Koen Rijnsent.*

Castle, Mayovka. *Photo courtesy of Leonardas Surgaila.*

Russian man, Vesnovo. *Photo courtesy of Leonardas Surgaila.*

Military and commercial ships in Pillau Harbor. *Photo courtesy of Joost Lemmens.*

Two Russian girls, Nagornoje. *Photo courtesy of Leonardas Surgaila.*

6

The EU and Kaliningrad

First European Efforts to Address
the Kaliningrad Question

IN MARCH 1993, Magdalene Hoff, a member of the European Parliament and chairwoman of its Delegation for the Commonwealth of Independent States, went on a fact-finding mission to Kaliningrad. Heinz Timmermann, a researcher at Cologne's German Institute for Eastern and International Studies, joined her.

They found speculation about the future of Kaliningrad in unofficial Russian circles and among neighboring states that suggested a host of outcomes. For example, Kaliningrad could become a "military outpost of Russia," "an autonomous republic within the Russian Federation," or a "Euro or Hanseatic region," or "part of a condominium with the surrounding states," or an independent "fourth Baltic republic."[1] The authors deemed all of these outcomes unlikely, barring the disintegration of the Russian Federation. However, all of them "underline the urgency of reflecting anew on the region's future: maintaining the status quo would . . . bring economic ruin on Kaliningrad and destabilize the entire Baltic area politically and militarily."[2] If existing conditions remained unchanged, the EC's policy of promoting stability in the Baltic Sea region (note: this is before the Maastricht Treaty and the introduction of the European Union or EU) would become a casualty of the Kaliningrad Question. On the other hand, were the EU to cooperate with Russia, the destabilizing forces spawned by Kaliningrad might be avoided. Neighboring governments believed a more benign outcome could be reached with a troop reduction in Kaliningrad, "the establishment of a special economic zone within the Russian Federation," and the oblast's joining the Baltic littoral states in economic development schemes. Hoff and Timmermann stated categorically that Kaliningrad should not be re-Germanized. "So far as Germany and the political parties in Bonn are concerned, Kaliningrad is not a German problem; it is a European one."[3] Both the Christian Democrats and the Social Democrats have embraced this prescription—consequently neither has aggressively addressed the Kaliningrad Question. This also helps explain why the EU over the years has been reluctant to do so.

Simultaneously, they reported, the Russian authorities did not have a clear picture of what changes in Kaliningrad's internal structure needed to be made to improve its economy. Nor were they sure about Kaliningrad's relations with neighboring states. Some Russian officials favored the creation of a free economic zone there with broad prerogatives; others advocated a closer relationship with the Center; and still others envisaged Kaliningrad as a military bastion that would help protect Russia from enemies to its west. Vladimir Zhirinovsky told a right-wing German gathering in August 1992 that he saw it as part of a German–Russian mutual alliance. In an obvious attempt to please his audience he said, "The northeast Prussian and Konigsberg question would, in any event, be solved to Germany's advantage."[4] Since then, other Russian ultranationalists have spoken about Russia getting Belarus and Ukraine back and the Germans receiving their old East Prussia territories in return. Such bizarre notions, of course, tell us more about the quirky psychological state of their authors than about a concrete and rational approach to the Kaliningrad Question. Hoff and Timmermann feared that the combination of maintaining a large number of Russian troops in the oblast, while Moscow struggled to provide Kaliningrad with the same high level of subsidies that it enjoyed during the Soviet era, was a formula for mischief. Moscow's most plausible option was to integrate Kaliningrad's economy with those of its neighbors. Some in the Russian Foreign Ministry realized that to deny Russia's regions the opportunity to cooperate with neighboring countries would in fact "stimulate separatist" tendencies. This prospect was cited in a discussion of Russia's Far Eastern and Siberian regions in the Foreign Ministry's November 1992 "Foreign-Policy Concept of the Russian Federation."

The German observers said it was in the West's interest to help integrate Kaliningrad into the Baltic area economy through regional cooperation with Russia. "It is precisely the EC that could make an important contribution here as participant, coordinator, and mediator, particularly since it is a focal reference point for the countries of the region and, as an integrative alliance, it stands above the parties concerned."[5]

The authors concluded, "Kaliningrad's opportunities lie above all in the fact that it is a relatively small and therefore manageable region, in which clear rules and responsibilities can be not only established but also implemented."[6] In the final analysis, however, the success of any campaign to prevent Kaliningrad from becoming a source of instability in Europe depended on the cooperation of authorities there and their superiors in Moscow. Here they identified a serious barrier to cooperation, since many officials in Moscow feared granting special economic status to Kaliningrad lest it encourage separatists in other parts of Russia. This fear was in keeping with another concern: that the devolution of power to the regions would only weaken Moscow's capacity to rule a country already riven by centrifugal political forces.

As early as 1993, the Hoff and Timmermann report provided a detailed account of the problems associated with the Kaliningrad Question and why it was imperative that the EC address them. But to better understand why the EC has been slow in developing a comprehensive development plan for Kaliningrad, a few words about the EC/EU's relations with "the East" are in order.

The EU and Eastward Expansion

In 1988, diplomatic relations were initiated between the EC and the Soviet-dominated Council for Mutual Economic Assistance. That same year, the European Commission with the support of the United States began to function as the main coordinator between the West and the Central and Eastern Europe (CEE) states. In response to rapid changes taking place in Poland and Hungary, the Polish and Hungary Aid for the Reconstruction of Economies Program (PHARE) was started under pressure from Germany. In May 1990, the European Bank for Reconstruction and Development (EBRD) was established by the EC and member states to provide loans to promote market reforms in the former Communist countries to the east. The campaign to promote democratic reform was not a new departure for the EU. In 1981, the EC enlarged southward, when it accepted Greece, and again in 1986 when Portugal and Spain became members. In each case the EC sought to convert autocratic regimes into democratic polities. Moreover, political and not economic considerations were the driving force behind this campaign.

As a result of these measures, the CEE states assumed quick membership in the EC to facilitate their "return to Europe." But the EC countries were unprepared for the collapse of Communism, and the task of making room for Europe's new democracies was seen as a daunting one. At this point, the EC became preoccupied with the ratification of the Maastricht Treaty (which did not come about until November 1, 1993), the creation of the European Monetary Union (EMU) and the process of deepening the organization through institutional reform. To complicate matters, Europe at midpoint in the decade was stricken by recession as it grappled with the aftershocks of economic globalization.

At the 1993 Copenhagen Summit, the EC presented potential member states with a set of political, economic, and legal requirements that they needed to comply with before they entered "Europe." The Poles et al. were somewhat put off by the fact that the East Germans gained membership in the EC effortlessly with the reunification of Germany. What's more, they were told by bureaucrats in Brussels that EC enlargement would not proceed until efforts to deepen the EC were completed. Naturally they were unhappy with what they correctly perceived as reluctance on the part of officials in Brussels to enlarge the organization eastward. The leaders of the constituent EU states, however, continued to assert that the door to the EU was open to all CEE countries. CEE officials chose to ignore conflicting messages from EU bureaucrats and leaders from the member states out of fear that this would feed the Euro-skeptics in their own societies. They also were reluctant to concede that they were prepared to accept any delay in their achieving EU membership.

After adoption of the Maastricht Treaty, political dynamics within the EU further compromised the CEE states' quest for membership as France lobbied for the EU turning its attention toward the Mediterranean and not the east. Paris feared eastward expansion would enhance Germany's influence within the EU, and Spain was not too happy about eastward enlargement, either. Madrid was worried that funds already going to poorer members of the EU would henceforth be earmarked for the new CEE democracies.[7]

As an analogue to PHARE, the EC established the Technical Assistance to the Commonwealth of Independent States program (TACIS) to help former Soviet Republics with technical assistance, although the three Baltic countries were designated for PHARE. Along with the TACIS program, PHARE would create the conditions for expanding the EU from Western to Eastern Europe. Many leaders and ordinary people in the existing EU countries, however, remained skeptical about the wisdom of eastward expansion.

"Enlargement is a declaration of war on all industrious and hardworking people in Austria. We demand that the question of enlargement be removed from the EU's agenda."[8] These harsh words belonged to the telegenic far-right Austrian politician, Jorg Haider, whose anti-immigrant Freedom Party came in third place in the 1999 parliamentary elections, when it captured fifty-two seats. In February 2000 an international uproar erupted when the Freedom Party joined a government formed by the conservative People's Party. In a show of solidarity the other fourteen states in the EU warned that Austria would suffer political repercussions by allowing Haider—who among other things had praised Hitler's "labor policies"—to enter the government.

But Haider stated openly what many politicians of all persuasions in Europe were thinking privately along with many of their constituents— although they were more prudent in hiding their real feelings.

The West Europeans' reaction to the collapse of Communism in Eastern Europe has been mixed. On the one hand, they have taken comfort in the disappearance of the Soviet threat, which preoccupied them for almost fifty years; but on the other hand they fear that with the USSR's collapse their countries will be subjected to a flood of refugees, hungry workers, and aggressive criminals. The Iron Curtain's disintegration, then, has not been an altogether happy event for them.

Today many Europeans, already in the EU, believe that its enlargement eastward will compromise their security as legal and illegal immigrants cross their borders and take their jobs or commit crimes against them and their communities. By 1989, an estimated 1.3 million former residents of the Communist lands in the East had fled to the West. Today that number is much higher.[9] The once tightly controlled borders separating East and West have become porous, and poorly regulated in the Cold War's aftermath. The Western news media has paid considerable attention to the refugees' criminal behavior; tales about the skill and daring demonstrated by "Eastern bloc" car thieves and the speed with which they work, in particular, have become legendary. For example, one may read about the owner of a Mercedes parking his car for a long lunch in Berlin and by the time he leaves the restaurant to retrieve it, the vehicle is in Poland being prepared for sale at a car auction. Indeed in one such case, an upscale Mercedes came into the possession of a Lithuanian minister. Appropriately, he was the minister of transportation. Even after the Lithuanian press disclosed its problematic origins, it was only with great reluctance that he returned the car to its rightful owner.

Farmers in Western Europe, who receive generous agricultural subsidies from their governments, fear cheap food imports from the CEE states and they have opposed expanding the EU for that reason. As mentioned earlier, poorer members of the EU, such as Greece, Portugal, and Spain, fear EU grants that now go to them will be earmarked for the CEE states should they become members. As Elizabeth Pond has observed, the income of the CEE candidate states is one-third of the EU average so they can make the case that they deserve the kind of help Portugal and Spain have received.[10]

Fears about economic competition and crime aside, there is another factor that explains misgivings in Western Europe about the Iron Curtain's collapse. "Like any other immigration wave, the great influx of foreigners could not only impose an economic burden on the EU countries, but also be perceived as a threat to national identity and culture."[11] Some Western Europeans, in other words, do not look upon their brethren from the East as being fellow Europeans but as representatives from another "alien culture." Recall that this is one of the reasons that the EU and NATO failed to address Yugoslavia's disintegration, and to prevent the awful killing that has occurred there.[12] This propensity to view people from the East as "aliens" was exemplified by the widely heard remark in Paris, Bonn, and London in the early 1990s that "those people in the Balkans have been killing themselves for centuries." The same could be said of the French and Germans but the idea that the "people to the East are radically different" from those in West Europe has died hard. The same sentiment was expressed in the United States to explain why Washington should not get entangled in the Balkans.

It is against the backdrop of fears about EU enlargement that the Schengen agreement must be evaluated. In 1985 five Western European states initialed an agreement to facilitate the free movement of travelers from the signatory states by removing visa and other barriers that previously obstructed transit beyond their home countries. Ten years later, the Schengen Implementing Convention clarified how it would be applied in practice as more states signed it. But facilitating free movement among citizens from the member states was only one incentive for additional countries becoming party to Schengen.

Tony Judt contends that when the Benelux countries, France, Germany, Portugal, and Spain, signed Schengen, much was said about the abolishment of frontiers and the harmonization of visas and immigration legislation. "A person allowed into Portugal would thus be free to roam as far as the Polish frontier, unquestioned and unmolested; the very incarnation of a postnational Europe." That is the positive side of the agreement, but there is another edge to it: "In practice, of course, the agreement means something quite different. It means that whichever state has the most draconian and exclusive immigration and/or labor laws will be able to impose its requirements on all others—a sort of highest common factor of discriminatory political arithmetic."[13]

By insisting that future members adhere to the strict acquis—rules—of Schengen, the EU is thrusting new barriers in their path. But does this really promote the internal security concerns of the EU states? Lykke Friis writes, "If the EU increases the membership threshold and sets unrealistic entry criteria, some applicants could be left outside the door for a long time. The result of this could be that the EU is confronted by exactly those internal security problems, which it set out to avoid—extra-territorial spillover, such as immigration and organized crime."[14]

The clear obstacles to eastward expansion notwithstanding, the CEE states assumed they would become EU members early in the first decade of the twenty-first century.

The EU and Its Programs for Kaliningrad

After the initial Hoff–Timmermann assessment of the Kaliningrad Question, a number of TACIS programs were funded in the oblast. They were designed with two major goals in mind: "to provide assistance in the transition to market economies and to contribute to the strengthening of democratic societies."[15] In the early 1990s, the European Parliament declared Kaliningrad a priority region for TACIS support and began conducting six major programs there. The individual projects were:

1. A program conducted at Kaliningrad State University to develop an undergraduate curriculum in business and economics.
2. A program conducted with the participation of Moscow's Gaidar Institute for Economies in Transition to develop an economic development plan for Kaliningrad.
3. A program designed to help restructure the oblast's fishing industry.
4. A project that provides consulting advice to newly privatized small and medium-size business enterprises.
5. A large project to develop Kaliningrad's transportation system—roads, rail, sea, and air—and to integrate it into the region's transports network.
6. A project with the regional administration to establish an economic development program consistent with the special economic zone.

In the spring of 1998, personnel from the TACIS program in Kaliningrad traveled to Moscow and warned their superiors in the European Commission that the oblast was in danger of becoming a black hole in Europe. In keeping with Hoff and Timmermann's report, they observed that the EU was the only body in Europe capable of preventing Kaliningrad from exporting its problems beyond its borders. It alone had the political influence and economic resources to develop a truly comprehensive systemic approach to the Kaliningrad Question.

In June 1998, the Kaliningrad TACIS team delivered a formal report to

Brussels. It addressed the question: Why is Kaliningrad unique? According to Stephen Dewar, who directed a TACIS program in Kaliningrad for several years, the report cited six reasons that Kaliningrad was special:

1. "Kaliningrad's exclave status, among other things, explains why Moscow deems one of its smallest regions so strategically vital to Russia."
2. The oblast's military/defense-dependent economy.
3. With the dissolution of the Baltic Economic Area, Kaliningrad has been cut off from economic linkages it enjoyed during the Soviet era.
4. Kaliningrad has been Russian a mere fifty years and it has a "lingering identity crisis."[16]
5. "More than any other Federal Subject in Russia, Kaliningrad is geographically close to numerous foreign states. . . ."[17] Indeed, it is surrounded by them.
6. NATO expansion to Kaliningrad has caused Moscow to see a military threat looming on the horizon that is exaggerated. But it "has obscured the far more serious threat of EU enlargement."[18]

To provide comprehensive assistance to Kaliningrad, however, the EU had to scale several obstacles. First, throughout the 1990s, Moscow did not display interest in working with the international community to address the Kaliningrad Question. Indeed Russian authorities deemed suggestions of this nature as attempts to interfere in their country's internal affairs. Consequently, officials in Brussels saw little reason for the EU to pay special attention to the region.

Second, as Dewar noted in a 1999 presentation in Moscow, "The only concrete offer in the EU–Russia Partnership and Co-operation Agreement (PCA) is the aspiration towards the creation of an eventual trade area. And this arrangement, understandably, will apply to Russia as a whole, not to selected Federal Subjects. Thus, Kaliningrad's eventual participation in this FTA (Free Trade Area) will depend on when—and if—Russia as a whole participates."[19]

On December 1, 1997, the EU and Russia signed the PCA. According to a TACIS publication, "The PCA commits the EU and Russia to intensify their political and economic relationships, to support the reform process in Russia and to strengthen political developments, as well as promoting Russia's integration into a wider European economic arena. Ultimately, the objective is to foster an economic rapprochement between the EU and Russia, which, after Russia's accession to the WTO, could possibly lead to the establishment of a free trade area. As a first step, approximation of Russian laws to European Community legislation will be of significance."[20]

But as Dewar has indicated, this agreement is restricted to trade and does not address crucial development issues. Nonetheless from 1991 to 1997, a total of 1,060.79 million ECUs were provided to Russia through TACIS in a variety of areas:

- nuclear safety and environment
- restructuring state enterprises and private sector development
- public administration reform, social services, and education
- agriculture
- energy
- transport
- policy advice
- telecommunications

A third obstacle was that the Kaliningrad watchers had not convinced EU officials that the oblast deserved special attention and they had doubts about the wisdom of introducing a major development program for Kaliningrad.[21] They also were unmoved by the threat that it could become a black hole. Moscow's apparent disinterest in the region was an additional reason that Brussels saw no urgent reason to address the Kaliningrad Question. What's more, they had grave reservations about enlarging the EU eastward, especially before the organization addressed its own problems such as crafting a more rational voting scheme and resolving other issues of governance. The simple truth was, that the EU had to "deepen before it widened."

Moscow's brutal assault on Chechnya represented a fourth obstacle to the EU providing major funding for the Russian TACIS projects and addressing the Kaliningrad Question in particular. Money for the TACIS programs was cut during the first war in the mid-1990s and the same thing happened with the onset of the second war in Chechnya beginning in 1999. Furthermore, the Council of Europe denied Russia voting rights in that body to protest Russia's brutal operations in Chechnya.

The Northern Dimension

As of mid-1999, while the EU bureaucrats remained opposed to any Kaliningrad Action Program, individual governments continued to adopt and implement programs that addressed Kaliningrad's problems. For example, Sweden's Foreign Ministry funded a study to determine how Kaliningrad might become a point of instability in the region. The Swedes also conducted work to provide clean water supplies and aerial-mapped Kaliningrad farmland as a first step toward its ultimate reclamation. Meanwhile, the Danes, through a variety of initiatives, provided funding amounting to $8 million, while the German Ministry of Interior provided humanitarian assistance to ethnic Germans in Kaliningrad.[22]

But two years earlier Finland proposed that the EU adopt a "Northern Dimension" to its activities that was potentially significant to Kaliningrad.

At the December 1997 European Council meeting in Luxembourg, the Finns submitted a proposal that "the Northern region is of particular significance to the EU. It is a region of great natural resources, with considerable human and economic potential. Aspects of its environmental situation are a cause for concern and will present a major challenge to future generations." Furthermore, "The Northern region is also the Union's only direct geographical link with the Russian Federation and, as such, is important for cooperation between the EU and that country."[23]

The Finns indicated they neither saw the need to develop a separate program nor did they deem it necessary to provide additional funds to the region. In an attempt to placate taxpayers in the member states, the proposal mentioned "adding value" to existing programs and activities but it indicated categorically that the new initiative was a vital part of the campaign to integrate Russia into the European community of states. "It can contribute to the strengthening of the Union's external policies and reinforcement of the positive interdependence between Russia and the Baltic Sea region and the European Union, notably by achieving further synergies and coherence in these policies and actions."[24]

The proposal also underscored the specter of a black hole about which the TACIS experts in Kaliningrad had warned. "Differences in border areas between the Union and the Russian Federation are considerable. In the Russian Federation the infant mortality rate is today approximately six times higher than in neighboring Finland. Life expectancy at birth is less than 57 years in Russia, 77 in Finland. Narrowing down the disparities in living standards is today one of the major challenges for the Northern region."[25] The proposal provided other reasons that the EU should be concerned about the situation in Russia. Its energy resources were critical to Europe and over time dependence upon Russia's oil and gas would grow, not diminish. Meanwhile, the region's environment was vulnerable to degradation and environmental problems in the Kola Peninsula—not to mention Russia's dependence on nuclear power, which produced the additional monumental task of dealing with nuclear waste.

Other areas of activity needed attention too. "The economic development and interdependency of the North will require the development of transport infrastructures and establishment of new connections with Europeanwide networks. Road and railway connections linking the European Community and the candidate countries in northern Europe (Estonia, Latvia, Lithuania, and Poland) as well as Russia, will require the further development of transport infrastructure and border crossing facilities."[26] Development of the northern region meant upgrading and expanding telecommunications throughout the area. Finally, "Illegal trafficking in drugs, nuclear material, illegal migration, criminal activities across borders, money laundering, social, training, and health issues, including reinforcement of consumer protection, veterinary, and phytosanitary control are problems to be addressed."[27]

Kaliningrad was not mentioned in the first draft of the proposal, and in the final one it was cited only once. "Programs of technical assistance devised to promote customs cooperation, future administration training and cooperation in the fight against organized crime should be considered through cross-border cooperation programs, for border areas, i.e., for the Kaliningrad region of the Russian Federation."[28] Both Lithuanian and Polish diplomats lobbied their Finnish colleagues to mention Kaliningrad in the document and in this campaign they were supported by Kaliningrad watchers from other countries.

The crisis in Kosovo, however, "partially scuttled Finland's plan to have its six-month EU presidency focus on the northeastern portion of Europe."[29] Then later in 1999, the Kremlin's brutal military operations in Chechnya were a further incentive for the EU to back away from developmental help to Russia. When France held the presidency in 2000, no further movement to advance the Northern Dimension initiative occurred given the French government's disinterest in expanding the EU eastward, that is, toward a region where German power was pronounced.

Once Poland entered the EU, Warsaw would add its voice to an EU-backed development program for Kaliningrad. Polish officials believed the EU had to address the "civilization gap" that existed in Eastern Europe, to wit: while economic conditions markedly improved in Poland and the Baltic states, adjoining territories and states—Kaliningrad, Belarus, and Ukraine—would experience economic stagnation and political drift and disarray. Poland did not want to serve as an EU "border-watch tower" as the first line of defense against the overflow of disgruntled and potentially dangerous migrants from the old Soviet Union.

Polish analysts warned their German neighbors that Berlin could not be indifferent to the threat from the eastern borderlands. "The issue of relations between the EU and CIS partners, especially Russia and Ukraine, should in the first place become a center of the Polish–German dialogue along with such fundamental questions as, e.g., the dates of Polish entry into the EU, mobility of labour force or other important bilateral issues."[30] The Poles feared that Germany, which supported their membership in NATO, would be satisfied with both EU and NATO enlargement after Germany no longer was a "frontline" state.

Poland claimed that the oblast's neighbors by themselves could not address Kaliningrad's problems and that a much more comprehensive effort had to be taken to address the Kaliningrad Question. Poland along with Lithuania, through roundtables and conferences, warned the EU that it could not ignore Kaliningrad as it moved east. Indeed, the specter of Kaliningrad being shut off from Poland and Lithuania once they both joined the EU was the subject of much debate among officials in Kaliningrad, and even ordinary folk, who appreciated that their economic welfare was closely linked to open commerce with both countries and easy access to them. Some special arrangement between the EU and Kaliningrad involving visa regimes and commercial relations had to be considered lest Kaliningrad be placed in an even more difficult situation than that it had already endured.

On May 21, 1999, the EU Council responded favorably to the Northern Dimension Initiative and the priorities it had outlined—transport, energy, environmental, educational, health, cross-border, trade, and investment programs. This decision to pay greater attention to Russia perhaps was linked to NATO's war against Serbia that spring, which led to discord between Russia and the NATO countries. Presumably, while some in the EU cited Moscow's attack on NATO to halt assistance to Russia, others believed just the opposite step was the more prudent course of action. But as Russian forces flattened Grozny, the EU curbed assistance to Moscow in general and the French later ignored the Northern dimension in particular after they took control of the presidency.

Second Thoughts about Eastward Expansion

By the spring of 2000 it was reported that both German industrialists and members of the ruling Social Democratic Party were having second thoughts about bringing a new group of CEE states into the EU by 2003. That was the date designated for the enlargement of the EU toward them. In private, some German commentators said that these states "were not ready for membership." Other European analysts, who had long argued that the EU should "deepen" before it "widens," could cite the Euro crisis as cause for halting the process. The Euro's worth by then had plunged about 20 percent in relationship to the dollar. Joshka Fisher, the German Foreign Minister, gave a speech in Berlin where he urged the EU to consider a fundamental change in its governance—creating a truly federal system was one of the options he said had to be considered.[31] Opponents of Fisher's "radical" idea exploited the publicity his speech had generated by once again stressing that the EU had to consolidate the position of its core states before providing membership to those countries in the former communist east who were seeking it. This was the position of the French government—in spite of public declarations to the contrary. As indicated earlier, the French were wary of eastward expansion because it would enhance Germany's influence in the EU, which was already considerable and Paris felt its interest lay in the south and not the east of Europe. Many British commentators did not need much coaxing to rethink the enlargement timetable since the "Brits" had doubts about the wisdom of doing so in the first place and the Thatcherites disparaged the EU altogether.

Another argument against EU enlargement eastward surfaced at this time—U.S. hegemony and Washington's capacity to dominate NATO. The dominant role that the U.S. played in the Kosovo conflict deepened European concerns about "U.S. power." Some CEE diplomats had informed their U.S. counterparts that "certain European colleagues" had told them that their accession represented nothing less than an American "Trojan Horse" in the EU. Still smarting from the embarrassment they had suffered during NATO's war on Serbia—when NATO had to rely so heavily upon U.S. military assets—the Europeans were not about to allow the Americans to have a voice in "matters EU."

In May 2000, the EU Summit was held in Portugal and presummit reports indicated that the questions of both "enlargement" and "deepening" would be treated at the high-level gathering. But in press reports afterward, it was learned that the issue of eastward expansion was mentioned only once and informally. Perhaps even more surprising, the delegates did not reach any new conclusions about the priority question of how the EU should make institutional changes necessary to address its governance and relations among the states already members.[32]

The fact that the major EU leaders could not address a question that they had declared pivotal to the organization's future further deepened concern in the CEE states about the EU's capacity to enlarge even assuming it wanted to do so. It was against this backdrop that Euro-skeptics in the CEE countries had reason to complain about another disturbing trend. Namely, while officials in Brussels asserted that "deepening" had to take priority over "enlarging"—meaning a delay in the next round was unavoidable—leaders like Chancellor Schroeder and President Chirac maintained that the "door to the EU" remained open to the former Communist lands of Europe.

Euro-skeptics in Prague, Warsaw, and Tallinn were wary of this discrepancy. They also had cause to challenge EU officials who maintained that the issue of membership rested solely on economic criteria. Even casual observers of the EU might ask: Were economic criteria alone responsible for Portugal's accession to the EU? What's more, were economic criteria the basis for the EU's Common Agricultural Policy (CAP), or did it exist largely because of the French agricultural lobby? Finally, the Germans demanded that any country seeking to adopt the Euro had to meet certain specific requirements—for example, limits on deficit spending—but even the Germans were said to have cooked the books so that they could meet the required limits.

In late June 2000, the EU held a conference in Brussels, "A New Iron Curtain? EU–Russia Relations in Focus." Some of the participants mentioned the gap between promises from member states' political leadership about eastward enlargement on the one hand and the reluctance of officials in the EU to move in that direction on the other hand. It made little sense for the political leaders to persist in making such promises when their advisers, and often they themselves in private, argued the new candidates in the east were not ready to comply with the EU's Acquis Communautaire. If a delay was in order, the CEE states should be told so at once. Failure to do so would strain relations between the Western and Eastern Europeans.[33]

But another reason for rethinking the enlargement timetable surfaced at the conference. EU officials and analysts reported that Moscow had begun to publicly display interest in the relationship between Kaliningrad and EU enlargement. Specifically, Russian officials voiced concern that once Poland and the Baltic States became EU members, Kaliningrad would be confronted with a new, strict visa regime that would have a profound impact upon the oblast's residents and business interests.

Officials and politicians in Kaliningrad had been making this observation for some time, but now their colleagues in Moscow realized that EU enlargement might not be as benign as they once thought—on the contrary, it could have a profound economic impact on all of Russia. Trade and commercial relations between the CEE states and Russia, in short, could be revised at Russia's expense.

As officials in Moscow began to display concern about the impact of EU enlargement upon their interests, opponents of the move exploited the Russians' skepticism to argue against it. They noted that about 40 percent of Russia's trade was with the EU and the Europeans were dependent upon Russia for much of their gas and oil. Trends indicated that the EU's dependence upon Russia's energy exports would grow over time. Why then take any measure that might cause friction with Russia? Did it make sense to enlarge the EU at the expense of harmonious economic relations with such an important energy partner?

Also, why rile the waters when Russia was still trying to achieve political stability. European leaders did not make public remarks to this effect but how could they ignore growing Russian concerns about enlargement?

Addressing the Kaliningrad Question

At the Helsinki European Council in December 1999, Kaliningrad was mentioned by both the Russian and European participants. Indeed, Vladimir Putin spoke of the oblast as a "pilot region." His wife Ludmila called Kaliningrad her hometown and her mother still lived there. In other meetings in the spring of 2000, for example, in Copenhagen, Danish diplomats concluded that Moscow at last was ready to work with the EU in addressing the Kaliningrad Question.

Nonetheless, European Commission officials based in Moscow remained skeptical about Russia working with the EU to address the Kaliningrad Question, but later in 2000, during a visit to Paris, Putin said he saw EU enlargement as an opportunity, not a problem, for Russia. In November during a conference in Moscow, Russian participants displayed a more positive attitude toward eastward enlargement. Natalya Smorodinskaya, an economist with special interest in Kaliningrad, urged the EU to act with greater dispatch in addressing the region's problems. Richard Wright, the European Commission ambassador to Russia, said, without singling out Kaliningrad, that the EU through the "northern dimension would provide $250 million to Russia's Northwest."[34]

On December 11 at the EU summit in Nice, the EU announced that the CEE countries next in line for membership—Estonia, the Czech Republic, Hungary, and Poland—would enter the organization by 2004. The CEE candidate states greeted this news with pleasure after they heard reports that the EU might delay the next round even further.

Early in 2001, Chris Patten, the EU official in charge of foreign relations encouraged Russia, Poland, and Lithuania to cooperate in addressing the Kaliningrad Question. Patten's words of encouragement were consistent with publication of an EU document that warned about Kaliningrad becoming a black hole in Europe. The economic prospects of the oblast and its neighbors were growing apart. For example, Kaliningrad's per capita gross domestic product was $500, five times less than Lithuania and forty times less than the EU average.[35]

A detailed discussion of what specific measures are needed to address Kaliningrad's economic, social, and ecological problems is beyond the purview of this book. Stephen Dewar, however, who has managed the special economic zone project for TACIS in Kaliningrad, has provided an outline of what must be done to develop its economy.

Economic development in Kaliningrad can rest neither upon exploitation of vast natural resources nor upon growth generated by a large domestic market. "Kaliningrad's future lies as an international trading city and region." That is the conclusion of the TACIS consultants who have been working there since the early 1990s. The region's development involves three things: "First, Kaliningrad must develop as a major transport centre—a 'conduit' or 'pipe' facilitating the flow of goods and services between Russia and the rest of the world."[36] But even if the oblast overcomes competition with other transport centers in the region or finds its own niche there, a second requirement is needed, international trade. The objective here is "to 'capture' opportunities to develop internationally traded goods and services industries in the Oblast. . . . This could take many forms, such as bulk-breaking of commodities passing through the ports right up to the introduction of brand-new industries, such as computer software development, which is one of several areas we are looking at in our project."[37]

"The third prong is to turn Kaliningrad into an international marketplace—to become the place which Russians and foreigners who do business together choose as their preferred location."[38]

To achieve these objectives, Dewar argues that Kaliningrad must work with what it already has and this means making the special economic zone viable, keeping in mind that it is not the only one in the region. Also, Kaliningrad must develop a special relationship with the EU. "Precisely what form this relationship should or could take remains to be determined, but many options are conceivable, from financial transfers to reduce the inequalities that the present situation is inadvertently creating through to various institutional arrangements." Finally, "as an international trading and transport centre we want to see Kaliningrad become the easiest part of Russia for people to enter."[39] For example, problems that foreign investors and business people currently encounter in other parts of Russia concerning visas, other travel restrictions, and currency controls will be eliminated as they will be more or less issued instantaneously or liberalized.

Writing elsewhere with Pertti Joenniemi and Lyndelle Fairlie, Dewar says that the EU faces three scenarios of indifference, isolation and integration.

Indifference

"In this scenario, the relationship between the EU and Kaliningrad continues as much as it has up to now." There may be programmatic changes but "they will, however, continue to lack a strategic framework that recognizes the special features of the region as the EU enlarges to encircle it."

Isolation

"In this scenario, the EU recognizes that Kaliningrad is falling far behind its neighbors in the Baltic region, both economically and socially. However, it decides that this is an internal Russian problem, partly because Russia itself insists that direct foreign involvement with the regions is not particularly welcome. . . ." Also, the EU may decide that "Russia as a whole is so far from reaching an acceptable level of sustainable progress in the transition to a market economy and a functioning pluralistic democracy, that further support would represent a poor investment of EU taxpayers' funds."

Integration

"In this scenario the EU recognizes that Kaliningrad is, de facto, a member of the European family. With or without the active cooperation of Moscow (though hardly possible in the face of formal opposition from that quarter), the EU actively cooperates with Kaliningrad in the construction and implementation of a Baltic regional development policy, within which Kaliningrad is treated as an equal partner." Kaliningrad would not be treated exactly as other states, but "Kaliningrad would receive the same level of assistance pro rata as the neighboring states."

The authors of these scenarios believe only the third course of action represents a relevant response to the Kaliningrad Question, and claim integration "is in the end the most probable scenario, although a challenging one and difficult to implement. This has also been the option that Russian central authorities seem to have had to some extent in mind during the first part of the nineties and which appears recently to have experienced something of a come-back."[40]

Even if the influential members of the EU become convinced that Kaliningrad deserves special attention—because of its unique place in Europe and the threats it poses to the region—advocates of an EU Kaliningrad initiative face some difficult obstacles.

In addition to those already mentioned, a major one is that Russia must adopt reforms that demonstrate to taxpayers in the West that the help they provide Kaliningrad will be used effectively and not wind up in the bank accounts of criminal lords. The factors discouraging private investors from risking money in Russia cannot be ignored by the EU or individual governments that are prepared to provide significant help. The reforms that Russia must adopt before the West provides extensive assistance and investments include the following:

1. Developing commercial legislation that protects both Russian and foreign investors including laws that guarantee contracts, property rights, and other safeguards that investors can customarily rely upon in mature capitalist countries.
2. Ending political corruption that has been responsible—according to some accounts—for the virtual disappearance of IMF and other funds provided to Russia, and which compels entrepreneurs to bribe officials at several levels of government to conduct even the most mundane business activities.
3. Seriously curtailing the power of organized crime to impose awesome costs upon doing business in Russia and placing the safety of foreigners working there at risk.
4. Adopting fiscal and monetary policies that protect investors against wild swings in ruble valuation and the transfer of funds within and outside of Russia.
5. Creating a federal system that is not based upon personal political deals between the Center and the regions but the rule of law; in other words, a federal system that provides the regions with the power to address regional issues in much the same fashion that states do in the United States or provinces do in Canada.
6. Establishing a sound banking system that strictly adheres to the principle of transparency.

The failure of Russia to adopt these reforms has been cited by European legislators and members of the U.S. Congress to justify the West's limiting help to Russia that is only humanitarian in substance or to prevent the spread of nuclear materials and missile components to pariah states. Support among the West European publics to fund an EU program to help Kaliningrad may become a reality should Putin provide investors with a safe climate for doing business. The programs that are being considered in this connection are all consistent with the goals discussed in the Northern Dimension proposal:

- to promote economic development, stability, and security in the region
- to address cross-border issues
- to contribute to narrowing the disparities of living standards and prevent and ward off threats originating in the region
- to contribute to reducing environmental and nuclear threats

By 2001, while the EU was considering how to address the Kaliningrad Question, Russian Foreign Minister Igor Ivanov indicated that how the EU treated Kaliningrad was seen by Moscow as a test of how the EU would treat Russia.[41]

Notes

1. Magdalene Hoff and Heinz Timmermann, "Kaliningrad: Russia's Future Gateway to Europe?" *RFE/RL Magazine* 2, no. 36, (10 September 1993): 37, 38.
2. Hoff and Timmermann, "Kaliningrad: Russia's Future Gateway," 38.
3. Hoff and Timmermann, "Kaliningrad: Russia's Future Gateway," 39.
4. Hoff and Timmermann, "Kaliningrad: Russia's Future Gateway," 39.
5. Hoff and Timmermann, "Kaliningrad: Russia's Future Gateway," 43.
6. Hoff and Timmermann, "Kaliningrad: Russia's Future Gateway," 43.
7. For an informative discussion of the EU and eastward expansion, see Clare McManus, "Poland and the Europe Agreements: the EU as a Regional Actor," in *A Common Foreign Policy for Europe,* ed. John Paterson and Helene Sjursen (London: Routledge, 1998), 15–132.
8. Lykke Friis, "Eastern Enlargement, Schengen, JHA and all that. . . ." *Working Papers, 1998/12* (Danish Institute of International Affairs), 1.
9. Friis, "Eastern Enlargement," 7.
10. Elizabeth Pond, *The Rebirth of Europe* (Washington, D.C.: The Brookings Institution Press, 1999), 108.
11. Friis, "Eastern Enlargement," 2.
12. One of the best qualified persons to criticize Western commentators who demonize the people of the Balkans is Richard Holbrooke, who played a pivotal role in negotiating the Dayton Accords in 1995. For example, see his *To End a War* (New York: Random House, 1998).
13. Tony Judt, *A Grand Illusion* (London: Penguin, 1996), 124–25.
14. Friis, "Eastward Enlargement," 21.
15. Stephan Dewar, interview, spring 1998.
16. Stephan Dewar, "Why Kaliningrad Is 'Unique' in the Russian Federation," unpublished document adapted from the June 1998 TACIS report to Brussels.
17. Dewar, "Why Kaliningrad Is 'Unique'," 4.
18. Dewar, "Why Kaliningrad Is 'Unique'," 5.
19. Stephan Dewar, "Russia and the West: The New Stage of Relations," paper presented at the Finnish Embassy, Moscow, 7 July 1999, 3.
20. TACIS, European Commission, *The TACIS Programme Annual Report 1997* (Luxembourg: Office for Official Publications of the European Communities, 1998).
21. By the late 1990s, the term *Kaliningrad watchers* had taken on a more specific meaning and did not merely refer to diplomats and scholars who displayed an active interest in Kaliningrad. In 1998, under the leadership of Lithuanian diplomats like Vygaudas Usackas—and those from Denmark, Finland, and Sweden, like Hans Brisk, Per Carlson, Rene Nyberg, and Ragnar Angbey, and colleagues and scholars from

Kaliningrad and Moscow as well as from other European states and the United States—a Roundtable on Kaliningrad was organized. By exploring various aspects of the Kaliningrad Question—for example, conditions there and in Moscow and the EU's policies toward the oblast—this group of diplomats and scholars lobbied their governments and the EU, urging them to address the Kaliningrad Question.

22. Off-the-record interviews conducted with diplomats from several countries in the Baltic Sea region.

23. "The Northern Dimension," undated document published by the Foreign Ministry of Lithuania, 1.

24. "The Northern Dimension," 2.

25. "The Northern Dimension," 2.

26. "The Northern Dimension," 3.

27. "The Northern Dimension," 3.

28. "The Northern Dimension," 7.

29. Charles M. Perry, Michael J. Sweeney, and Andrew C. Winner, *Strategic Dynamics in the Nordic-Baltic Region: Implications for U.S. Policy* (Dulles, VA: Brassey's, 2000), 199.

30. "The Year 1998! The End of Illusions," a report from the Centre for Eastern Studies, Warsaw, March 1999.

31. *New York Times* (25 June 2000).

32. *Washington Post* (31 May 2000).

33. European Commission, "EU Conference on a New Iron Curtain? EU–Russia Relations in Focus," (Brussels, 26–27 June 2000).

34. Sophie Lamboschini, "Russia: Moscow Conference Focuses on EU Ties," *RFE/RL Magazine,* 24 January 2001.

35. "EU Fears Kaliningrad Becoming "Black Hole" in Europe," *Russia Today,* 10 January 2001.

36. Stephan Dewar, "Future for Kaliningrad," unpublished paper, May 1998, 1.

37. Dewar, "Future for Kaliningrad," 2.

38. Dewar, "Future for Kaliningrad," 3.

39. Dewar, "Future for Kaliningrad," 4.

40. Pertti Joenniemi, Stephen Dewar, and Lyndelle D. Fairlie, "The Kaliningrad Puzzle: A Russian Region within the European Union," unpublished paper, spring 2000, 11–12.

41. RFE/RL *Russian Security Watch* 2, no. 10 (13 March 2001).

7

Moscow and Kaliningrad

THROUGHOUT THE 1990s, Moscow's approach to the Kaliningrad Question involved three policy orientations.

Kaliningrad as an Imperial Bastion
(The "Russian Imperialists")

Among the competitors for political power in Moscow were the hard-liners bent on reclaiming Russia's imperial past. They perceived Kaliningrad as a Russian bastion in Europe.

After the Soviet Union collapsed, the Communists, with the help of the ultranationalists, dominated the Duma's Lower House. The Reds included the Russian Communist Party leader, Gennady Zyuganov, and the speaker of the Duma Gennady Seleznev. Among the Browns were Vladimir Zhirinovsky, the head of the Liberal Democratic Party, and other neofascists, like General Albert Makashov. The last was not so well known to Western observers as Zhirinovsky, but was potentially more dangerous than the loud-mouthed Zhirinovsky, whose wild antics and rhetoric attracted the attention of the global media. From time to time he railed against the Kremlin, but in the final analysis generally provided the votes he possessed in the Duma in a manner favorable to the government.

But Makashov was a true believer who wanted to crush Russian democracy. In 1993, he provoked a violent showdown with Yeltsin's government when he urged his supporters to storm Moscow's Ostankino TV station. In the wake of the August 1998 economic crisis, he blamed "the Jews" for Russia's economic plight and only after a long pause did his former Communist colleagues, Zyuganov and Seleznev, speak openly in opposition to his racist pronouncements. He split with them and formed the Movement in Support of the Army, a neofascist party.

At that time, many Russian watchers deemed it an even bet that an alliance of Reds and Browns could wrest control of power from the democrats in Moscow. The ultranationalists sought to achieve electoral victory as disgruntled voters turned against not only Yeltsin but the West as well. They were among the people who protested NATO's bombing of Serbia in March 1999 loudest. The younger among them in a demonstration of pan-Slavic unity threatened to join their Serb brothers in Serbia's war against the West—only a small number actually did so. Indeed a wide range of radical extremists on both the left-wing and right-wing fringes of the Russian polity hoped to win the hearts and votes of disgruntled Russians who reviled the democratic reformers and their champions in the West—Anatoli Chubais, Boris Nemtsov, et al.

Representatives of the Red–Brown coalition had two things in common. The first was their commitment to the reconstruction of an imperial Russian state, one that would reabsorb all the territory the USSR lost when it imploded in December 1991. The second was a political strategy based on attracting those despondent and humiliated Russians whose lives had been ravaged in the aftermath of the Soviet Union's collapse. They were susceptible to claims that "traitors" within Russia and "dark" forces outside of it were responsible for the country's desperate economic, social, and political situation. Russia's plight was attributed by them not merely to the reformer's ineptness but to the fact that they were in league with evil Western forces bent on destroying Russia in much the same fashion that they destroyed the Soviet Union.

The two groups did not work together in a cohesive and purposeful fashion but they prevented the reformers around Yeltsin from passing legislation to advance a market economy in Russia. Nor did they enjoy leaders with popular appeal, but it was from such circles that the toughest and most provocative threats were made in opposition to NATO enlargement and in reaction to alleged foreign claims on Kaliningrad.

In 1995, *Komsomolskaya Pravda* reported that according to Russian military doctrine, if the Baltic democracies were included in NATO "then Russian Federation armed forces will be sent into Estonia, Latvia, and Lithuania. Any attempt by NATO to prevent this action would be regarded by Russia as the prelude to a worldwide nuclear catastrophe."[1] This was precisely the kind of language that caused Senator Daniel Patrick Moynihan to warn in 1998

that NATO enlargement would provoke the Russians and justified his reject-
ing the process as imprudent.

U.S. officials and American Russian watchers alike generally characterized
such threats on the part of hard-liners—to use force to protect Russians in
the near abroad or in response to the Baltic countries entering NATO—as
mere hyperbole. The Reds' and Browns' angry rhetoric aside, they knew that
any attempt to threaten the security of Kaliningrad's neighbors would set
Russia on a collision course with the West. This was especially true of any
perceived threat to the Baltic countries, which had influential supporters in
the American media, among policy makers, and in the U.S. Congress. Furthermore, the notion that Russia had the capacity to implement such threats
was ludicrous given the financial crisis that had wracked Russia since August
1998.

Threats of this nature were worrisome, however, because some prominent
members of the Russian political and military elite had voiced them—people
who held responsible positions or individuals who one day conceivably could
do so. For example, in the summer of 1999, the Russian military occupied
the Pristina airport before NATO's forces could enter Kosovo. This bold
move was calculated to provide Moscow with leverage in the conflict's aftermath. With their forces in places—albeit a small contingent of troops—the
Russians hoped to create a district under their control in Kosovo. This incident suggested to some Western observers that the military had acted independently of Russia's political leadership and sent a signal to the world that
it would no longer bow to the Kremlin as was common in the Soviet Union.
Moreover, representatives of hard-line circles, and people who courted their
support, had a real prospect of gaining political power in Moscow. Their rising political fortunes were based upon existing trends and not a worst-case
scenario hatched by overzealous Western defense analysts. Russia's weakened
position would last well into the twenty-first century, thereby making it
dependent upon Western assistance. The hard-liners, however, would reject
assistance and in an attempt to mask the country's frailties take actions that
provoked the West. They simply did not care how the West reacted to their
policies; indeed, they welcomed Western hostility. They could take comfort
in the fact that such bluster did have an impact upon Western statesmen even
if Russia did not have much to back its threats. (Of course, for many in the
West, the fact that Moscow still possessed a massive nuclear arsenal was sufficient reason for them to "listen" to Russia's concerns.) Such outside pressure would help the hard-liners consolidate their position at home. This is
what Slobodan Milosevic did when he provoked the NATO attack upon Serbia in March 1999. Thousands of people were killed as a result, and about
one million were forced from their homes, not to mention the havoc the war

created in American–Russian relations, but Milosevic consolidated his power within Serbia.

In contemplating Russia's future behavior at midpoint in the 1990s, one could ignore a pivotal fact: Russia was caught in a revolutionary maelstrom and would be wracked by crisis for at least another decade. While only a prophet could predict the future, the trends there—political, economic, and social—were cause for alarm and there was no early resolution to them— political gridlock, economic stagnation, and social upheaval. Since these problems were systemic, one could not assume, for example, that when prog- ress was made on the economic front—or when the hard-liners experienced a political setback—Russia was on a firm track of recovery.

It was quite plausible then that reactionary, antidemocratic groups would achieve power in the near future, or at a minimum help shape the future course of Russia, regardless of who the next president was or the Duma's composition after the December 1999 elections. The hard-liners saw the Kali- ningrad Question in very clear-cut terms. In considering the choice of "a free market or tanks" they choose the latter. Recall Sergei Shakhrai's warning about the expansionary designs of foreigners on Kaliningrad and his conclusion: "We have again to declare clearly the priority of Russia's military-strategic interests in the Kaliningrad region."

Some Russian defense analysts downgraded Kaliningrad's military signifi- cance but the hard-liners deemed it vital to the country's security. In defense of their position they cited twentieth-century Russian history and saw it as providing lessons for the twenty-first century. Following the Nazi's example during World War II, future foreign aggressors could use Polish and Lithua- nian territory as a corridor to facilitate attacks on St. Petersburg and Moscow. Even if that worst-case scenario never materialized, the Reds and Browns figured with good reason that the mere presence of "hostile" troops on Rus- sia's western borders could influence the course of political developments in Russia at their expense.

The conviction that Russian control of the Baltic Sea region was a vital security goal was held not only among the radical fringes of the Russian defense establishment. Military analysts in Moscow, who represented more moderate and reasonable opinion, felt this way as well.

For example, in his survey of Russian–Baltic history, Alexander A. Pikayev of Moscow's Center for Geopolitical and Military Forecasts, said five lessons presented themselves:

1. Every time a Baltic territory emerges under the dominance of a West- ern power, it becomes a *platzdarm* for invasion of Russia's mainland.

2. Russia's isolation from warm-water Baltic ports always invites Moscow's aggressions into the Baltic territories.
3. Without Russian participation, Baltic security can never be viewed as reliable or sustainable.
4. Democracy in Russia represents a main source for modern Baltic independence and provides important security guarantees in and of itself.
5. Interruption of economic cooperation with Russia would necessarily undermine Baltic economies and their domestic stability.[2]

Recognizing Russia's weakened condition, the imperial-minded there might accept foreign assistance and seek an accommodation with the West but only as a short-term, tactical compromise. It would be an error to interpret it as an ideological conversion. Indeed as indicated above, some radicals on the right and left might reason that they could promote their political fortunes within Russia by provoking the West. Both the Reds and Browns rejected Western liberalism in either its political or economic formulations. Furthermore, activists in both camps were convinced that the West, led by the United States, was bent on destroying Russia in much the same fashion that it devastated the Soviet Union.

It was not only the old men and women—their chests adorned with medals earned in the Great Patriotic War and who gathered on Red Square to distribute Marxist-Leninist tracts to visitors from the provinces—who deemed the West responsible for Russia's plight. Many Russians with university degrees were puzzled that the Soviet empire collapsed while it remained the only country on earth that could devastate the United States in a nuclear strike. These views, latent for years, became manifest as the Russian people vented their outrage over NATO's bombing of Serbia in 1999. Hostility toward the West was fed later that year when U.S. and West European leaders scolded the Russians for their indiscriminate use of force in Chechnya. Indeed, many Russian hard-liners believed that the West wanted Russia to experience another humiliating defeat in the Caucasus so that Western business interests could dominate the region's energy wealth.

Products of a despotic political culture, many Russians believe fundamental shifts in power are often a product of hidden machinations, not overt ones. Many have concluded that alien "dark forces" demoralized the Soviet political elite and disarmed them psychologically; how else could one explain the empire's implosion at the very time Western defense analysts expressed alarm about the USSR's vast nuclear arsenal. The young people, who face a bleak future in Russia—and middle-age men and women, without the skills, contacts, or entrepreneurial instincts to prosper in the new economy—may not perceive the past with the nostalgia of their parents, but they are unhappy with their existing circumstances. They have tried to blind themselves to reality through vodka and drugs and are likely candidates for radical demagogues who blame Russia's plight on the Jews or the Americans. They represent a twenty-first-century *lumpen*-proletariat—not victims of a blighted capitalist order but of a failed communist experiment.

Gennady Zyuganov has been pointed in blaming the West for Russia's difficulties in an attempt to mobilize popular support behind the Communists and their nationalistic allies. In his book, *The Geography of Victory*, Zyuganov espoused the philosophy of "Eurasianism"—a worldview that proclaimed— prior to the second war in Chechnya—that Orthodox Russia must forge an alliance with its "philosophical cousins," the Islamic fundamentalists—and other peoples with a collectivist tradition—in a struggle against the Western imperialists whose celebration of unbridled individualism and insatiable materialism are poison to a communitarian ethos. With this wide vision, Zyuganov has tried to win the hearts and minds of the Russian people through an appeal to their unique Russianness—but in lock step with their southern neighbors. This campaign of inclusion clashes with the strictly narrow Russian nationalist approach of General Aleksandr Lebed.[3]

During the Yeltsin years, the Reds' and Browns' overriding foreign-policy objective was to resurrect an imperial Russian state, one that would incorporate into it most, if not all, of the territory that once was controlled by the USSR. For them, the issue was not demilitarization but the remilitarization of Kaliningrad and they felt this way prior to talks about enlarging NATO. They welcomed Russia's union with Belarus as a step toward the resurrection of a new Russian empire to which all the former Soviet Republics would belong. They saw a strong Russian military presence in Kaliningrad as an asset to intimidate the Lithuanians and the Poles. As Dmitri Trenin wrote: For the "imperial-minded" in Russia, the Baltic states "are regarded as a lost part of the Russian Empire and Soviet Union. Baltic independence during the period between the two World Wars, as well as today, is considered the result of a temporary weakness of Russia."[4]

Even after the Lithuanian government provided humanitarian assistance to Kaliningrad in the wake of the August meltdown, and encouraged other countries to do the same, Vladimir Zhirinovsky remained unimpressed. On the contrary, he proposed that Russia take Lithuanian and Polish territory to make possible a corridor that would connect Kaliningrad with Russia proper. In return Vilnius and Warsaw would be given territory in Russia's Smolensk region.[5]

Finally, in considering how the hard-liners would respond to an EU offer of extensive economic assistance to Kaliningrad, one need only consider what is a truism. The unreconstructed Communists reject outright efforts to build a capitalist economy in the oblast and the ultranationalists are inclined to see Russia's economic future in neomercantilist terms where there is little, if any, room for cooperation with foreigners.

Kaliningrad as a Gateway to the West
("The Regionalists")

Unlike the hard-liners, who opposed a free-market economy, and glorified an all-powerful imperial state controlled by Moscow, the regionalists realized that it was neither prudent nor possible to return to a Soviet-style system dominated by Moscow. The regions had to have real political power to operate a political system that was congruent with a free-market economy. Also, unlike the Reds and Browns who balked at working with the West, they welcomed the opportunity to do so. Indeed, economic logic dictated that they do so. Of course, the actions of many governors contradicted their proclamations to be democrats, and their support for regional power did not necessarily represent a commitment to democratic federalism. Many favored both for a simple reason: they served their parochial self-interest.

Initially most of the elite in Kaliningrad were happy with the status quo and wanted both "a free market and tanks." They and ordinary folk alike favored a heavy military presence in the oblast, but not necessarily because they harbored aggressive intentions. No, their preferences were based on pragmatism; since so many of them were in active service, military retirees, or depended upon the military to make a living, it would be odd if they welcomed the rapid decommissioning of Russia's military in the oblast. Residents of military enclaves, whether they be somewhere in Virginia or Gibraltar, are more inclined to favor a strong military than do their fellow countrymen who work in civilian occupations. In Kaliningrad, such sentiments were especially strong since nondefense-oriented jobs in the oblast were scarce or deemed economically risky. In the mid-1990s, polls indicated that while 64 percent of Kaliningrad's residents favored Kaliningrad serving as a bridge to Europe, 55 percent still supported the existing level of troops and equipment there.[6]

Over time, as the troops declined in number and the Russian defense budget shriveled, it made little sense to ignore one unique feature of Kaliningrad—its exclave status; that's what attracted Western attention to the oblast in the first place. Governor Matochkin and his associates saw a special relationship with the West—with investments from that source—as a way to compensate for Moscow's declining economic support. But with Gorbenko's election, the new governor celebrated self-reliance—in part, one surmised, because he feared that too much outside involvement would lead to a level of transparency that would endanger him politically and economically. Like the economic oligarchs in Moscow, many regional elites exploited nationalism to protect their own economic interests, not because they were true patriots.

Gorbenko persisted in stressing economic self-reliance for Kaliningrad even after the August 17, 1998, crisis—if only for a while. He said in an early 1999 interview, "We consider the main principle of our economic policy to be the support and protection of local manufacturers." Later that same day, however, he told a gathering of CBSS delegates that Kaliningrad would "establish and maintain mutually beneficial relations with an expanding EU."[7] From Gorbenko's perspective, then, the problem was how to attract Western economic investments without losing control of the reins of political power that allowed him to translate political authority into hard currency "profits" for himself and his compatriots.

Gorbenko demonstrated his new thinking, when in contrast to the Russian and Kaliningrad Duma, he adopted a more pragmatic position on the sale of land. In November 1998, the Kaliningrad Duma passed a law that restricted the buying and selling of land to Russian citizens. Several months later, Gorbenko said he favored legislation that allowed foreigners to purchase land in the oblast. "I believe our land should be sold to citizens of other countries just as long as they do not build dangerous plants there."[8]

After the "August Crisis," Gorbenko's political opponents and other politicians in Kaliningrad were even more insistent in their support of Yuri Matochkin's Western orientation. That is, Kaliningrad must develop a special relationship with the EU or continue to suffer an economy in crisis. After August, even officials in Moscow who rejected Matochkin's argument found it difficult to dismiss the "regionalists" position on the Kaliningrad Question. It involved the following observations:

1. Russia does not have the funds necessary to jump-start the oblast's economy that is a prerequisite to social and political stability there. And it is Kaliningrad's economic crisis, not "hostile neighbors," that is the primary source of Russia's security problem there.
2. Russia must maintain harmonious relations with Kaliningrad's neighbors whose commercial activities and political cooperation are vital to the daily lives of the oblast's residents.
3. Russia must work closely with the EU because it has the economic resources to provide Kaliningrad with significant public assistance and the prestige to encourage private foreign investments there.
4. Kaliningrad, through cooperation with the West, can become a bridge that facilitates Russia's economic integration into Europe.

Although not all of Kaliningrad's politicians favored close relations with the West, most of them lobbied Moscow for greater control over the oblast's affairs. They posited that Russian Federalism would become a reality only after the regions enhanced their authority over their economic activities. This included the freedom to control commercial activities, to retain a larger share of tax revenues generated by the region, and the ability to engage in economic activities independent of Moscow's oversight. The power-sharing agreement that Tatarstan signed with Moscow on February 15, 1994, was seen as a model for them. Under the agreement the republic gained control of taxes generated by the sale of alcohol, oil and gas, and Moscow and Tatarstan split the proceeds from the value-added tax (VAT), fifty-fifty. This split contrasted with the 25 percent share other regions had received and that had declined to 15 percent in 1999.[9]

But while advocating greater power for their region, officials there continued to argue that Kaliningrad's exclave status placed it at a decided economic disadvantage requiring heavy subsidies from Moscow. Officials in the Center responded with a curt "we simply don't have the money." Nonetheless, this was a statement of fact: Kaliningrad's geographical location made it a unique entity requiring special consideration.

Also, politicians in Kaliningrad were intrigued by the activities of peers like Sverdlovsk Governor Eduard Rossel. Early in the 1990s Rossel was removed from office by Yeltsin but later was elected to that post and afterward fought for greater freedom from Moscow. Like several other governors, Rossel had formed a regional party, the Transformation of the Urals Party, and had avoided membership in larger political blocs, such as the one Samara's governor, Konstantan Titov, had formed.

In anticipation of the December 1999 Duma election and the year 2000 presidential election, Titov established Russia's Voice (Golos Rossii) to mobilize the regions and give them a greater voice in political matters at all levels of government. Leonid Gorbenko allied himself (for a time) with Titov along with other governors who sought greater political power for their regions. Through their membership in the Federation Council they had sought with some success to influence federal policy. The council was able to wield considerable influence, given the deadlock between the Duma and government. But the regional elites were searching for new ways to promote their interests. Having failed to register in time to place its own candidates up for election, however, Russia's Voice would have to work with a party that had already done so.

On February 17, 1999, thirty members of the Federation Council called for public support of Titov. They also signed an appeal that attacked the existing state for behaving as a unitary and not a true federal system, for taking taxes from the rich regions without giving them to the poor ones, and for refusing to work with them to achieve common objectives.[10] In the process of forming his governor-based coalition, Titov in early 1999 was in competition with Moscow's Mayor Luzhkov, who was striving to build a political base Father-land (Otechestvo) in the regions in the hope that it would catapult him into the presidency in 2000. As spring approached, he was not having much success in this venture because the governors feared that if elected president, he would concentrate power in the Kremlin. Snubbed by the governors, Luzhkov then began recruiting mayors of large cities who were often in conflict with regional authorities over how revenues were dispersed. Mayors bridled at the thought that they were net contributors to regional budgets but their constituencies were not fairly compensated by the governors who redistributed the funds to the rural areas. This practice was associated with what is an anomaly; that is, in contrast to voting behavior in many Western countries, in Russia voting turnout is higher in rural districts than in urban ones.[10]

In early August, however, Luzhkov and Mintimer Shaimiev, Tatarstan's president, appeared in a televised press conference to announce that Luzhkov's Fatherland party would join Shaimiev's All Russia to form a political bloc that became known as OVR. In tandem they would compete for votes in the upcoming Duma elections. As mayor of Moscow, Luzhkov controlled a large municipal budget. But he also had access to private funds because he had the authority to make private ventures profitable or by not issuing licenses and taking other measures critical to an enterprise's commercial success. Given his political and economic base in Russia's largest metropolis, Luzhkov was long considered to be one of the front-runners for the presidential race. What he lacked, however, was support outside of Moscow; hence his campaign to court regional elites.

Shaimiev had two powerful assets going for him. First, he controlled a large republic with abundant natural resources (petroleum among other commodities that produced hard currency) and benefited greatly from preferential economic rights. Consequently he was a natural leader of those regional elites who wished to have an impact upon the Federal Duma and Russia's president. And second, he was arguably Russia's most powerful Muslim politician. In 1999, Muslims represented an estimated 15 percent to 20 percent of the federation's population and, unlike the ethnic Russians, they were not suffering from a zero population growth rate—so in the twenty-first century, their numbers would grow in relationship to the Russians.

This alliance between two such powerful politicians alone was cause for a buzz in Moscow, but it created even more excitement when they announced that Yevgeni Primakov would join them. With Primakov on board the alliance was expected to do very well in the Duma elections. Also, with an electoral base both Primakov and Luzhkov were front-runners in the 2000 presidential race. One reason Boris Yeltsin fired Prime Minister Sergei Stepashin in August 1999 and replaced him with Valdimir Putin, was his failure to prevent the alliance from being forged. After Primakov joined it, Yeltsin and "his family" had good cause to look to the future with anxiety.

In addition to the political heavyweights who had become associated with OVR, Vladimir Gusinsky was the group's financial supporter. Head of the powerful Most-Media empire and a bitter rival of Boris Berezovsky, who was a member of Yeltsin's "family," Gusinsky's deep pockets were deemed an important asset that enhanced All Russia–Fatherland's electoral prospects. They were deemed positive of course because the man who replaced Stepashin, Vladimir Putin, was a relatively unknown entity without a political base. Moreover, pundits considered his prospects poor since anyone associated with Yeltsin suffered from widespread hostility toward the Kremlin.

In assessing OVR's chances, however, a caveat was in order. Ever since the Soviet Union collapsed, politicians and political factions had combined in short-term alliances, and proved to be incapable of developing long-term political blocs (with mass-based support) that survived more than one election season. The Communists were the only exception to this rule. Political analysts in Russia and beyond deemed this to be the likely fate of OVR even if its candidates did well in the 1999 Duma elections. Should they also elect a president in the summer of 2000, moreover, the alliance's long-term prospects would improve markedly.

Individual political fortunes aside, one thing was clear. Displays of regional autonomy had surged as Moscow's ability to provide subsidies to the regions declined. Indeed, in many regions federal officials and members of the armed forces had become dependent upon regional authorities to pay their salaries and to fund their agencies. Consequently, Moscow harbored doubts about the loyalty of federal personnel in Kaliningrad who were beholden to Gorbenko for their livelihoods. Indeed, Gorbenko had not been shy in attempting to coopt them and according to political analysts in Kaliningrad he had been, to a significant degree, successful.

In the new post-Soviet economy, regional authorities depend upon hard currency and often must use market-driven criteria in their decision making. For example, in early 1999 a Kaliningrad shipyard launched an unfinished warship to make room for a Norwegian cargo vessel. The latter needed repairs and, unlike the Russian Navy, its Norwegian owners paid hard currency for the refurbishing of their ship and they were not in arrears for work already conducted.

Students of Russian regionalism concluded, therefore, that as a free market grew in Russia and state control over economic affairs declined, there would be a diffusion of political power to the regions as well. Perhaps the best indicator of expanding regional power was the following observation: during the Soviet era, ambitious politicians campaigned to secure posts in Moscow and advance their political careers, but in the 1990s like-minded people were staying in the regions because they saw real opportunities to advance there.

Playing the Kaliningrad Card ("The Unitarists")

Unfortunately for those in Kaliningrad, who deemed their future hopeless without a close relationship with the EU, there were powerful personalities and interests in Moscow who opposed this relationship. These people, who might be labeled the "Unitarists," did not wish to return to a twenty-first century version of the old Soviet Union, but saw little reason for the regions to enjoy real political power or control over their economic affairs. They deemed the regions as administrative units that followed the dictates of the policy makers in Moscow and sought to concentrate power at the center of the polity.

From their perspective, Kaliningrad was merely one of eighty-nine regional entities and it represented a card to be played in Russia's relations with its neighbors and the West in general. To wit, Yeltsin, and the various prime ministers who had served under his stewardship, used Kaliningrad to check Western initiatives Moscow opposed, or to advance policies it favored. As indicated earlier, during the first round of enlargement some defense analysts claimed that Russia would deploy tactical nuclear weapons in Kaliningrad after Poland entered NATO.

The card had failed to halt enlargement, and Moscow had presumably accepted the first round of ascension. But in the future it might use Kaliningrad as a pretext to argue that the introduction of a small number of non-Polish troops into Poland constituted a provocation. After all, Poland shared a border with Russia's Kaliningrad and defense analysts there asserted that Russia and not Poland should be worried about the military balance between Poland and the oblast. According to one Russian analyst, "Poland enjoys predominance in all conventional arms and manpower categories. It is decisive in such key categories as manpower and combat aircraft. The Kaliningrad group of forces is too weak to launch any offensive against Poland. Conversely, Poland possesses sufficient military predominance to launch a successful offensive operation against the exclave."[11]

At mid-point in the 1990s, the following (Russian provided) figures supported this claim. Poland had a manpower advantage of 188,200 to 24,000, a tank advantage of 2,017 to 870, and a combat aircraft edge of 412 to 32. Under these circumstances, Warsaw's complaints about excessive "troops in Kaliningrad" were either a display of profound ignorance or a calculated provocation. Also, Alexander Sergounin noted that some Russian defense analysts recognized major security problems to Russia's south and east: "There are other experts insisting that Russia is able to cope with the threats from South and East, but what really needs attention is a new Western 'Drang nach Osten', i.e., NATO and EU enlargement." Polish forces by themselves did not pose a threat to Russia, but Polish troops aligned with nuclear-armed allies did.[12]

NATO's war with Serbia in 1999 gave new velocity to this perceived threat among Communists and ultranationalists. Meanwhile Russian moderates, who saw NATO enlargement as a tool to pressure Russia into accepting U.S. efforts to undermine governments that Washington labeled "pariahs," like those in Libya, Iraq, and Iran, opposed it for that reason alone. Desperate for hard currency, the Russians saw no reason that they should not sell weapons to these states while the United States was the world's leading arms merchant.

The prospect that Poland would soon enter the EU also was cited as evidence that Kaliningrad would suffer as Warsaw accepted the strict visa regime associated with the EU Acquis Communautaire. Commerce between Poland and Kaliningrad would become a more difficult and expensive enterprise for businessmen in the oblast. As has already been mentioned, this concern had merit.

Turning to Kaliningrad's other neighbor, Lithuania, a spectrum of Russian political elites had opposed the U.S.–Baltic Charter and were even more outspoken in opposition to the Clinton administration's favoring Lithuanian membership in NATO. To prevent this humiliation to Russia, they were prepared to play the Kaliningrad card.

Western defense analysts cited Lithuania as the best prepared of the three Baltic countries militarily; besides, unlike Estonia and Latvia it did not have a "Russian problem." Some Russian analysts did not believe that Lithuania's prospect for NATO membership were good, so it was senseless for Moscow to complain about it. Others realized that to put any pressure on Lithuania would provide ammunition for Lithuania's supporters in the United States who were demanding that Washington waste no time accepting Lithuania into the alliance. Still others did not give a fig about Lithuania's chances; they simply opposed the idea. In discussions with members of the Russian Foreign Ministry this writer was treated to a vivid example of the Kaliningrad card in play when he was told, "If the U.S. agrees not to allow the Balts into NATO, then we can talk about the Americans working with us in Kaliningrad."[13]

One thing was clear: should Lithuania be selected in a second round of enlargement, one could anticipate the Kaliningrad card being played again. Putting aside the threats from fringe elements, which have advocated an attack on Lithuania were it invited to join NATO, even moderate members of the Russian political elite would respond with anger. They might even be inclined to resurrect the transit issue and threaten Vilnius with economic reprisals if it did not provide Russia with a formal corridor through Lithuania to Kaliningrad.

After Yeltsin signed a border treaty with Lithuanian President Brazauskas in 1997, members of the Kaliningrad City Council wrote Yeltsin a letter of complaint. "This treaty should be considered alongside the treaty on the transit of cargo and passengers to the Kaliningrad region, taking into account Russian security, which means ensuring that Lithuania will not join NATO."[14]

While Moscow launched rhetorical attacks, Lithuanian officials claimed the Russian government would make no serious effort to block Lithuania's entry into the alliance. President Adamkus had cited the close relations between his country and Russia and Russian officials had spoken openly and frequently about the harmony that both countries enjoyed. Members of the Lithuanian diplomatic corps, and some members of parliament, also indicated that in private discussions with their Russian counterparts they were told in effect: "We must continue to oppose your membership publicly but we do not really think that your joining NATO represents a security threat to us."[15]

Turning to the issue of Western assistance for Kaliningrad, some Unitarists conceded they could use help in addressing the Kaliningrad Question, but they feared, in the process, Russia's losing control over the oblast. Many European and U.S. diplomats were pessimistic about Russia welcoming outside assistance and cited Moscow's dispute with Japan over the Kurile Islands to explain their pessimism.

Western observers deemed it senseless for Moscow to rebuff the Japanese request to return the Kurile Islands to Japan. Russia possessed vast stretches of territory in the Far East and was not land-poor like Japan. Tokyo had indicated that it was prepared to provide Moscow with significant economic assistance, in addition to lucrative commercial opportunities, should the Russians return the islands to their original owners. But the Russians continued to see the Kurile Islands as a justified reward for their conflict with Japan during World War II. That sentiment was even more strongly felt in the case of East Prussia, given the awful carnage that the Nazis visited upon the Soviet peoples during the war.

Even though they deemed East Prussia as a World War II trophy, other Western diplomats, who discussed Kaliningrad with their Russian counterparts, reported that they had little real interest in the oblast and its problems. From their perspective, Kaliningrad was just one of eighty-nine regions, and its economic problems were not much different from those that other regions were enduring throughout the federation. Also, preoccupied with the crushing problems confronting the Russian government, they had little time to devote to the Kaliningrad Question. Growing interest in regional political power aside, many of Russia's political leaders remained preoccupied with Moscow, where they believed the struggle to determine the future of Russia would unfold, not in the hinterland.

However, Russia's economic plight, the dismal condition of its army, and the fact that its most pressing security problems were internal and to its south and east, strengthened the case of pragmatists who advocated that Moscow accept any outside help it could get to revitalize Kaliningrad. There were indications that some Russian authorities were thinking in such terms. It is noteworthy that in mid-December 1998, the Russian Security Council devoted special attention to Kaliningrad demonstrating that some officials in Moscow were ready to address the Kaliningrad Question. Furthermore, in January 1999 at the annual Russian ambassadorial meeting, a separate session was devoted to Kaliningrad. The contents and outcome of that meeting are unknown, but on April 12, 1999, a press release from Yeltsin's office indicated that the president urged renewed efforts be undertaken to advance progress on a 1998–2005 development program designed for Kaliningrad.

There was reason to believe that security, not economic considerations were responsible for Moscow's revived interest in Kaliningrad. But perhaps the August crisis had provided further evidence to skeptical Russian leaders that they desperately needed outside help if they were to grapple with their daunting economic problems. In the case of Kaliningrad, there were two compelling reasons that federal authorities ought to be forthcoming in joining the EU, and the United States, in addressing the Kaliningrad Question.

First, Kaliningrad could serve as a test case and show how the West could cooperate with Russia in helping build a democratic society and free-market economy. Here the issue of scale was relevant. With a population of a little less than one million in an area the size of Northern Ireland, Kaliningrad was small enough to conduct and assess programs, and that could provide insight into how the West could help Russia at large. This prospect was a compelling incentive for officials in Moscow to work with the West in addressing Kaliningrad's problems.

Second, Kaliningrad could provide insight into another critical question: "How might Russia cooperate with the EU while remaining outside of that organization?" Moscow in the 1990s indicated that it had no problem with EU enlargement since it was an economic organization. But by the close of the decade, the Russian government displayed concern about enlargement; specifically how might Russia's economic relations be affected once its neighbors joined the EU and began adhering to EU policies. This concern grew in January 1998 when Poland, in anticipating EU membership, adopted a strict visa regime that resulted in a curtailment of traffic to and from Kaliningrad. What's more, Moscow anticipated that the EU would press the Lithuanians to adopt a stricter border regime with its neighbors as well.

The diplomats and analysts who belonged to the Kaliningrad watchers used these arguments to encourage Moscow to be more forthcoming in welcoming international efforts to address the Kaliningrad Question. They noted also that it was imperative that the Russians gain a comprehensive understanding of how the EU worked and the substance of its rules. A heightened understanding of the EU would help facilitate more extensive relationships between Brussels and Moscow and between the former and individual Russian regions. Expanded interaction between the EU and Russia would develop constituencies in both Brussels and Moscow for more extensive cooperation than had been the case to date. This, in turn, would create incentives for an enlargement in staffs to conduct such work.[16]

The Putin Revolution

In the fall of 1999, Muslim fighters from Chechnya sent a force into nearby Dagestan led by Moscow's old nemesis, Shamil Basayev. The Chechen warlord said that he would drive the Russians from Dagestan and create a new Islamic Chechen–Dagestan Republic. From this redoubt Basayev and his supporters—including Islamic fighters from outside the region—then could set their sights on the oil wealth of the Caspian Sea. Basayev reasoned that once the Russian forces began to take casualties, the Russian people and many of the political elite in Moscow would grudgingly accept his bold campaign to create his Islamic Republic in Russia's North Caucasus.

But Prime Minister Putin and his defense minister, Igor Sergeyev, culled the best (allegedly) troops available from the ranks of the Russian Army in an effort to construct a fighting force that would destroy the estimated 1,200 rebels that invaded Dagestan. Included in this number were units of marines from the Baltic Sea Fleet in Kaliningrad. In face of a larger and better-armed enemy, Basayev pulled his forces from Dagestan and relocated them in Chechnya. But his assault on Dagestan gave the Russian military the pretext to embark on a campaign of retribution that they had dreamed about since being driven out of Chechnya four years earlier.

Basayev was wrong also about Russia's political elite and people supporting a tough Russian response to the attack. Indeed, the liberal Grigory Yavlin-sky supported the government and said that the fighting in Dagestan represented a "concerted attack by international Islamic extremists, separat-ists, and terrorists against Russia." Washington's favorite "Russian reformer," Anatoli Chubais, joined him, as well as one of the West's most reviled reactionaries, "Comrade" Zyuganov, in supporting Putin's policies.

Moreover, after several apartment houses were bombed in Moscow and other cities, killing three hundred people, Putin's tough policies toward the "bandits in Chechnya" received overwhelming support from the Russian people. (The Chechens denied they were responsible for the bombings.) Pub-lic opinion surveys noted Putin's positive ratings climbing, then reaching the level enjoyed by "the most popular politician in Russia," Primakov, and soon Putin surpassed the former prime minister.

After the fighting returned to Chechnya itself in September and 100,000 Russian troops with tanks, artillery, and helicopter gun ships began to level several cities, including the capital, Grozny, the international community expressed its outrage. Leaders like Bill Clinton, Tony Blair, and Jacques Chirac urged Yeltsin to rein in his troops who were "indiscriminately killing civilians." In an attempt to reduce army casualties, the Russian forces did not meet and defeat the Chechen fighters in close-in actions but stood back and fired artillery rounds and dropped bombs on suspected rebel units. As in the 1994–95 conflict, most of the casualties were civilians. Most could not escape the venue of the fighting, fearing that if they left their cellars they would fall victim to Russian bombs or be cut down by disapproving Chechen fighters who did not deem it patriotic to flee the scene.

The international community's criticism, however, helped bolster Putin's popularity with the Russian people and the forty-seven-year-old former KGB agent became a national hero. Having suffered years of humiliation and enduring the leadership of a sickly old man for a decade, the trim and fit Putin provided the Russian people with a new sense of national self-esteem. At long last, a strong leader had appeared and perhaps there was some hope for Russia's future after all.

Meanwhile commanders in the Russian Army greeted Putin, and his tough line and promises to provide the military with more funding, with open arms. Fearing that the Kremlin might reach an accommodation with the Chechens again—with further humiliation for the Russian Army—some commanders had spoken openly about mutiny. Putin said he would not negotiate a cease-fire because there was no viable Chechen leader with whom he could negotiate.

As the Duma elections approached, Putin became the Russian leader with a "Midas touch." In an attempt to match efforts on the part of Luzhkov and

Primakov to attract regional elites to the OVR, the Kremlin established Yedinstvo, Unity. Its leader, Sergei Shoigu, a member of Putin's cabinet, portrayed Unity as a regional voting bloc and a significant number of governors allied themselves with it. But critics noted that they represented the weakest and poorest regions, and Unity's prospects for electing candidates under its banner in the December Duma elections were deemed poor.

But as Putin's popularity soared so did Unity's stock. Furthermore, as the election approached the Yeltsin "family's" friendly media lords—led by Boris Berezovsky—began to improve Unity's visibility and popularity. Predictably, the fortunes of OVR began to slide, and evidence to this effect surfaced when OVR leaders suggested that they might join Unity in a common voting bloc.

After the December 19, 1999, elections, Unity placed a close second behind the front-running Communists and captured almost 24 percent of the vote. OVR came in third with 13 percent of the vote. The results indicated that the Communists and their Brown allies would no longer dominate the new Duma—indeed, most of the far-right radical parties did poorly in both "party list" and single-member seats.

Putin's support not only helped Unity but his favorable comments about the Union of Right Wing Forces also helped that party in December. After the election, powerful governors like Shaimiev and St. Petersburg's Yakovlev—whom Putin held in disfavor—openly endorsed Putin as president and soon they were joined by a majority of regional leaders. After Boris Yeltsin shocked the world and announced his retirement on New Year's Eve, and the date for the presidential elections was moved up from June to March, it was clear that Putin would become Russia's next president. In recognition of Putin's improved prospects, Primakov said he would forgo a bid for the presidency. Putin won the contest in March in the first round, and immediately after being inaugurated in May he began to restore Moscow's power over the regions.

This was not an unexpected move. Upon being selected prime minister, Putin announced that his number one priority was to restore the authority of the Russian state. This goal was popular with Russians from all walks of life. For many of them, Putin helped restore their faith in the state when he adopted the brutal campaign in Chechnya. His promise to strengthen Moscow's oversight of the regional political and economic barons, who had blatantly ignored federal authority, was welcomed by many Russians as well. He insisted that all regional laws must become consistent with federal law and the Russian constitution. Who could disagree with this legitimate goal?

When Putin was in charge of Kremlin relations with the regions in 1997, he was seen as "one of the radical bureaucrats who took an extremely tough line against regional barons."[17] Early in 2000 while prime minister, Putin took a number of initiatives that suggested he would tighten Moscow's control over the regions:

1. He indicated that he would place constraints upon the regions' borrowing from international creditors. He complained that Moscow was liable to reimburse foreign creditors because of the failure of dead-beat governors to pay their debts.
2. In a sign that Moscow intended to squeeze more revenues from the regions, the Tax Ministry announced that the regions had to provide the federal government with detailed information about all potential taxpayers in their jurisdictions.
3. Putin signed a bill designating that funding for newspaper print used by the regional press would pass through federal and not regional channels.
4. In February 2000, federal officials announced that all criminal police in the regions henceforth would report to law enforcement authorities in Moscow and only traffic and other mundane activities would be the exclusive responsibility of local authorities.
5. Yegor Stroev, the chairman of the Federal Federation Council, announced in January that he favored an amendment to the constitution that would allow direct presidential rule in any part of the country. Governor Ivan Shabanov of Voronezh said he favored this measure with the proviso that the person selected by the Kremlin must have the support of regional legislatures. The fact that such important regional officials were making these concessions indicated that they and their colleagues were ready to give Yeltsin's powerful successor whatever he wanted.

On the basis of these actions, one could conclude that Putin would not engage in the practice of "asymmetrical federalism" that highlighted ad hoc deals between Moscow and the eighty-nine regional bodies under Yeltsin. In looking at other federal systems, one finds asymmetry at work: for example, in the United States, California is seven times larger in population than Wyoming. But the critical feature of asymmetrical federalism in the Russian case that attracted attention was Moscow's making deals with the regions not dictated by or consistent with the Russian constitution. Also some republics were conducting activities that violated their own constitutions.

Putin was not abusing his authority when he said that the Center must force the regions to pay taxes and thereby restore the power of federal authority. Nor was he out of line when he said Moscow would hold regional elites accountable for crime and corruption in their jurisdictions. One could also make the case that the number of regional bodies should be decreased.

In short, there were a number of measures that the Center could take that the regional elites would resist but that were justified politically and administratively and represented a legitimate exercise of federal authority. Clearly, the legal relationship between the Center and the regions had to be codified in law and not continue to be determined by political deals, as had been the case under Yeltsin.

Within a week after being inaugurated Russia's second popularly elected president, Putin moved quickly to reassert Moscow's control over the regions. First, he divided Russia into seven large districts and appointed a "governor general" to oversee each one of them. Thus, the Kremlin could keep a closer watch on what was going on in the vast hinterland of Russia. Russian democrats expressed concern about the plan since the boundaries of the seven districts were similar to the seven military districts that existed in the country. Also, five of the governor-generals were former military men, one was a former security official, and only one was a politician. That man was Sergei Kirienko, the former prime minister whose political base was in Nizhni Novgorod. As a consequence, the Russian political analyst Henry Piontkovsky characterized the move as "part of a trend toward the militarization of our country."[18]

Kaliningrad was placed within the Northwest District where the governor general would operate out of St. Petersburg. The man selected for the job was Viktor Cherkesov, like Putin a former KGB operative. Unlike the president, Cherkesov's duties involved prosecution of Soviet-era dissidents, and even after the USSR imploded, he continued to function in a similar capacity. For example, in the 1990s he carried out a five-year campaign to prosecute the environmentalist Alexander Nikitin. Charges against Nikitin were dropped in 1999 but revived in 2000. Ruslan Linkov, an opposition politician, said Cherkesov's appointment was "the worst thing that can happen. The old ways are coming back."[19]

Putin scored another victory against the regional executives when he introduced a decree that would bar the governor and regional legislative leaders from serving on the Federation Council. This meant that the regional officials no longer would enjoy the cover of immunity from prosecution. Indeed, the Kremlin could remove regional authorities who were accused of violating federal law from office.

These actions were endorsed overwhelmingly by the Duma but rejected by some members of the council. Ingushetia's Governor Ruslan Aushev said the plan meant the country was returning to "the Soviet era" when Moscow controlled all levers of power in the so-called federal system.[20] Some political analysts claimed Putin could not make this change in the polity by decree, but only a revision in the 1993 constitution could achieve that objective legally. The Duma, however, supported Putin and overturned the Federation Council's attempt to maintain its status.

Simultaneously, Putin created a state council designed to coordinate relations between Moscow and the regions. Only twenty appointees would serve on the council, and it was assumed those seats would be given to representatives from the regions that wielded considerable economic and political power. Clearly, the new body would not provide the regional authorities with access to federal deliberations in the same way that the Federation Council did. Some commentators in Russia and abroad cited changes in the old council as further proof that Putin was resurrecting a new dictatorial state.

But even some foreign scholars deemed the Federation Council as inconsistent with the workings of a democratic federation. "The Federation Council has most often acted to disrupt the development of a normal federation by seeking to retain and expand regional powers far beyond that envisioned in any effective federal system."[21]

To make certain that the regions did not withhold taxes from Moscow, Putin appointed former Prime Minister Sergei Stepashin to head an agency auditing them. Also, Putin ordered that henceforth Interior Ministry personnel in the regions would be hired and fired by Moscow; regional officials would have nothing to do with the matter. To drive home the fact that Moscow would no longer tolerate regional executives issuing illegal decrees, Putin negated such actions in several areas.

In a move to further restrict regional independence, the Kremlin announced that regions planning to do business with a foreign power had to register with Moscow before doing so. Changes in the tax code also denied the regions the same level of revenues that they had enjoyed during the previous decade. For example, a flat 13 percent tax on income was adopted, and since the regions relied largely upon this source of revenue, they in particular would be hurt by the move to reduce the revenues it generated. Moscow's Mayor Luzhkov calculated that as a result of changes in the tax code, the federal government would control 65 percent of the country's taxes and the regions only 35 percent. Before the revision, the percentages were 52 percent and 48 percent respectively.[22]

Luzhkov suffered another blow when the Constitutional Court ruled that Moscow's residential registration system was unconstitutional because regional authorities had no legal right to dictate where Russians could reside.[23]

For many observers both in and outside of Russia, Putin's actions represented proof that he was not prepared to allow the regions to function as similar bodies did in other federal systems. Others concluded that only time would tell just how far Putin intended to go in eliminating anomalies in the

Russian federal system that obviously had to be changed. Indeed, he did not go as far as some feared he would. For example, Putin did not make changes in how regional executives were selected. On the basis of statements that he had made while prime minister, it was deemed certain that as president he would end the direct election of regional executives, but he said that would not be a wise move since the people now expected to select their regional leaders.

While there was cause for pessimism about Putin's actions, one could conclude that in the first months of his presidency he was testing the waters. He himself was not sure how far he wanted or could go in reimposing Moscow's total control over Russia's regions. If he truly tried to emasculate them, he would face resistance both within and outside of Russia. As a pragmatist, it could be surmised, he would not go that far.

Notes

1. Stuart J. Kaufman, "The Baltic States in Post–Cold War U.S. Strategy," in *The Baltic States in World Politics,* ed. Birthe Hansen and Bertel Heurlin (Surrey, England: Curzon, 1998), 59–60.

2. Alexander A. Pikayev, "Russia and the Baltic States," in Hansen and Heurlin, eds., *The Baltic States,* 137.

3. See, for example, Charles Clover, "Dreams of the Eurasian Heartland," *Foreign Affairs* 78, no. 2 (April 1999), 9–13.

4. Dmitri Trenin, *Baltic Chance* (Washington, D.C.: Carnegie Endowment for International Peace, 1997), 14.

5. *Baltic News Service,* 5 October 1998.

6. Steven Main, "The Prospects Posed by the Kaliningrad Oblast and Possible Solutions for the Future," paper, June 1997, 5.

7. RFE/RL *Newsline,* 10 February 1999.

8. RFE/RL *Newsline,* 19 January 1999.

9. EWI, *Russian Regional Review* 4, no. 2 (21 January 1999): 4.

10. EWI, *Russian Regional Review* 4, no. 7 (25 February 1999): 3–4.

11. Pikayev, "Russia and the Baltic States," 150.

12. Alexander Sergounin, "Russia's Security Policies in the Baltic Sea Area," (NUPI, Conference on Long-Term Security Prospects for the Baltic Sea Area, Oslo, 23–24 May 1997), 467. For a discussion of Poland's relations with Russia since 1989, see Sarah Meiklejohn Terry, "Poland's Foreign Policy Since 1989: The Challenge of Independence," *Communist and Post-Communist Studies,* 33 (2000), 7–47.

13. Interviews with Russian officials in the spring of 1998 in Kaliningrad and Moscow.

14. "Kaliningrad Against New Border," *The Baltic Times,* 20–26 November 1997, 6.

15. Interviews with Lithuanian diplomats in 1998 and 1999.

16. European diplomats who favor this kind of relationship nevertheless concede

that widespread ignorance about the EU among the political classes in Moscow represents a barrier to such cooperation. They make the same complaint about ignorance about the EU in Washington. This remark is in keeping with the widely held view among foreign diplomats, who have worked with the Russians for decades, that many "Russians do not do their homework" and without a common knowledge base, fruitful discussion is extremely difficult. There are, of course, world-class diplomats and analysts in Russia, but in many Russian ministries and institutions the remnants of Soviet-era work habits—and preoccupation with protecting one's turf and not embarking upon difficult or controversial programs—remain in place. Mastering the agency's political culture therefore takes priority over mastering the substance of one's job. This condition is not uncommon in the West but it is not as prominent, because the political environment is less volatile and innovative workers enjoy the protection of a functioning legal system. Therefore, Western officials can devote more time to mastering their jobs and less energy to preventing hostile or arbitrary forces from placing their positions at risk. Western officials and others who work in Russia's regions, of course, have had the same experience.

17. Stephen E. Hanson, "Ideology, Interests, and Identity" in *Center Periphery Conflict in Post-Soviet Russia,* ed. Mikhail Alexseev (New York: St. Martin's Press, 1999), 15–46.

18. *Globe and Daily Mail,* 13 May 2000.

19. *Washington Post,* 3 August 2000.

20. RFE/RL *Newsline,* 19 May 2000.

21. Alfred Stepan, "Russian Federalism in Perspective," *Post-Soviet Affairs* 16, no. 2 (spring 2000): 161.

22. *Nezavisimaya Gazeta,* 21 July 2000.

23. EWI, *Russian Regional Review,* 2 July 2000.

8

The United States and Kaliningrad

America's Grand Design in Europe

W HAT POLICIES SHOULD the United States adopt toward Kaliningrad? In the twenty-first century, the answer to this question must be assessed against the backdrop of the two major U.S. policy objectives in Europe. The first is to safeguard the zone of democracy that has appeared with the collapse of the Soviet empire. The second is to integrate Russia into the Euro-Atlantic community while building new security architecture there.

The Clinton administration issued a grand design for U.S. foreign policy in February 1996: "While democracy will not soon take hold everywhere, it is our interest to do all that we can to enlarge the community of free and open societies, especially in areas of greatest strategic interest, as in Central and Eastern Europe and the new independent states of the former Soviet Union."[1] Afterward President Clinton stated more cryptically, like George Bush before him, that the U.S. goal is to create a Europe "whole and free." This means empowering people who endorse the cherished values of liberal democracy and a free-market economy and establishing an institutional framework that enhances the prospects of democracies throughout Europe.

President George W. Bush entered the White House in 2001 supported by foreign-policy advisers who indicated that the new administration would devote less time and resources to Europe than the Clinton administration did. But like his father, the younger Bush remains committed to a Europe that is whole and free.

Among NATO planners there is confusion about the precise reason the alliance should be enlarged now that the Soviet Union has been lost in the mist of history. In considering candidates for membership, NATO planners assert that any new member must be a military asset and not a liability to the alliance. Why insist on this requirement? The answer is simple. It assumes NATO's primary mission is to deter, and if necessary defeat, an aggressor that possesses the conventional military capability—or something close to it—of the former Soviet Union. Yet there is no country in Europe that will acquire that capability for a long time, if ever.

NATO today, without the addition of a single new tank or soldier, has the ability to deal with any existing or future military threat to Europe for many years. The most imminent and serious threat to European stability is the economic upheaval, social disarray, and political discord spawned by the collapse of the Soviet empire and the difficult transition of its former satellites and republics from closed to open societies. This condition not only contributes to instability in Eastern and Central Europe, but it also may hamper member states there from making the transition from communism to democracy.

After World War II, the United States provided the British, French, and Germans with the military protection that enabled them to rebuild societies ravaged by war. It is unlikely that they would have achieved those objectives with Marshall Plan assistance alone. The overarching security that NATO provided them was pivotal to the restoration of their economies and to sustaining their democratic polities.

Safeguarding the Zone of Democracy in Eastern and Central Europe

NATO's primary mission in the post–Cold War world is to provide the new democracies of Central and Eastern Europe with military safeguards that enable them to revitalize societies ravaged by communism. Membership in the EU alone will not achieve that objective.

NATO knows how to put many more divisions in the field armed with the world's most sophisticated weapons, but it does not know how to build democracies. As James Goodby has reminded us: "The essence of European security lies in the process of creating an inclusive community of democratic nations. In this sense, free elections are as much a security measure as are ceilings on the number of tanks."[2] Therefore it is a vital security objective to safeguard those open societies that have appeared with the collapse of the Soviet empire. They must be carefully nurtured, because like Russia, they too are experiencing the aftershocks of transition. Indeed, future economic setbacks may place democracy at risk in those former communist countries where the drive toward democratization thus far has proceeded smoothly. NATO then should provide them the stability acquired through membership as soon as possible. NATO membership alone may not directly promote their economic welfare but it will reduce the real and imagined fears that the people in the region harbor about their future prospects. Such fears, in turn, can exacerbate the daunting economic, political, and social problems that they all are enduring. Their biggest fear is being left out of the Euro-Atlantic community and NATO in particular; in their minds it is the only meaningful link that Europe enjoys with the United States.

NATO's 1999 war with Serbia provides another rationale for promoting democracy and accelerating the enlargement process. In contemporary Europe, states that rule largely by political power (force) and not political authority (that is, with the popular legitimacy acquired through democracy) are inherently unstable. Without the rule of law, they can achieve order at home only by resorting to force. Simultaneously, they are prone to settle problems with their neighbors in a similar fashion and/or to encourage anti-democratic elements in those countries. The very prospect of joining NATO has helped settle border questions such as those between Hungary and Romania, and Germany and Poland. It also has encouraged a host of countries to ensure the rights of minority peoples within their own countries, for example the Russians in Estonia and Latvia, and the Roma in several Central and Eastern European countries.

Some Washington critics of democratization retort that the United States can neither impose democracies on the peoples of the world nor have the resources to embark upon such a Herculean campaign. There are merits to both of these objections, but they ignore two trenchant facts.

First, the focus here is upon Europe, not the entire world. In contrast to some peoples in the world, those living in what was once the Soviet Union's "outer empire"—the satellites in Eastern Europe (and many of them in the USSR's "inner-empire"—the former Baltic republics) are eager to join the European community of democracies. They do not see strict requirements for membership in European institutions as an imposition upon them of "alien" Western values as do many people in Africa, the Middle East, the Far East, and Russia.

On the contrary, they share "organic—historical, cultural, political, and religious—linkages" with their cousins in the Euro-Atlantic democracies. These organic linkages are assets, not liabilities, in protecting the zone of democracy in Central and Eastern Europe. It behooves U.S. military planners to exploit them as the Bush administration devotes more time and resources to trouble spots in the Middle East and Asia. By protecting the zone of

democracy in Europe via organic forces, U.S. armed forces can be redeployed
to the Far East where similar organic assets are not in place.

Should autocratic governments replace failed democracies in the region,
the costs of coping with this setback will be awesome. Consider in this connection the burden that Western taxpayers have had to endure after their
leaders failed to anticipate and prevent the Balkan wars. For example, by
1999, the bill for the peacekeeping troops that first arrived in Bosnia in the
aftermath of the 1995 Dayton Accords had reached $9.4 billion.[3] The expen-
ditures for NATO's war against Milosevic's Serbia and the cost of rebuilding
Kosovo, and eventually Serbia, will certainly exceed the Bosnian bill. And, of
course, the financial burden is only a small part of the larger picture. "The
four years of battles and massacres had claimed some 200,000 lives, made
refugees of half of the Bosnian population of 4.3 million, and displaced the
largest number of children since World War II."[4]

Critics of NATO's first-round enlargement opposed membership for the
Czech Republic, Hungary, and Poland because all three were deemed militarily deficient. But the stability the three new members have contributed to
Central Europe, by the virtue of their being democracies, far exceeds any military contribution they conceivably could have made to peace in the region.
In short, democratic political assets are far more important to the alliance
than another shipload of smart bombs.

The three Baltic countries seek the safe harbor of European institutions,
the EU and NATO, because they deem themselves Europeans and celebrate
the values of their European heritage. They are wedded to NATO membership in particular because it is explicitly a security organization to which the
United States—a European nation in North America—belongs.[5] Friendly
commentators, who urge the Balts to forget NATO and concentrate on EU
membership instead, should keep this in mind and not forget that for a half
century they lived under a cruel dictatorship that threatened their existence
as a people.

In the same way that the British, French, and Germans relied upon U.S.
military power to help foster stability in Western Europe, the Balts see their
security primarily in terms of U.S. protection. Europe's failure to develop a
common foreign and security policy, and its inability to prevent the awful
wars in the Balkans, is just another reason that they look to the United States
for security guarantees.

But what about Russia's opposition to the inclusion of the Balts in NATO
with a second round of enlargement? NATO's bombing of Serbia has heightened this concern among some Western officials and analysts. Opponents
of enlargement in Washington in particular have deemed growing anti-

Americanism in Russia, spawned by NATO's action in the Balkans, as an asset in their campaign to keep the Balts out of the alliance.

What both opponents of enlargement in the West and Russia blithely ignore is that the Baltics are sovereign states and have a right to join any alliance of their choosing. Furthermore, the pivotal role they played in the Soviet empire's implosion has earned them a place in the alliance—and the gratitude of Americans and Russians alike.

In late March 2001, Vladimir Putin met with Lithuania's President Valdas Adamkus, and acknowledged that every country had a right to become a member of any security system that it wanted to join. But in a joint statement, the presidents also agreed to the following caveat: No state could "strengthen its own security at the expense of other countries." Putin argues that Russia's security will be jeopardized should Lithuania become a member of NATO.[6]

However, those in Russia who object to Baltic membership cannot ignore the fact that Moscow stands to gain by the expansion of NATO's border eastward. As indicated earlier, having stable democracies on its western borders is an asset as Russia deals with truly dangerous security problems in the Caucasus, the former Soviet Central Asian Republics, and braces for the mounting presence of China in its Far Eastern territories. For example, an estimated 2.5 million Chinese "illegals" now live in Russia's Far East.[7]

Democratic-minded Russian officials and intellectuals—and ordinary folk as well—have been reminded of this truism as President Lukashenko maintains a Soviet-style dictatorship on the border. Lukashenko has arrested opposition politicians and Belarussian and Russian journalists for publishing the truth about developments in Minsk. Would the Russians really feel more secure were their Western neighbors wracked by internal upheaval and governed by dictators?

Also, history has demonstrated that weak and unstable governments in Eastern and Central Europe ultimately contribute to disharmony, not harmony, between Germany and Russia. This is one of the most compelling reasons that the Baltic countries must not become a gray zone in the borderland separating the old Soviet Union and the new democratic Europe. As Russian observers like Mikhail Alexseev and Vladimir Vagin have demonstrated, areas of Northwest Russia stand to benefit economically as the Baltic states are integrated into Europe's major institutions—NATO as well as the EU.

The prospect that Ukraine may retreat from democracy and a market economy is additional cause for Russian democrats to look with favor upon stable democracies in Central and Eastern Europe to countervail that eventuality. Prospects for the development of a stable democracy with a viable free-market economy in the Ukraine are not good. Democratic institutions and a democratic political culture alike are weak in Ukraine, and one could make the case that the prospects for democracy are better in Russia than in Ukraine. In spite of the reelection of Leonid Kuchma in 1999—characterized as pro-West—instability in Ukraine threatens the zone of democracy throughout Eastern and Central Europe and is a further incentive for expediting both EU and NATO enlargement. Meanwhile, sober-minded practitioners of realpolitik in Moscow cannot long ignore the fact that Russia has limited resources to deal with its real security problems in other parts of the old empire and not imagined ones in the Baltic Sea region.

Finally, the residents of Kaliningrad, who are seeking to build a prosperous democratic society founded upon the rule of law, can be benefactors of democratic neighbors who are experiencing economic growth. Economic disparities between Lithuania and Poland on the one hand and Kaliningrad on the other hand may cause friction, but consider the plight of the Kaliningraders were they to be located in a territory surrounded by antidemocratic regimes and neighbors who were enduring the same economic and social problems that plague their oblast. Kaliningrad's residents live rather in one of the most stable areas of Europe with (mostly) prosperous, peaceful neighbors who are prepared to help them revitalize their economy and address the social and ecological problems that blight their lives.

Integrating Russia into Europe

The second major U.S. objective in post–Cold War Europe is to integrate Russia into Europe, and through cooperation with NATO build new security architecture there. It was perhaps possible for the first Bush administration, in league with America's European allies, to have begun working with Russia toward this end in the early 1990s, but both lacked the vision to do so. There was no guarantee of success, but no attempt was made at all and this was a serious blunder. At any rate, in the twenty-first century the prospects of integrating Russia into the Euro-Atlantic community can be achieved only through incremental steps. There are, however, three major obstacles to the successful accomplishment of this objective and one is pivotal to stability in Eurasia.

A Difficult Transition

A major barrier to Russia's integration into the Euro-Atlantic community is the awesome problems Russia faces as it make the difficult transition from a closed to an open society. The economic, social, and political dislocations associated with the transition have been discussed at length in this book and they will continue to foster instability in Russia for many years.

As a result of these dislocations, and persistent fears that President Putin might resort to antidemocratic policies to treat them, leaders of the Western democracies face serious political opposition from their constituents as they adopt programs designed to enhance Russia's economic prospects. Critics ask how it can be justified when commercial, banking, and other laws that safeguard investment are not in place—not to mention that criminals and corrupt officials have stolen funds from private investors and the international community.

Upon replacing Clinton in the White House, President George W. Bush and his advisers have stated on numerous occasions that unlike their predecessors they will not get entangled in Russian internal affairs.

Russia Isolates Itself

Many politicians and military leaders in Moscow are distrustful of the West. Reasons for this condition have already been cited: NATO's war with Serbia, and European and U.S. criticism of Russia's brutal military operations in Chechnya being two recent examples. Many ordinary Russians, and not only those associated with the military or power ministries, are distrustful of the West. In November 1999, a poll indicated that 41.1 percent of the Russian people believed the West wanted to transform Russia into a Third World country, and 37.5 percent said the West wanted to split Russia apart.[8] Because of U.S. power, Russians are deeply suspicious of Washington and are inclined to see the United States in particular as feeding Western enmity toward Russia.

During the last years of Yeltsin's presidency, Russian foreign-policy officials warned of America's "uni-polar hegemony" in much the same fashion that Chinese and French officials did. Indeed, Putin has sought to exploit concern about Washington's "imperial reach" to drive a wedge between the Americans and Europeans. After he became president, Putin demonstrated that Russia under his stewardship would be even more forthright in pursing international policies that the United States would not like. Among other things, this included playing a larger role in the Middle East and reaching out to regimes—such as Iran—that Washington has labeled "pariah states."

There is no cause for alarm that Russia is playing a more active role in world affairs under Putin than Yeltsin. It is disturbing, however, that many Russian elites have not yet come to grips with the fact that Russia will never be as powerful as the Soviet Union. Under the spell of this delusion, Russia's leaders refuse to recognize that their empire is lost forever and that it behooves them to look inward, that is, to concentrate on building the resources of the rich society in which they live.

Vladimir Putin's efforts to restore a powerful state in Russia and to project power abroad lends credence to those in the West who fear that he too may be under the delusion of "empire envy." Indeed, in the spring of 2000, the Russian Foreign Ministry continued to insist that the Baltic countries voluntarily joined the USSR in 1940 and were not forced into the Soviet empire. The people living in those democracies and their leaders were appalled by this action, although the European and U.S. leadership chose to ignore it.[9]

During the 2000 U.S. presidential campaign, George W. Bush cited a related problem: the propensity of the Clinton administration to treat Russia (rhetorically, at least) as if it wielded power equal to that enjoyed by the United States. In part, during the 1990s, under Presidents Bush and Clinton, Washington avoided humiliating the Russians, certainly a prudent course to follow. But Republicans charged that President Clinton acted upon the belief that unless Washington supported Yeltsin, people less friendly to the United States would replace him. One concrete result of this policy was that it encouraged Russian elites in the belief that Russia will one day enjoy the same prerogatives of "big power" status that the USSR once enjoyed.

Those in the West who would give Moscow a veto over NATO enlargement further encourage Russian leaders to cling to exaggerated notions about Russia's place in the world. The West should not demonize Russia, but it should not patronize the leaders in Moscow either, when its self-interest collides with Russia. It must not remain silent when Russia engages in self-destructive behavior. Most importantly of all, like the leaders of other former great empires the Russians must recognize that the non-Russian peoples, whom the czars and Soviets once subjugated, no longer will accept Russian hegemony. If Moscow persists in this ill-conceived idea, the very integrity of Russia itself may be placed at risk. Among other things, it may result in Russia's adopting a policy of virtual self-isolation from the rest of the world.

The West Isolates Russia

The view among some Western statesmen that Russia cannot ever become a part of Europe is a companion to the failure of Russian leaders to recognize their country's power limitations.

Henry Kissinger has written: "Russia is in, but not of Europe; it borders Asia, Central Asia, and the Middle East, and it pursues policies along these borders that are difficult to reconcile with NATO objectives."[10] Kissinger's major premise that Russia is not a European society is one supported by other Western commentators who assert that any campaign to integrate Russia into Europe is quixotic. This is the flip side of the argument that Russians like Zyuganov make that Russia is an Eurasian power and should turn inward, not toward the West, to find solutions to its problems. The logic of both arguments dictate that Russia will become isolated in the twenty-first century—not integrated with the West.

Whatever the historical and cultural divide that separates the West and Russia, there is no reason that it cannot be crossed and a positive relationship forged between Moscow and Washington in addressing matters of vital self-interest. James E. Goodby has documented that during the Cold War the enmity between the West and the Soviet Union was far greater than existing cleavages between the West and Russia. Nonetheless, rules of behavior were crafted that spared the world a nuclear holocaust.[11]

Since the USSR's implosion, an even larger number of Russians have had contacts with the West and have embraced a decidedly European, and not Eurasian, identity. Most younger, better-educated Russians look toward Europe, not Asia, when they talk about Russia becoming a "normal country." They are not uncritical of the West but they clearly hope to build the same kind of open society that they have experienced during their travels to Europe and North America or know from books, TV, and the Internet.

At the same time, Russia's fractious relations with its neighbors to the South have prompted many Russians to leave those areas and to seek new homes in Russia. That out-migration will continue as anti-Russian feelings spread through predominantly Muslim areas of the former Soviet empire. The hostile rhetoric that has been leveled at Russia and Russians from people of the South have disabused many Russians of the idea that they have more in common with their southern neighbors than they have with their "fellow Europeans."

The failure of Russia to knit together a viable Moscow-dominated CIS, compels clear-thinking Russian leaders to focus upon the revitalization of Russia. The latest fighting in Chechnya demonstrates that the costs of maintaining imperial hegemony may place the very integrity of Russia itself at risk.

Those in the West who perceive Russia, by design or inadvertence, as hopelessly wedded to an anti-democratic heritage should not forget that Germany and Japan had little experience with democracy, too, yet both have embraced democratic values and institutions. Of course, unlike Russia, they lost World War II and were occupied by democratic forces, which helped them make the transition from autocracy to democracy.

Still there is no reason that Russia cannot become a democracy over time as more and more Russians interact with people from democratic societies and democratic values are flashed before them via modern technology. Nostalgia for the Soviet Union remains strong but it is largely a phenomenon associated with older Russians who are passing from the scene more quickly than their longer-living cohorts in the West. Just like the "class of '38" (those young people in the USSR who were thrust into positions of influence at an early age due to Stalin's purges of their elders in the 1930s), younger Russians today have been more adroit than their elders at exploiting the new economic opportunities that have arisen with the Soviet Union's collapse. Many of them are unhappy with their existing living standards but they do not favor a return to the past. Prolonged deprivation could drive them into the arms of anti-democratic demagogues and end Russia's quest to build a democratic society. But no one who has closely watched Russia can deny a very compelling fact: it is a far more open and democratic society today than it ever has been.

In the twenty-first century, relations between Moscow and Washington can improve through step-by-step cooperative measures that build confidence on both sides and set the stage for the adoption of even more ambitious cooperative efforts. In this fashion, the Russians and Americans may achieve other common goals that are vital to both of them: for example, the reduction of nuclear weapons through the START process, curbing the global proliferation of weapons of mass destruction, building a missile defense system, combating terrorism, and helping Russia build a democratic society with a healthy free-market economy.

The United States and Russia must find areas of cooperation—no matter how modest they might be—because there are numerous areas of dispute separating them that will persist. Even assuming the bad feelings—which appeared on both sides over NATO's war with Serbia and Russia's brutal assault on Chechnya—subside, there are many areas of friction between Washington and Moscow that are likely to persist for years:

1. Disputes over Russian arms transfers to Iraq, Iran, and other countries that Washington, D.C., deems to be pariah states.
2. Differences over political and economic policies toward such states.
3. Competition over access to and control over the Caspian Sea region's gas and oil riches.
4. The conviction on the part of many Russian leaders and ordinary citizens, who harbor nostalgic feelings about the Soviet system, that the Americans want to emasculate Russia so that the United States will reign as the world's only superpower.
5. The suspicion on the part of many Americans that, after the Russian economy rebounds, the old Communist apparatchiks still controlling Russia have no intention of maintaining good relations with the West.

6. Friction between Washington and Moscow over the Bush administration's campaign to build a national missile defense system.

Joint Western–Russian programs that alleviate Kaliningrad's problems can serve as a positive counterpoint to these areas of discord between Washington and Moscow. Through a demonstration of good will, Washington can help ameliorate the fear of many Russians that the United States wants to isolate their country. Kaliningrad hardly looms large in the minds of the Russian people, but by helping address the oblast's problems, a culture of cooperation between the two countries may be promoted. In the final analysis, truly harmonious and trusting American–Russian relations will not materialize overnight in a single grand leap forward but incrementally through a series of modest measures such as those envisaged in U.S. assistance to Kaliningrad.

Also, Western developmental efforts in Kaliningrad may provide answers to the pivotal question: How can the West help Russia resolve the problems which threaten the creation of both a democratic polity and a free-market economy?

Skeptics in the U.S. Congress and the White House are right in remarking that Russians in the final analysis must take measures and make sacrifices to build democracy and capitalism in their country. They must develop an effective legal system and the capacity to enforce it, collect taxes and protect the needy in society against further deterioration in their living conditions, and fight crime and corruption while building a strong democratic state.

Russia is far too large for the United States to provide economic assistance that will have a significant impact upon its development prospects. But Kaliningrad, with a population of less than one million people and a territory the size of Northern Ireland, may serve as a testing ground and provide insight into ways the West can better help Russia as it moves from a closed to an open society.

All these arguments are proffered in favor of Washington directing its attention to Kaliningrad with appropriate policy responses. Ironically, the stability that northeastern Europe has enjoyed since the collapse of Soviet Communism accounts for its relative neglect—for example, in contrast to the West's preoccupation with the fractious Balkans. In a Council on Foreign Relations task-force report, "U.S. Policy toward Northeastern Europe," Zbigniew Brzezinski and his colleagues proposed that the U.S. government develop a coherent approach to northeastern Europe. On the basis of their deliberations, the task force reached seven conclusions, which U.S. authorities should consider in developing a "Kaliningrad policy" within the framework of an overall policy toward northeastern Europe.[12]

1. During the Cold War, northeastern Europe was a strategic backwater and received relatively little attention in U.S. policy. However, since the end of the Cold War, the region has become an important focal point of U.S. policy.
2. Northeastern Europe is also a test case for the administration's policy toward Russia.
3. Three critical areas of U.S. policy interest—the Baltics, the Nordics, and Russia—intersect in northeast Europe. [Furthermore] the Baltic region is the one region in Europe where a U.S.–Russian confrontation is still conceivable.
4. The United States faces a number of critical challenges in the region. One of the most important is managing the security aspirations of the Baltic states.
5. The policy challenges in northeastern Europe—particularly those in the Baltic subregion—directly touch on Russia's security interests and have important implications for U.S.–Russian relations.
6. The issue of security in northeastern Europe directly affects U.S. relations with the Nordic states, especially Sweden and Finland.
7. Security issues in northeastern Europe pose important dilemmas for U.S. policy toward NATO. The Baltic issue is the trickiest and most sensitive part of the enlargement puzzle.[13]

The task force recommended that the U.S. Department of State appoint a senior official for regional cooperation in northeastern Europe; that the Clinton administration provide more resources to implement its policies in the region; that the "United States should differentiate between the Baltic states based on their performance and should admit them into Euro-Atlantic institutions individually rather than a group"; that one Baltic country, Lithuania, be considered in the next round of NATO enlargement; that the Clinton administration impress upon Congress the rationale for a Kaliningrad policy; and that it should seek greater support on this score from its European allies.[14]

This "Northern European" initiative is the U.S. analogue to the EU's "Northern Dimension" and the fact that a number of influential U.S. foreign-policy analysts have rallied around it suggests that Washington may be ready to address the Kaliningrad Question. On the basis of the analysis that has been conducted in this study, what specific policy guidance can we offer U.S. policy makers?

Adopting a Low Profile

The United States must adopt a low profile in any assistance program for Kaliningrad lest fears in Moscow about separatism, and mischief making on

Washington's part, are exacerbated. America's role should be one of supporter, not leader. Some Russian political elites, stung by the U.S.–Baltic Charter and the Clinton and Bush administrations offering NATO membership to Lithuania, have interpreted both as evidence that the United States is bent on dictating the terms of Western assistance to the oblast.

Russian commentators, even those of a liberal bent, remind their U.S. colleagues that Russia may no longer dominate the Baltic Sea area as it did during the Cold War, but Moscow's weakened position will not last forever and Russia will naturally reassert its presence there when it is revived. After all, it is in Russia's and not America's back yard! In the meantime, the Americans have no business mucking about there. "How would you feel if we made our presence felt in Mexico?" they proclaim.

Many other Russians not of a liberal bent are even more vocal in claiming that the United States is insincere about helping Kaliningrad: Washington is feigning interest in the oblast but its real intentions are to open NATO's door to the Baltics. NATO's crossing the so-called Red Line, therefore, not only precipitates hostile outbursts from the Communists and ultranationalists, it even prompts some of their Western-oriented Russian opponents to respond with heat.

As previously indicated, trepidation about a heavy U.S. presence in the region is exhibited not only by Moscow, but by Bonn as well, and by some of the Scandinavian countries, too. The Germans supported NATO enlargement to remove Germany as a "front-line" state, but Washington's promising the Balts membership in NATO has unsettled the German government. (Some German diplomats claim that they do not oppose the idea but they are at odds with the notion that it should be accomplished in the year 2002.) When Helmut Kohl was chancellor, he feared this promise would place his special relationship with Yeltsin's Russia at risk and he preferred that the United States not make its presence felt in the region. It appears that Kohl's successor, the Social Democrat Gerhard Schroder, is of the same opinion.

Scandinavian analysts, who believe a Baltic rim identity can be established along with functional regional organizations that promote the welfare of all of the region's inhabitants—the Balts, Germans, Poles, Russians, and Scandinavians—look warily upon Uncle Sam's presence there. The Cold War served as an artificial barrier to both, and assertive U.S. activities could place them at risk; it would spook the Russians and diminish the prospects that they would cooperate in accomplishing regional priorities—such as regional economic development, decontaminating the Baltic sea, and dismantling nuclear power plants, fighting crime, and curbing illegal immigration.

Some Baltic and Scandinavian governments, which otherwise welcome a U.S. presence in the region, worry that the Americans are prone to dwell upon the security implications of most issues. And even when they do not, given their awesome military might, it is difficult not to think of hard security issues when they are present.

American authorities have indicated that they see U.S. involvement in any program devoted to Kaliningrad as supportive and not U.S.-directed, as unobtrusive and not assertive. All indications are then that Washington is prepared to adopt a low profile should it participate in a joint Western–Russian development program for Kaliningrad.

Focusing on Soft Security Issues

U.S. diplomats agree with their European and Russian counterparts that any Western assistance program to Kaliningrad must treat soft (not hard) security questions—for example, ecological restoration, resolving economic and social problems, providing technical assistance in public administration and border control, crime, and sickness prevention, and so on.

In June 1999, Marc Grossman, the assistant secretary of state for European affairs, addressed the Council of Baltic Sea States, the first time an American had appeared before CBSS as an official observer. Grossman indicated that one of his first acts as a newly appointed assistant secretary two years earlier was to launch in Bergen, Norway, the U.S. government's Northern European Initiative. Its six priorities were:

1. Strengthening civil society
2. Promoting business
3. Protecting and restoring the environment
4. Seeking safe and efficient energy sources and use
5. Promoting public health
6. Preventing transnational crime[15]

A year earlier, Grossman had told the same group: "The United States cannot—and should not—become involved in all areas in which you are building regional cooperation. But there may be areas where we can provide what we call 'value added' and make a contribution that will help achieve your goals."[16]

The U.S. government has supported a variety of programs in the region. For example:

1. An HIV/AIDS information and drug prevention program in Klaipeda schools that Washington is considering for other cities in the region, including Kaliningrad.

2. A $200,000 disease control program that has been developed for Latvia to prevent the spread of an especially dangerous strain of drug-resistant tuberculosis.
3. With the Soros Foundation, and through the Baltic American Partnership Fund, $400,000 has been earmarked to support the work of NGOs in helping build civil societies in the region. The fund has a total budget of $15 million to develop and sustain NGOs in the area.
4. An additional $300,000 has been allocated to help Lithuania and Estonia develop energy programs.
5. $500,000 to help Latvia implement its new citizenship law.
6. The United States has provided $600,000 to sponsor a Great Lakes–Baltic Sea partnership program that rests upon the Environmental Protection Agency's expertise in cleaning up polluted waterways.
7. The United States also has provided $500,000 for nuclear fuel containment vessels in Murmansk.
8. The U.S. Environmental Protection Agency is also conducting clearwater programs for the Nemunas River; at some points it serves as a border between Lithuania and Kaliningrad.

The help provided, however, does not represent the kind of extensive and strategic assistance that Kaliningrad watchers deem necessary to address the daunting problems facing Russia's westernmost region.

Providing Help through a Variety of Channels

U.S. assistance to Kaliningrad may be canalized in a variety of ways.

The U.S. government, for example, should exploit Lithuania's special relationship with Kaliningrad to provide assistance to the oblast. Lithuania's assistance to Kaliningrad has received favorable attention in both Washington and Moscow.

A move in this direction has already been made. For example, the National Endowment for Democracy has funded a project to help local officials in several Kaliningrad cities develop public administration skills. The program is being carried out through Kaunas-based Vytautas Magnus University and is being conducted by Lithuanian consultants who have been working with local Kaliningrad officials. The latter have complained that they have not received any help from the governor's office to develop budgetary, human resource, and skills needed to run a city or town.[17] They apparently feel a greater comfort level working with Lithuanian than with Western trainers, because the Lithuanians were once part of the Soviet empire and know from whence their Kaliningrad colleagues are coming. What's more, they speak Russian and live in close proximity to the Kaliningrad officials, whom they can visit in trips that take hours at most, not days, in planning and execution. Consequently, it is neither time-consuming nor expensive to conduct follow-up activities. Meanwhile, federal officials in Moscow welcome Lithuanian help, because they have no fears about the motives of a small, weak neighbor that they have praised for its positive and cooperative relations with Kaliningrad.

The U.S. government should provide funding to American NGOs that are capable of providing a range of assistance—educational, medical, business development, computer skills, and so on—to Kaliningrad individuals and organizations. As Marc Grossman has indicated, the U.S. government has been working with the Soros Foundation to help build civil societies, promote regional energy programs, curb crime, and address ecological problems in the Baltic countries and northwest Russia. Among other programs, Soros has provided funds to help former Russian Army officers start businesses in Kaliningrad. More help of this nature is required, and American, German, Lithuanian, Polish, and Scandinavian NGOs should develop a network of relationships that help resolve Kaliningrad's problems.

Another channel for U.S. assistance, which should reduce Moscow's concerns about a strong U.S. presence, is to work through subregional organizations such as the Council of Baltic Sea States, to which Russia belongs. By definition, CBSS is not configured to treat hard security questions and it is well-suited to foster cooperative efforts that address a range of serious problems—ecological, economic, crime, and so on. In this connection, Ian Bremmer and Alyson Bailes write, "Sub-regional groups in Europe do not and should not attempt to be primary providers of security." But they can "cushion or mediate the tensions of NATO/EU enlargement." Furthermore, "regular meetings and the creation of personal ties encourage esprit de corps, create channels of communication which might also be used to defuse crisis; and should at least unconsciously strengthen taboos against the use of force."[18]

Unfortunately, some Scandinavian diplomats report that Russian participation in CBSS activities has been episodic; that may be a function of Moscow's propensity to ignore entities it does not believe are deserving of serious Russian participation. This "big-power" mindset has represented a barrier to Russian cooperation with smaller states in the Baltic Sea region, but the 1998 crisis may have induced beleaguered Russian political leaders and analysts to recognize that they need help from whatever quarter it can be secured.

The EU, of course, is a different matter because Russia recognizes it as a powerful economic organization with vast resources and expertise that Russia badly needs. The EU consequently is in a position to play the role of Russia's major partner in developing and managing significant Western programs earmarked to revitalize Kaliningrad's economy. One would hope the EU decides to undertake the kind of far-reaching development program for Kaliningrad that its TACIS experts have recommended. Although the United States is not a member, it has the capacity to lobby the EU states and urge them to support the kind of comprehensive development program which TACIS experts in Kaliningrad have requested. U.S. influence would take on greater resonance, of course, should Washington demonstrate a willingness to contribute both financial help and technical assistance to the program.

EU officials argue that one problem here is that the U.S. foreign-policy community displays considerable ignorance about the EU—how it is governed, its programs, its rules, and its current problems and future prospects. The American journalist Elizabeth Pond, a close student of the EU, has documented that U.S. commentators have been both pessimistic and largely wrong about the EU's prospects and performance.[19] Like their Russian colleagues it behooves the Americans to acquire such knowledge to enhance the U.S. government's effectiveness in working with the EU in addressing the Kaliningrad Question. In keeping with the growing understanding that economic questions—that is, soft security issues—will continue to have a significant impact upon promoting European stability, the United States and the EU must establish a more comprehensive relationship than there has been up to the present. The prospect that the EU will become a serious economic competitor to Washington—made most resonant by the introduction of the Euro in 1999—has provided an incentive for such cooperation. A further incentive for Washington paying closer attention to the EU is justified by concern among U.S. defense analysts that the EU's Euro-Force might compromise NATO.

There is already a consensus on the part of EU and U.S. officials that they must cooperate more closely and more extensively in fighting crime in the Baltic Sea region. The problem of organized crime, in particular, is obvious, and Western governments and legislatures realize it deserves more attention than it has received. The economic viability of the former communist countries in the region, and their civil societies, are all at risk in the face of well-organized, financially powerful, and ruthlessly led criminal organizations. Moreover, these Mafias, which have established networks in the region, have global outreach and have attracted the attention of law enforcement officials in Europe and North America. But much more needs to be done to fight them; and given the limited resources of the authorities in Kaliningrad and their neighbors in Poland and Lithuania, both the EU and the United States must provide them all with a lot more financial and technical assistance than they currently receive.

Governments and their legislatures, however, should realize that the specter of Kaliningrad as a black hole and all the other problems associated with it—ecological, social, and economic, and not just crime—must be treated as well. This means the EU and the United States should consider the prospects of undertaking a major development program in Kaliningrad, one that treats all the daunting problems that exist in the oblast. Such help, of course, is predicated upon Moscow's cooperation.

The U.S. Acknowledges Russia's de Jure Possession of Kaliningrad

During the Clinton administration, officials in the U.S. Department of State often mentioned Kaliningrad, but, rhetoric aside, they did not deem it important to U.S. relations with Russia, and some leading officials were ignorant about Washington's legal position on Kaliningrad. For example, early in 2000, at the second anniversary celebration of the U.S.–Baltic Charter, the event's sponsors—the Joint Baltic American National Committee and the Council on Foreign Relations—invited Strobe Talbott to deliver a luncheon address. During his remarks, the deputy secretary of state and the Clinton administration's point man on Russia stressed the importance of Kaliningrad in U.S.–Russian relations. But when this writer asked him why, in light of such comments, the United States continued to deny Russia's de jure control of Kaliningrad, he answered, "But we do!" [recognize Russia's control].

When it was brought to his attention that this was not the State Department's position, Talbott asked for a comment from Ron Asmus, who was the department's official responsible for NATO enlargement. Asmus conceded that this happened to be true. Both Asmus and Talbott quickly added, however, that this was not significant, because the United States recognized Moscow's de facto control of Kaliningrad.

This exchange suggested several things. First, it supported one of the major contentions of this book that even otherwise well-informed U.S. officials possessed only sketchy knowledge of Kaliningrad. Second, this condition existed because, in spite of pronouncements to the contrary, the Kaliningrad Question remained a distant issue in the halls of the U.S. Department of State. And third, it had not been a major topic of concern in U.S.–Russian diplomatic discussions because if it had, the Russians would have made known their displeasure with the U.S. position on the exclave's legal status.

In keeping with U.S. efforts to placate fears in Moscow about separatism, the time has come for the Bush administration to consider revising the U.S. government's position on Kaliningrad's legal status. The existing position, that Kaliningrad is under the "legal administration of Russia," while stopping short of acknowledging Russia's de jure control over the territory, is a barrier to addressing the Kaliningrad Question. As previously indicated, some international law experts claim this position is insupportable and Russia indeed enjoys de jure control of Kaliningrad.

Also, since no government has claims on the oblast (and the prospect of absorbing almost one million Russian speakers is unappealing to Kaliningrad's neighbors), why not state categorically that it is sovereign Russian territory? Washington's current position only reinforces fears in Moscow that the United States is disingenuous about helping Russia develop Kaliningrad and that talk about integrating Russia into Europe is mere propaganda.

Presumably the U.S. position rests on the desire not to foreclose a future change in Kaliningrad's status or to secure some concessions from Moscow in exchange for recognizing Russian sovereignty over the region. But any change in Kaliningrad's status must be accepted by Moscow, so there is no reason not to acknowledge that Kaliningrad belongs to Russia. Indeed, this admission may facilitate any conceivable change in Kaliningrad's status. Recall that Vladimir Shumeiko, a former candidate for governor in Kaliningrad, who once was a Russian deputy prime minister and served as chairman of the Russian Federation Council, made this suggestion in July 1998. He argued that if Kaliningrad were not given this preferential status, the oblast could be wracked by a social explosion and therefore "become a protectorate of a neighboring country or even an area managed by the Council of Europe."[20]

Regardless of the U.S. pledge not to recognize Stalin's annexation of the Baltic countries, the people residing in Kaliningrad are Russians and Russian-speakers and they do not claim that a foreign government has been imposed upon them. Should they ever try to bolt from the Russian Federation, they will be unable to accomplish that objective without Moscow's cooperation. Indeed, U.S. recognition of Russia's de jure control over Kaliningrad may help the oblast achieve republic status within the federation. It also may facilitate greater EU–Russian cooperation on addressing the Kaliningrad Question.

Finally, concessions that can be wrested from Russia in exchange for recognizing its de jure rights in Kaliningrad may be less substantial than the benefits that can be derived from demonstrating that the West does not wish to isolate Russia. Indeed, since no foreign government claims Kaliningrad, it is difficult to identify what benefits can be derived from withholding de jure recognition.

Acknowledging Regional Power in Russia

Putin has sought to curb the power of Russia's regions, but as the country adopts a market economy, the regions will play a larger role in the affairs of Russia than they have in modern Russian history. U.S. policy must acknowledge this development, and the Bush administration has indicated that it favors working directly with Russia's regions. If the relationship between the Center and the regions can be governed by the rule of law and not political deals, that is a plus for democratization in Russia. Devolving power from the Center to the regions also is consistent with grass-roots democracy and not a polity, where power is concentrated in a unitary state that has been the case throughout Russian history. It is also consistent with the EU's support for the principle of "subsidiarity," in other words, to encourage decisions being made at the lowest level of government possible.[21]

Of course, Russia's regions suffer from the same problems that are associated with the Center—corruption, criminal control of the economy, a weak state unable to collect taxes or enforce commercial laws, and so on. It is a mistake therefore to glorify the growth of regional power unless it is accompanied by the rule of law and other features of a truly open society with a functioning free-market economy.

These caveats aside, the United States should consider ways to work directly with the regions where it makes sense to do so. Given the special circumstances that exist in Kaliningrad, a regional focus is justified and it might become a testing ground for U.S.–Russian cooperation on a range of fronts.[22] Once again, the culture of confidence that may be promoted among both U.S. and Russian foreign-policy elites can have positive consequences for both countries and make it easier for them to cooperate in other critical areas of self-interest, such as arms control.

Preparing for the Resumption of Hard Security Issues

While U.S., European, and Russian analysts are in agreement that U.S. involvement in any international efforts to aid Kaliningrad must be low-key and restricted to soft issues, future circumstances may change both the focus and the involvement of Washington in the Baltic Sea region. At some point in the near future, the Kaliningrad Question may once again become entangled with hard security issues and create tensions there. Such points of potential discord must be anticipated so measures can be taken to prevent them from becoming serious sources of friction.

Military analysts in Washington have been concerned about Russian nuclear weapons and the proliferation of weapons-grade material supplies and knowledge about delivery systems passing to pariah states and terrorists. But weapons of mass destruction and delivery systems aside, Russia's massive domestic problems—and their leading to further disintegration of the Russian state and society—have not been seen as the dangerous security problems that they represent.

Many U.S. defense analysts do not acknowledge the truly ominous situation that could arise with further deterioration in the Russian economy and the prospects that it will be stricken by political gridlock and/or anarchy. One is reminded in this connection of the refusal of U.S. officials on the eve of the USSR's collapse to take seriously the trends that indicated it was about to implode. Anyone who suggested that outcome in U.S. defense circles was reminded—with marked impatience and often scorn—that Moscow still possessed a vast nuclear arsenal. Its fleet of 304 Mirved, SS-18s alone could strike the United States with more than 3,000 nuclear warheads.

This misguided preoccupation with Soviet military power blinded most realists to domestic trends in the USSR that indicated the empire was in an advanced stage of disintegration. The propensity to ignore domestic factors and to dwell upon the structures of the international political system is consistent with academic realist theory and helps explain why so many Western scholars and foreign-policy practitioners failed to anticipate the USSR's collapse. Currently, because Russia is militarily weak, like-minded defense analysts are downgrading the significance of Russia in crisis, ignoring the fact that its disintegration could become a source of instability over a vast area of the world. Indeed, we cannot forget that most of the people who live on Earth, and much of the globe's resources, can be found in and around the borders of Russia.

During the first decade of the twenty-first century, Russia will continue to be wracked by economic, political, and social problems that may keep it from achieving political stability and steady economic growth. Consequently, Russia could take on aspects of a failed state, ending the democratic experiment there and thrusting into power antidemocratic leaders who also are hostile to the West. Leaders of this kind conceivably could gain power even if Russia is spared this awful outcome; that is, existing circumstances may precipitate a return to autocracy in Russia and thrust into power those leaders who wish to rebuild an imperial Russian state. Under these circumstances they will adopt more confrontational policies toward the West in general and respond even more concretely to the expansion of NATO. For example, the following Russian responses are plausible:

1. Moscow will revisit the issue of NATO enlargement and protest NATO-related infrastructure improvements in Poland, or at the appearance of

a small number of NATO troops there, and take countermeasures. They may include an effort to upgrade Russia's military assets in Kaliningrad.

2. Should Lithuania be invited to join NATO in 2002, Moscow may impose an economic embargo upon Vilnius and resurrect the old issue of transit through that country to Kaliningrad.
3. Encouraged by hard-liners in Moscow, Lukashenko may close his border with Lithuania and deploy a large concentration of troops at the border, while demands that eastern Lithuania really belongs to Belarus are aggressively promulgated in Minsk.
4. Moscow may demand renegotiations of the CFE Treaty citing the claim of some Western analysts that the treaty was signed by two defense blocs, not individual states. Consequently, with three former Warsaw Pact states in NATO, the weapons limitations that were allocated under CFE will have to be renegotiated.[23] Also, since Kaliningrad is the only remaining part of the former Soviet Union's Baltic Military District, and the Baltic states have not acceded to CFE, an even larger number of inventory of weapons can be deployed there than is currently the case.

One cannot forget that even during the Yeltsin–Putin years, Russia took measures that were provocative. For example:

1. In the spring of 1999, in a direct challenge to NATO, Russian paratroopers left their base in Bosnia and traveled by road to occupy the airport in Pristina. They did so to arrive ahead of the NATO forces, which were entering Kosovo under a cease-fire agreement, and stake a claim for a sector of their own in Kosovo. This ploy provided Moscow with leverage over developments there, even though they did not have the means to stop NATO forces were they inclined to throw their weight around. Yeltsin said, after the fact, that he had approved of the provocative action, but many analysts believe the Russian generals moved of their own volition.
2. This incident, along with efforts to undermine the government of Eduard Shevardnadze in Georgia and to provide weapons—and men—to various pro-Russian groups elsewhere in the Caucasus, has forced many Western analysts to reconsider the old notion that Russian generals will not move without first getting permission from their civilian superiors.
3. In late June 1999, with the full support of President Yeltsin, the Russian military conducted maneuvers in the Baltic Sea region (and beyond), which were depicted by the code name "West 99." About 10,000 troops from northeastern Russia along with thirty ships, two submarines, and a squadron of long-range bombers took part in the exercise. According

to *The Baltic Times,* "During the military games, Russian soldiers will stage mock missile and air strikes on Baltic air and sea ports. Under the scenario developed by the Russian Defense Department, Russian paratroopers would be deployed to Latvia and Estonia after the air raids, while Belarussian troops would enter Lithuania to push out the NATO aggressors."[24]

4. In November 1999, when the Russian military began a brutal attack on Chechnya's cities with high civilian casualties, many Russian commentators expressed concern that the military commanders were getting out of hand. Writing in *The Moscow Times,* Yevgenia Albats cited the threats of Defense Minister Igor Sergeyev and a commander in Chechnya, General Anatoly Kvashnin, that they would resign if the politicians in Moscow called a cease-fire. Indeed, another prominent general, Vladimir Shamanov, warned of a civil war if that happened. Albats concluded, "Having vented their revenge on Chechnya" they might want to vent it elsewhere. "Like for instance, on the Moscow politicians about whom they couldn't care less and whom they are in no hurry to obey."[25]

Russia's future is unclear. What is clear is that concerns about security questions associated with the Kaliningrad Question may reappear and become a source of friction between Russia and its neighbors and the Euro-Atlantic community. One cannot assume that Russia's economic and political problems, and the plight of its military, will preclude some future Russian government from adopting confrontational policies in the region. As indicated earlier, some imperial-minded Russian leaders may actively seek a confrontation with the West to enhance their political prospects within Russia—for example, exploit the specter of an expanding, "rapacious" NATO—to turn voters away from more moderate candidates and toward people like themselves.

Concerns about security questions associated with the Kaliningrad Question, however, may remain latent and not become manifest if the West and Russia anticipate them and take measures to prevent them from becoming future points of friction. Under existing circumstances, fears that Russian security will be jeopardized with NATO enlargement, and the concerns of Moscow's neighbors about existing Russian troops and/or equipment in Kaliningrad—or attempts to restore those assets in the oblast—can be assuaged by time-honored arms-control principles: transparency, the provision of information about military assets, and the creation of inspection regimes to verify troop movements. Furthermore, cooperative Russian–Western efforts to address nonsecurity issues may serve as confidence-building measures and facilitate the resolution of thorny security issues which may emerge in the future.

Indeed, some areas of cooperation that involve security per se should be considered. For example, why not establish a Partnership for Peace (PFP) Center in Kaliningrad, which would attract troops from all participating PFP countries? Additional activities may be linked to the center, such as the coordination of mine-clearing operations, the training of border guards and other personnel to check the flow of arms, drugs, illegal immigrants, and contraband that is coursing through the region.

Of course, if hard security issues do reemerge in northeastern Europe, and in Kaliningrad in particular, officials in Berlin, Moscow, the Nordic capitals, and certainly Poland and Lithuania will agree uniformly that the United States must play a pivotal role in addressing them.

Notes

1. The White House, "A National Strategy of Engagement and Enlargement," in *America's Strategic Choices,* ed. Michael E. Brown et al. (Cambridge, Mass.: MIT Press, 1997), 32.

2. James Goodby, *Europe Divided: The New Logic of Peace in U.S.–Russian Relations* (Washington, D.C.: U.S. Institute of Peace, 1998), 183.

3. *Washington Post,* 3 April 1999.

4. Elizabeth Pond, *The Rebirth of Europe,* (Washington, D.C.: The Brookings Institution Press, 1999), 64.

5. A growing number of Americans do not come from Europe, but the civic values they embrace in becoming an "American" have their roots in European ideas and values. U.S. nationalism, in other words, is not based upon blood ties, but on civic values and ideas that first surfaced in Europe.

6. Press release, Lithuanian Foreign Ministry, 31 March 2001.

7. RFE/RL, *Newsline,* 30 July 1999.

8. Reuters, 23 November 1999.

9. Lithuanian Embassy, e-mail, 6 May 2001.

10. Henry Kissinger, "NATO: Make It Stronger, Make It Larger," *Washington Post,* 14 January 1997, A15.

11. Goodby, *Europe Divided.*

12. Zbigniew Brzezinski et al., eds., *U.S. Policy toward Northeastern Europe* (New York: Council on Foreign Relations, 1999).

13. Brzezinski, *U.S. Policy,* 2–3.

14. Brzezinski, *U.S. Policy,* 20.

15. Remarks by Marc Grossman, assistant secretary of state for European affairs, presented at Council of Baltic Sea States, Palanga, Lithuania, 14 June 1999.

16. Remarks by Marc Grossman, U.S. Department of State press release, 25 June 1998.

17. Interview with Jurgita Siugzdiniene, Lithuanian project director at the Municipal Training Center of Kaunas University of Technology, spring 1998, and personal correspondence.

18. Ian Bremmer and Alyson Bailes, "Sub-regionalism in the Newly Independent States," *International Affairs* 74, no. 1 (winter 1998): 133.

19. This is a major thesis of Elizabeth Pond's book, *The Rebirth of Europe.*

20. Paul Goble, "A Fourth Baltic Republic?" RFE/RL, *Newsline* 2, no. 138 (21 July 1998).

21. Pond, *The Rebirth of Europe*, 45.

22. Brzezinski, *U.S. Policy*, 41.

23. See, for example, Jeffrey D. McCausland, "Conventional Arms Control," *Adelphi Paper 301* (London: International Institute for Strategic Studies, 1996). For a Russian perspective on CFE and Kaliningrad, see Alexander A. Pikayev, "Russia and the Baltic States," in *The Baltic States in World Politics,* ed. Birthe Hansen and Bertel Heurlin (Surrey, England: Curzon, 1998), 147–50.

24. Daniel Silva, "Russian Troops Stage Mock Invasion of Baltic States," *Baltic Times*, 8–14 July 1999, 3.

25. Yevgenia Albats, "Power Play: Moscow Fears Disarming Its Own Generals," *Moscow Times*, 12 November 1999.

Epilogue

Kaliningrad and the Future

WHAT ABOUT Kaliningrad's future? Will the oblast remain part of Russia or will it become a fourth Baltic republic with the independent status that Estonia, Latvia, and Lithuania enjoy? Observers of Kaliningrad have been asking such questions ever since the collapse of the USSR. In considering them, four plausible scenarios present themselves:

The Status Quo

This scenario rests on the persistence of prevailing conditions in the oblast:

- The economy remains stagnant with high levels of unemployment, low rates of growth, and little foreign or domestic investment.
- Kaliningrad continues to suffer high rates of AIDS and drug abuse.
- Violent crime remains high and criminal gangs in league with corrupt politicians continue to play a dominant role in the economy.
- The political system remains deadlocked between the oblast's Duma and the governor.
- Moscow remains financially unable to provide Kaliningrad with significant help and the military there remains financially stricken.

Meanwhile in Moscow:

- The officials there do not have a coherent Kaliningrad policy.
- The central government remains weak and the danger of balkanization is spreading.

- Russia's economy is at best growing slowly and a large segment of the population lives in poverty.

This is a plausible outcome and whatever help is provided under these circumstances will be ad hoc. Neither significant public support from abroad nor foreign private investment is possible. Under these circumstances the specter of Kaliningrad becoming a black hole will materialize sometime early in the twenty-first century.

Kaliningrad Becomes Independent Fourth Baltic Republic

Whenever the subject of Kaliningrad arises, this outcome is often discussed, but no one explains how it will materialize. When pressed, those who proffer this scenario seem to be talking about Kaliningrad gaining the status that ethnic republics like Tatarstan enjoyed during the Yeltsin years. But unlike Estonia, Latvia, and Lithuania, Tatarstan is not an independent country; it is a republic within the Russian Federation. And, as we have observed, Putin has been reducing the privileges that the republics have enjoyed.

Kaliningrad would become a fourth independent Baltic country only after it achieved de jure independence and disaffiliated with the Russian Federation. President Putin would not allow this to happen, and on this matter he has the support of all political elements in Russia.

At present there is no significant groundswell of separatist support in Kaliningrad among the elites or ordinary folk there. Commentators, who cite Chechnya as a reason for Moscow to anticipate grass-roots support for separatism in Kaliningrad, ignore important factors that distinguish the two regions.

Scholars employ two theories—the "instrumentalist" and the "essentialist"—in evaluating the prospects for separatism in Russia. The instrumentalists posit that economic self-interest will constitute the driving force behind any secessionist movement in Russia. Essentialists, on the other hand, stress cultural or ethnic identity as providing the energy necessary to bolt from the Russian Federation.[1]

According to instrumentalist theory, the basis for separatism in Kaliningrad would be widespread and pervasive concern among the population about their economic welfare. In short, Kaliningraders would bolt from the Russian federation in the expectation that independence would improve their living standards and economic prospects.

By contrast, the essentialist argument for Chechnya's secession is rooted in cultural and identity politics, not in mundane economic concerns. In

Chechnya, the ethnic Chechens have a long and honored tradition of resisting Russian imperialism. The common bond of ethnic national identity there has been historically entangled in their Islamic faith and their resistance to Russian hegemony. But there are no essentialist factors in Kaliningrad that would precipitate separatist tendencies there.

While in power, both Matochkin and Gorbenko had tried to squeeze financial aid from Moscow by implying that foreigners would exploit secessionist tendencies that were driven by economic discontent. Early in 2001, university students in Kaliningrad took to the streets in protest of a change in the tax code that would emasculate SEZ indicating their displeasure with Moscow. But in spite of such statements and activities there are no indications that influential politicians or economic barons want to secede from the federation. Most ordinary people in the oblast identify themselves as Russians and they too want to remain tethered to the federation.

Kaliningrad Becomes a Russian Republic

Under this scenario Kaliningrad acquires the extensive privileges that ethnic republics like Tatarstan enjoyed after the USSR collapsed. This means gaining greater control of economic affairs, revenues, and the authority to enter into extensive commercial relations with foreign countries—not only foreign business interests.

Politicians and members of the business community in Kaliningrad favor the oblast acquiring similar powers. One of the major complaints that authorities in Kaliningrad have made is that it is impossible to attract foreign investment in the face of ever-changing laws that jeopardize the profitability of enterprises investing in the region.

Were Kaliningrad to have more extensive control of its economy, taxes, laws, and policies governing investment and banking, its commercial climate would improve. Of course, this is predicated upon the expectation that the governor and the regional Duma honor regional laws and policies. Also, assuming that Moscow displayed less paranoia about foreign revanchism, the EU would be more inclined to provide the aid the TACIS experts have recommended. The same would hold true for the United States.

As indicated earlier, however, Putin has reduced the ability of the regions to operate independently of Moscow, and the likelihood that Kaliningrad will acquire powers associated with republic status are dim. There is reason to believe, nonetheless, that Putin will entertain modest changes in Kaliningrad's status as it encounters difficulties associated with EU eastward enlargement.

Kaliningrad Becomes an International Protectorate

Some pundits have suggested that Kaliningrad could become an international entity that remains affixed to Moscow but enjoys far greater control over its affairs than is the case today. And unlike a republic within the federation, it would function like a trustee of the EU. In other words, think of the United Kingdom's administration of Hong Kong in the last years before that colony became a political entity of China.

The oblast's governmental bodies would remain under Russian authority but the EU—or some other international entity—would have authority over commercial activities. Russia would retain the right to maintain a moderate military presence in the trustee territory and dominate the law-enforcement agencies.

Because the EU would oversee commercial activities, one would expect Kaliningrad to receive more public and private investments than is presently the case. Russia meanwhile would be spared the expense of taking primary responsibility for the region and its residents, including the integration of Kaliningrad into existing and projected transportation and power grid programs. This is no small asset at a time when Moscow is faced with the enormous task of revitalizing the rest of Russia.

The problem with this scenario is that no one of authority in Moscow has indicated interest in any such scheme. Furthermore, developments in Chechnya have exacerbated fears among the Russian elite and common people alike about the specter of separatism. And the humiliation suffered by Putin and the military with the Kursk disaster has made both sensitive to any perceived demonstration of weakness on their part. Clearly, to place any part of the federation under outside control would compromise Russian sovereignty.

Putin has no reason to fear that centrifugal "essentialist" forces will threaten the federation's integrity except in those areas where there is a significant non-Russian population. But he has expressed concern that "instrumentalist" factors may loosen ties between Moscow and Siberian regions.

Vladimir Ivanov, who heads the Siberian Accord—an economic association that includes nineteen regions—has stated that economic hardship feeds secessionist tendencies in Russia's Far Eastern provinces. Siberia comprises 80 percent of Russia's territory with only 20 percent of its inhabitants. Most significant of all, living standards in Siberia are 20 times lower than those enjoyed by residents of Moscow.[2]

Days after he was sworn in as Russia's president, Putin toured Russia's Far East and indicated that he was concerned about separatist tendencies in this vast area east of the Urals. He clearly feared that separatism could spread like a virus in poverty-stricken regions and had to be exterminated wherever it appeared to be aborning.

Strobe Talbott, President Clinton's principal Russian expert, has observed that most Russian politicians believe that the Baltic countries set into motion events that eventually led to the Soviet empire's dissolution when they bolted from the USSR.[3] With this specter in mind, Moscow's ruling classes will not sacrifice any territory lest that precipitate events that ultimately lead to Russia's disintegration.

In January 2001, however, the *Sunday* (London) *Telegraph* ran a story claiming that Germany's Chancellor Gerhard Schroeder and Putin signed a secret agreement giving German business interests a free hand in Kaliningrad in return for Berlin forgiving Moscow's $22 billion debt to Germany. Authorities in both capitals denied the story, and logic would suggest it was false. Kaliningrad does not have extensive business opportunities to justify such a trade, and both Schroeder and Putin would have to be politically tone-deaf not to hear the negative reaction of other Europeans to "another secret German–Russian" agreement; recall the Molotov–Ribbentrop Pact of 1939.[4]

A fifth possibility is suggested by the Russian government's concern about how EU expansion will effect Kaliningrad. Given the unique conditions prevailing there, and its strategic location, there are some Russian commentators who believe the EU should give the oblast associate status. Of course, EU officials might suggest, in turn, that if Brussels did so, Moscow would have to make some concessions as well, for example, empower the officials in Kaliningrad with the authority to cooperate with their neighbors in a manner that is not possible under current circumstances.

The EU and Kaliningrad

By early in 2001, the debate that had occurred within the EU the prior year ended with the consensus that the EU had to address the Kaliningrad Question. In addition to meetings and statements cited earlier, the European Commission submitted a report to the European Council in January that recommended that the EU look at the Kaliningrad region as a special problem area within Russia.

The report said that enlargement would actually be in Russia's overall interest but conceded that with Lithuanian and Polish membership in the EU changes would occur that could harm Russia. "Some of these changes will have an equal impact on all Russian regions while others will have specific implications for Kaliningrad, mainly on the movement of goods, people, and the supply of energy." The paper explored these problems and others not directly related to enlargement, but that would affect Kaliningrad—"areas such as environment, the fight against crime, health care, and economic development."[5]

The report's main suggestions included the following:

1. The EU and Russia examine the trade impact of enlargement on Kaliningrad.
2. The EU and Russia, Poland, and Lithuania discuss the functional management of border crossings.
3. The EU–Kaliningrad fisheries relations be reviewed in the light of the consequences of enlargement on fishing access and of future fisheries agreement between the EU and Russia.
4. The EU and Russia discuss key issues of environmental concern in Kaliningrad.[6]

The flurry of EU activity revolving around the Kaliningrad Question was closely linked with Sweden's six-month EU presidency beginning in January 2001. Sweden, like Denmark, has been active in diplomatic efforts to address the problems of its Russian neighbor. In particular Sweden has been concerned about Kaliningrad's contribution to Baltic Sea pollution. Indeed, Swedish analysts concluded in 2001 that if Kaliningrad's environmental problems were fully addressed, the cost would amount to $3 billion over a four-year period.[7]

Further EU interest in Kaliningrad was indicated with the publication of a book of readings on *The EU and Kaliningrad: The Consequences of EU Enlargement on Kaliningrad,* published early in 2001. Kaliningrad watchers such as Finland's Rene Nyberg and Pertti Joenniemi, and Lithuania's Vygaudas Usackas, and EC consultant Stephen Dewar were contributors to the book, which carried an introduction by Christopher Patten, the EU's External Relations Commissioner.[8]

Kaliningrad watchers, who argued that Kaliningrad deserved a special economic development program of its own, however, could not be heartened by the EC's report to the European Council, for it carried the following caveat: "It is sometimes suggested that a special fund should be established for the development of Kaliningrad. However, the Commission rather believes that the first priority is to work with the Russian and local authorities to identify priority areas for support and then to help them find appropriate grant and/or loan funding for these activities."[9]

This caveat aside, the EU has clearly indicated that it is prepared to work with Russia and member states to address the Kaliningrad Question with greater purpose than has been the case up to this point. The EU is not likely to create a special development program for the oblast but instead funnel assistance to Kaliningrad through the Northern Dimension.

Putin's Role

Any consideration of Kaliningrad's future, however, is academic without first considering the big question: Is Putin serous about building a democratic polity in Russia with a market economy, or will he—in the face of protracted, and possibly mounting, problems—revisit Russian despotism? Because of his brutal policies in Chechnya, his assault on the press, and what some regional officials deem draconian efforts to reimpose Soviet-style control over their activities, many Russians fear they have been witnessing a return to autocracy.

As Putin has correctly observed, democratic principles dictate that relations between Moscow and the region must be codified by law. But democratization likewise is advanced when popularly elected regional executives and stable political and governmental infrastructures are in place. Any effort to prevent this from happening will undermine Russian democracy. The restoration of a strong Russian state is vital to the revitalization of Russian society, but in a democratic federal system the Center does not dictate to the regions on all matters.

In Russia's drive to develop a free-market economy, viable regional political systems are assets. Observers of regional economic development cite Novgorod as an example. Under Governor Mikhail Prusak: "Novgorod has jumped to second in Russia in terms of foreign investment per capita behind only Moscow, and third in terms of economic development." More than half of the region's industrial output is from foreign investment. Prusak has passed investor-friendly provisions, but so have other regions. So what has he done differently? One commentator says: "What makes Novgorod unusual among Russian regions has been the local elites' embrace of cultural traditions that stress self-government and openness to foreign investment."[10]

Those authorities in Moscow wishing to dominate economic activity in the regions will hamper Russia's economic development. Even the imperialminded in Moscow cannot ignore a trenchant fact: given Russia's desperate economic plight, any economic setback will be detrimental to the country's security. Unfortunately, many continue to do so perhaps out of ignorance or simply because they deem political power more important than economic growth.

On January 6, 2000, Putin signed off on Russia's new national security doctrine. As secretary to the Security Council the previous spring, he had worked on the document, so he was familiar with its contents. Foreign commentators characterized it as "alarming." Among other things, it indicated that the West—in contrast to a 1997 statement—was deemed a security threat and not a partner, and that Russia would lower the threshold on the use of nuclear weapons by scrapping its "no first use" doctrine. This tough statement, along with Russia's brutal destruction of Grozny, convinced many observers that hard-liners dominated the Kremlin. It was foolhardy to expect these same people to adopt a more liberal policy toward the regions.

The document indicated, however, that restoration of the Russian economy was a major security goal. Putin has stated on several occasions that a strong military and economic stagnation are mutually exclusive phenomena. In foreign evaluations of Putin after he became acting president, all concluded that he favored a free-market economy. Presumably his service in Germany convinced him that if Russia expected to enjoy economic prosperity, it had to develop a vibrant capitalist economy.

While acting as deputy mayor to Anatoly Sobchak, Putin worked closely with Western business representatives, and they gave him high marks for understanding their needs. As a pragmatist and intelligent man he could not ignore a pivotal lesson of the Cold War's outcome—the road to national wealth and power in the twenty-first century rests on a free, not a command, economy.

Putin also must recognize that one of the major reasons why political influence has shifted from Moscow to the regions is the diffusion of economic power with privatization. Under the Soviet system, Moscow prevailed as both the dominant political and economic force in the USSR, and that condition contributed to the Soviet Union's eventual disintegration. Today Putin must beware that in his quest to tighten vertical control over the regions he does not harm Russia's economic prospects. Under existing circumstances, thousands—nay tens of thousands—of entrepreneurs are making economic decisions that were once the province of party hacks and managers in Moscow.

In the economic universe of the twenty-first century, state control over economic affairs has declined dramatically with the passing of economic autarky. Today modern business enterprises operate independently of their own political authorities as they achieve multinational status. The global market has eroded international sovereignty and there will be no return to state sovereignty as exemplified by the Treaty of Westphalia. As Benjamin R. Barber has written: "Markets abhor frontiers as nature abhors a vacuum. Within their expansive and permeable domains, interests are private, trade is free, currencies are convertible, access to banking is open, contracts are enforceable . . . and the laws of production and consumption are sovereign, trumping the laws of legislators and courts."[11]

Meanwhile, bureaucrats and foreign political leaders who operate and control the World Bank and International Monetary Fund have the power to supercede the preferences of elites in Moscow as Russian commerce becomes entangled in the global economy. Russian leaders need only look to disputes between the Europeans and Americans within the WTO regime to accept a stark truth: in the global economy even the world's richest countries no longer possess true sovereignty. Attempts to recreate an economy dominated by Moscow will lead to a cul-de-sac—there is no going back!

In assessing Putin's first year as president, some commentators faulted him for not moving quickly and dramatically to reform Russia's economy. For example, after promising that he would pass a law that would allow investors to buy and sell agricultural land, he backed off that promise and said he would let the regions handle it.

But other observers were more positive in their assessment of his economic performance, suggesting that while he was moving slowly, he was moving in the right direction. In an evaluation of Putin's first year, a Carnegie Foundation report concluded: "On the economic front Putin has surprised many observers. He has assembled the most pro-reform team in the government since the early 1990s. This team already has some accomplishments, including a major tax reform package and a balanced budget."[12]

In assessing Putin's political performance, there was greater consensus among Russian watchers in the West. They deemed it worrisome. For example, on the eve of the 1999 Duma elections Michael McFaul was optimistic about the prospects for democracy in Russia. Several months later, after watching Putin closely, McFaul was less sanguine. In the *Washington Post,* he wrote: "Not since the August 1991 coup attempt has the future of Russian democracy been more uncertain than it is today."[13] In this connection, McFaul mentioned the brutal Russian campaign in Chechnya; the kidnapping of Radio Liberty reporter Andrei Babitsky, and efforts to revise the election law that would outlaw proportional representation and thereby undercut the political survival of the reformers in the Duma.

Amy Knight, who has documented the pivotal role that former KGB officials and operatives have played in both the Yeltsin and Putin regimes, also provided a pessimistic appraisal of Putin's first months as president. She claimed Putin conducted the brutal crackdown in Chechnya to advance his political position. "With the economy in a shambles, corruption rampant, and the Chechen problem still unresolved, it is not difficult to understand why Russians would find someone like Putin so attractive." In the process, "They appear to have lost sight of the fact that the Soviet state deteriorated and collapsed precisely because men like Putin were running the show." She qualified her pessimism when concluding, however, that "this is not to say . . . that Putin cannot change and discard some of his KGB heritage."[14] Like most foreign observers of Putin, Knight was not ready to claim categorically that Putin had restored autocracy to Russia. Perhaps it would take several years before a final determination could be made on this count.

Many Russian democrats, however, were less circumspect in their assessment of Putin's first year in office. Andrei Piontkovsky, the director of Moscow's Institute for Strategic Research, observed: "Putinism is no more than the impoverished philosophy of absolute power shared by the security service and the oligarchy close to them."[15] Putin also was criticized by some of the economic oligarchs who had helped him get elected president. Boris Berezovsky in a trip to the United States indicated that he was unhappy with developments in Moscow. And Vladimir Gusinsky—the latter accused of crimes by Russian prosecutors, leading to his arrest in Spain—warned that Putin was reversing Russia's path toward democracy.

Since both men had gained their wealth through questionable practices and perhaps deserved to be in jail, they are not the best judges of Putin's activities. But the assessment of Grigory Yavlinsky, the head of the Yabloko Party, was another matter. His critics accused him of arrogance but not economic dishonesty. On January 30, 2001, he authored a provocative piece in *The Moscow Times* titled, "Sham Reform Leads to National Bolshevism."

Yavlinsky claimed, "People are beginning to understand that we have a sham freedom of speech, which really only allows us to systematically praise the bosses. . . . We have sham elections" because the government, not the people, selects candidates. He said the same thing about sham federalism, since the Center dominated the regions. Thus Yavlinsky concluded that Putin's rule was most appropriately labeled "National Bolshevism, i.e. an attempt to build capitalism without civil society."[16]

Both Russian and foreign analysts saw Putin's efforts to combine Unity with the Fatherland Party of Luzhkov and Primakov as a campaign to gain full control of the Duma and to restore a powerful Russian state. In Western capitals, however, the fear was expressed that he would accomplish this objective at the expense of Russia's historical drive to democratize a country that had been ruled by autocrats throughout its existence.

While lamenting the disintegration of the democratic experiment in Russia, more far-seeing Western analysts feared that even if Putin consolidated power in Moscow, the oligarchs in league with corrupt officials and the Mafia would in fact control the country.

In the process, Russia would suffer further economic stagnation, widespread social discord, and the virtual balkanization of political authority.

Furthermore, Putin might adopt measures that in the short run would enhance Moscow's power but in the process prevent Russia from building a truly democratic and stable society over the long term.

The Center and the Regions

By the second half of the 1990s, Russia's economic and political elites outside Moscow wielded considerable economic and political influence in their regions. Even Russian nationalists, who were strong supporters of the Center's authority and those who preferred that the president appoint regional executives, could not ignore regional power. Nor could they ignore positive aspects to this condition. Nikita Mikhalkov, the Russian filmmaker who directed, wrote, and starred in the highly acclaimed *Burnt by the Sun*, spoke before a forum of the World Policy Institute in New York City, and refuted claims that Russia was disintegrating. An outspoken nationalist, Mikhalkov observed that the real healing process in Russian society was taking place in the regions.[17]

Boris Nemtsov, the former Nizhni Novgorod governor and Yeltsin aide, provided another reason for Russia's adopting a true federal system. "Trying to make Russia a unitary state is senseless. It's impossible to run such a vast country from one center, and will inevitably lead to Russia's break-up."[18]

But Putin was convinced that the regional barons had wielded too much power and perhaps some of them even agreed that this diffusion of power to the hinterland had helped weaken the Russian state. Also many democrats agreed with him that the number of regions should be reduced. For whatever reason, most regional officials quickly consented to Putin's efforts to limit their authority and to reform the Federation Council out of existence. But by the fall of 2000, some of them indicated that they were unhappy with Putin's reforms. Aleksandr Lebed, the governor of Krasnoyarsk protested changes in the tax code that would deny the region's critical revenues. For example, the 15 percent share of the value-added tax that had gone to the regions henceforth would remain in Moscow. Yuri Luzhkov, the mayor of Moscow, warned that Putin's reforms indicated that he intended to replace Russia's federation with a unitary system.[19]

In spite of protests from the regions, Putin continued to expand the Center's control over them. With the onset of the fall 2000 elections, some governors like Kursk's Alexander Rutskoi were prohibited from running for reelection and federal authorities began to arrest regional officials for criminal activities. In light of the fact that many regional officials—like their counterparts in Moscow—had abused their political authority to enrich themselves during the stormy 1990s, additional arrests were expected and in many instances warranted.

Nonetheless, today Putin has to realize that regional bosses in league with powerful economic barons will fight to maintain their influence. Indeed, a number of oligarchs have followed the lead of Boris Berezovsky, who sought both the authority and shelter that was afforded a regional executive by getting elected to regional office. Thus in 2001 when both Berezovsky and Gusinsky had fled Russia for fear of being prosecuted, Roman Abramovich became governor of Chukotka. Oligarchs-turned-politician have discovered that rather than paying huge "fees" for facilitating their commercial endeavors, they can achieve the same objective by sitting in the governor's chair.

Putin's record on disciplining recalcitrant regional leaders has not gone unblemished. To cite a glaring example: Putin tried but failed to remove Vladimir Yakovlev, the governor of St. Petersburg, from office. This failure was all the more telling since Putin's political base is located in Russia's "second city."

Likewise efforts to impose Moscow's control over regions like Tatarstan—where the authorities are non-Russian, and/or control an area with considerable wealth—are being resisted. And as an indication that Putin has felt regional resistance, he passed a resolution allowing governors to run for a third term and indicated that regional and not federal officials should determine how the sale of agricultural land should be handled. On this last matter, regional authorities might view that gift of authority skeptically, since the sale of farmland has been such a fractious issue in Russia.

While Putin's efforts to crush regional power has received lots of attention by journalists and some Russian watchers, those in the latter category who are students of Russian Federalism disagree with the assessment that he has succeeded in his campaign. For example, the East-West Institute's Robert W. Orttung concluded by the spring of 2001 that "Putin's reforms of the federal system have not been very effective." In addition to evidence that has already been cited to support this conclusion, Orttung has identified the sources of regional executive power:

> First, strong governors have been able to block the rise of any serious opposition candidates from among local politicians. Second, the governors in office now in contrast to the Yeltsin appointees who ran in 1996 have considerable experience in public politics and had to win an election to secure their current office. Third, the governors have by now mastered the use of so-called administrative resources, the mechanisms which make up the arsenal of their power on the ground. These weapons include extensive influence in regional electoral commissions.

And finally, "a key source of the governors' power is their relationships with regional, and increasingly, national business."[20]

In the future, it is likely that regional authorities will oppose efforts by some in Moscow who want to spend massive sums of money to maintain a Soviet-size military establishment and thereby deny funding for Russia's daunting domestic problems. The Kursk disaster in the summer of 2000 and the Ostankino TV tower fire a week later forced the imperial-minded in Moscow to accept a bitter truth. Russia is a poor country beset with many economic problems, and even after they are resolved Russia will never project power globally the way the Soviet Union did. Unfortunately many old Soviet-era authorities still in power have not yet acknowledged this fact: it is not altogether clear whether Putin himself has recognized this truism.

Yet, Russia's roads, bridges, and other infrastructure can no longer be neglected. The plight of Siberia's residents in the winter of 2000–2001 whose flats and buildings were unheated in one of the region's coldest winters suggests more of the same in the future. If Russia is to avoid serious and widespread social and political upheaval at home, the Russian economy must be revitalized. That daunting task cannot be accomplished if Putin attempts to restore an all-powerful Soviet-style state that dominates both the political and the economic realms of society and seeks to project its influence globally in a manner consistent with the USSR.

It was in partial recognition of this truism that Putin announced in January 2000 that within three years Russia would reduce its 1.2 million member armed forces by 350,000. Earlier he had indicated that he would let Russia's nuclear arsenal shrink below 1,500 warheads—in other words, a figure lower than that allowed by the START II agreement that the Duma had not yet signed.

In the twenty-first century, the weight of reality will force those in Moscow who choose to play the Kaliningrad card to recognize that "big power" ambitions may constitute a barrier to the development of Russia's regions. And stunted economic development in the country's hinterland spells trouble for the federal government. Turning to Kaliningrad and other regions in the country's northwest, Moscow should welcome developments on its western borders that enhance the economic capacity of Russian regions adjacent to them.

As Mikhail Alexseev and Vladimir Vagin have demonstrated in their study of Pskov, while the imperial-minded in Moscow may savage the Estonians and Latvians for their so-called mistreatment of their Russian population, closer commercial relations between those two countries and Pskov are in its self-interest. As the economies of Estonia and Latvia grow and the commercial and transportation sectors expand and provide outreach to the West, it is vital that Pskov become integrated into that expanded economic network.

"After the Soviet collapse, political players in Pskov have had many opportunities to see that the West—even with NATO expansion—is not coming to the region with a sword, but with trade carts." Alexseev and Vadin continue: "If Pskov looks up only to its legacy as geopolitical barrier against the West, it risks ending up as a backwater province with fewer trade carts to and from Europe passing through."[21] Pskov's governor, Yevgeni Mikhaylov, the only member of Vladimir Zhirinovsky's "Liberal Party" to win a gubernatorial seat in Russia, fully understands this. During the 1996 elections, Mikhaylov distanced himself from Zhirinovsky who spoke about regaining Russia's patrimony in Alaska and the Baltics. Mikhaylov instead dwelled upon regional economic concerns.

If Russia is to join the global economy and work with and through the IMF and WTO, Moscow must adopt economic practices that are consistent with a free-market economy and prevailing international economic practices and norms. Putin may choose not to bow to the dictates of economic globalization, but the price Russia will pay in turn will be monstrous—economic stagnation.

Most of Kaliningrad's economic and political elites realize that their oblast's problems will not be resolved via misguided attempts to throw Russia's weight around in the Baltic Sea region but by cooperating with Kaliningrad's neighbors. In short, they realize that it is not in Russia's vital interest to play the Kaliningrad card. Consequently Vladimir Nikitin, Kaliningrad's Duma chairman, in March 2001 urged the Russian Duma to ratify the 1997 Lithuanian–Russian border treaty claiming it would benefit the oblast.[22]

Also John P. Willerton has observed: "A once relatively monolithic political establishment has given way to an increasingly fragmented and diverse array of elite elements. The popular election of regional officials changes those officials' perspective of political responsibility from an exclusive focus on Moscow to regional constituencies."[23]

Those words were penned before Putin's rise to power, but the circumstances that allowed the Moscow elite under the Soviet Union to impose its policies upon the regions no longer obtains. One need only mention the passing of the command economy as a reason that it will be impossible to return to a bygone era.

At the same time, Dmitri Gorenburg has found that non-Russian ethnic groups see their control of regional governments as a device to advance their group interests.[24] This represents another reason that they have significant cause to resist Putin's attempts to deny them the prerogatives of power. The turmoil among Muslims in the North Caucasus is an incentive for Moscow to make concessions to Islamic citizens who live elsewhere in Russia. At the same time Russian citizens living in "non-Russian" regions have economic incentives for supporting regional authorities in clashes with Moscow. Here we see a blending of "essentialist" and "instrumentalist" factors explaining why both ethnic minority groups and Russian communities in the regions will resist attempts on Moscow's part to reimpose tight central control over their activities.

The August 1998 economic crisis forced the regional elites to look for local answers to their economic problems. Moscow simply did not have the resources to help them even assuming officials there were inclined to do so. Indeed, political leaders from Kaliningrad indicated that the crisis actually helped local business firms in at least two ways. First, it spared them foreign competition, and second, it forced them to rely upon their own resources, and not upon foreign partners, in conducting their business affairs.[25] It is likely that expanding regional economic and political influence will serve as a countervailing force to the imperial-minded in Moscow who refuse to shed their expansionary ambitions.

Still, the region's pragmatists realize that as long as Moscow dominates the revenue pools in the country, the Kremlin has a big stick to keep recalcitrant regional elites in line. Traditional practices such as relying upon Moscow to provide assistance will die hard as well. But as a larger part of the Russian economy becomes a market economy, the regions will become less dependent upon Moscow as they generate wealth of their own. Having said this, however, it is clear that Russians of all political persuasions will oppose separatist efforts to bolt from the federation from whatever their source.

The creation of a viable state, including regional governmental bodies, rests upon a rationalization of relations between them and the Center. In the Western democracies, the principle of subsidiarity characterizes federal relations and has been adopted by the EU as well, that is, where feasible decisions are made at the lowest level of government possible and only those that need to be made at the Center should occur there. The example of the United States is relevant here. Recent efforts to reform the U.S. welfare system originated in the states. It was governors and state legislatures that first experimented with the welfare reforms that were eventually adopted at the federal level in Washington.

It is perhaps too facile to attribute the popularity of the subsidiarity principle to the end of the Cold War. But during the Cold War, the prominence of the national government was justified by the threat emanating from opposing capitals—Moscow and Washington. With the declining rationale for the "warfare state," the logic of concentrating power at the national level of government has been subverted as people in both the United States and Russia dwell upon mundane problems and no longer preoccupy themselves with affairs of state and world politics. Chechnya is an exception, but from the Russian perspective, this is an internal and not an external matter.

The Baltic Sea Region

Looking beyond Russia, the end of the Cold War has provided the opportunity for the Baltic Sea littoral countries to think of themselves as members of a region and to seek regional solutions to their problems. Through organizations like the Council of Baltic Sea States, and other regional and subregional bodies, public and private actors from countries throughout the area have begun to search for solutions to problems that they share because of the common bond of geography. Also the logic of modern commerce, communications, and transportation dictates that they cooperate; it is in their self-interest to do so and is not merely a product of abstract ideals.

The Scandinavian countries have demonstrated that they are prepared to provide money and expertise and to use their contacts in the EU to address the Kaliningrad Question. As even a casual glance at this book's notes shows, Scandinavian scholars and diplomats have been active in publishing information about Kaliningrad and bringing the Kaliningrad Question to the attention of their fellow Europeans.

The same can be said of German scholars and to a lesser degree of German officials. Still wary of ruffling Moscow's feathers over Kaliningrad, the government in Berlin remains cautious and staunchly maintains the posture that any Western programs directed at the exclave must first go through Moscow. There is no indication that Germany will change this posture any time soon. Indeed, German leaders in both the Christian Democratic and the Social Democratic parties are having second thoughts about the wisdom of EU eastward expansion—their public comments to the contrary. Should Putin indicate that he welcomes German support in Kaliningrad, however, Berlin is likely to be forthcoming in extending a helping hand to the oblast.

Poland, of course, has powerful incentives to provide assistance to the only Russian region with which it shares a border. Via Kaliningrad, the government in Warsaw can demonstrate that it wishes to cooperate with its counterpart in Moscow. The Russians in both Moscow and Kaliningrad simultaneously realize that Poland is an important economic partner for the oblast. Neither have they been unmindful of the fact that the government in Warsaw has lobbied the EU on behalf of Kaliningrad.

The capacity of the Polish and Russian governments to maintain harmonious relations, however, may be put to the test by NATO enlargement. Since

Poland is NATO's front-line state, any future move on Moscow's part to play the Kaliningrad Card may place Warsaw right in the middle of the dispute—say, for example, over the second round of NATO enlargement that welcomes Lithuania into the alliance.

Lithuania continues to play a leading role in reaching out to Kaliningrad in an effort to facilitate more extensive commercial relations and agreements on border issues but also to prevent it from being isolated. In January 2000, a Lithuanian–Kaliningrad regional business consortium was established. By that time there were 321 Lithuanian–Russian joint ventures registered with Kaliningrad's special economic zone, and they accounted for 22 percent of all joint ventures there.[26] Also, representatives of Vilnius and Kaliningrad City signed a protocol proclaiming that they are prepared to cooperate in various political and economic activities.

On February 9, 2000, the deputy foreign ministers of Lithuania and Russia met in the Lithuanian resort town of Nida and issued a joint statement of cooperation. They agreed to coordinate activities associated with the EU's Northern Dimension in the areas of trade, investments and the environment. They also discussed ways the U.S. government, through its North European Initiative, can cooperate with both countries in addressing the Kaliningrad Question.[27]

But in the spring of 2001, Lithuanian diplomats observed to their dismay that their Russian Moscow-based counterparts suddenly stopped talking about an issue that previously had preoccupied them—the provision of a visa-free regime for residents of Kaliningrad after Lithuania entered the EU. The Lithuanians were dismayed because they had concluded that while some influential political leaders in Moscow favored opening up Kaliningrad to foreign investment, there were others who opposed this policy. They reasoned that extensive foreign investment in Kaliningrad and involvement in its affairs might loosen the region's ties to Moscow. They favored, then, policies that would tighten Moscow's control over the exclave and, in effect, indicate to foreigners that they were not welcome there.

While there are mixed views in Moscow about the wisdom of working with foreign states in Kaliningrad, one thing is clear: efforts of individual states in the Baltic Sea region to address Kaliningrad's problems can play an important part in their resolution. Since 1991, Denmark—the most active country in providing assistance to Kaliningrad—funded fifty programs that amount to 10 million Euro. Sweden has provided 4 million Euro and Germany 1 million Euro.[28] But only the EU has the resources, expertise, and political authority to develop a truly comprehensive and systemic approach to the Kaliningrad Question. The Brussels bureaucracy and like-minded people in the capitals of member states have resisted a massive Kaliningrad-directed approach of this kind but the EU's support to the oblast is likely to grow.

Is Moscow Ready to Address the Kaliningrad Question?

As prime minister, and in his early months as president, Putin's position on this matter was unclear. In an October 1999 meeting of Russian and EU officials, Putin allegedly used the words *pilot region* in reference to Kaliningrad. Afterwards some observers cited them to justify their claim (hope) that he was now ready to work with the EU and address the Kaliningrad Question.

In May of the following year, Danish diplomats were heartened by a conference that was devoted to Kaliningrad. They concluded that Russian authorities were now eager to work with the EU on this issue. In Brussels that summer, representatives of the Russian Foreign Ministry informed me that this was an accurate assessment of their government's intentions.

On July 30, however, Putin visited Kaliningrad, his wife, Ludmila's, home region and his mother-in-law's residence today. In his comments there, he seemed to back away from his earlier words. "We do not need pilot regions. We need self-sufficient regions that are developing steadily and efficiently, closely integrating into (the) national economy, taking into account specific regional features, of course. The Kaliningrad oblast is undoubtedly a special region, and its peculiarities will be taken into consideration while drafting federal policies."[29]

In subsequent meetings with representatives from the Baltic Sea states and the EU, however, Russian diplomats indicated growing interest in the EU's cooperating with Moscow in efforts to address the Kaliningrad Question. Analysts in the Kremlin feared that EU enlargement could have a negative impact upon Russia's commercial relations with Europe. Putin expressed such concerns in his meetings with EU officials and leaders from EU member states.

Moscow's growing interest in the EU also could be interpreted as part of Putin's drive to foster close and harmonious relations with the British, French, and German administrations. The Kremlin delighted in discussing Putin's "summits" with Tony Blair, Jacques Chirac, and Gerhard Schroeder during his first year in office.

Among other goals, Putin hoped to exploit growing concerns among the West Europeans about the U.S. propensity to snub Washington's allies rather than consult them. During the 2000 U.S. presidential campaign, the Europeans expressed alarm about comments emanating from the Bush camp, for example, that the United States should withdraw its peacekeepers from the

Balkans and turn the job over to the Europeans. Nor were they happy about Bush's determination to build a U.S. National Missile Defense system even if that meant scrapping the 1972 ABM Treaty.

On October 31, 2000, Putin traveled to Paris to meet with high-level EU officials and French president Chirac. In days prior to the meeting some commentators reasoned that the trip might be embarrassing for Putin in light of the French public's unhappiness with Russia's policies in Chechnya. But the Russian president received a warm welcome in part because during the summer, France—like the rest of Europe—was stricken by rising energy prices. The United Kingdom's North Sea oil resources would soon be depleted and Russia's energy would become even more critical to Europe.

After Bush was sworn into office, the U.S.–British bombing raids on Iraq spawned growing concern in West European capitals that the Americans would embark upon further "potentially dangerous crusades" without first consulting their NATO allies. Afterwards, it could not have escaped Putin that by working with the EU in addressing the Kaliningrad Question, he served both his domestic and foreign-policy interests.

In his April 2001 State of the Nation address, Putin ignored the United States in his foreign-policy remarks, but mentioned that he sought close relations with Washington's European allies.[30]

But even if Putin indicates he is prepared to work with the EU in joint programs in Kaliningrad, what about the political situation in Kaliningrad itself? On the eve of the 2000 gubernatorial election in the oblast, many observers there indicated that the prospects for joint efforts to develop Kaliningrad would be compromised were Gorbenko reelected governor. Some even recommended that all external aid to the region be terminated should he be returned to office.

The New Governor in Kaliningrad

At the time of Putin's visit to Kaliningrad in the late summer of 2000, political opponents of Gorbenko were confident that they would turn him out in the upcoming gubernatorial election. A promising start took place in late 1999 when all political groups in Kaliningrad joined in a common alliance against Gorbenko.[31] New revelations about Gorbenko's corrupt practices surfaced at this time.

On December 5, 1999, NTV's *Itogi* reported a link between criminal activities in Kaliningrad and Gorbenko's administration. Specifically, it was alleged that Gorbenko had undermined efforts on the part of a special anticrime unit that was investigating his first deputy governor, the notorious Mikhail Karentnyi.

The report also made allegations that Gorbenko bolted from All Russia–Fatherland (OVR) in favor of Unity on the condition that Moscow fire the head of the anticrime unit in the oblast. Furthermore, the reporter, Yekaterina Vasilieva, alleged that Karentnyi offered her $300,000 if she did not run the story.[32]

The day after it appeared, Kaliningrad Mayor Yuri Savenko, Duma speaker Valery Ustyugov, and presidential representative Aleksander Orlov announced that they had formed a coalition to oppose Gorbenko in the fall 2000 election, and that among other things they blamed him for the oblast's economic slide. Polls indicated that Savenko was most likely to be Kaliningrad's next governor. In October 1999, a survey of potential gubernatorial candidates revealed that voters there favored him over Gorbenko by 22 percent to 13 percent. And whereas only 4 percent of the respondents identified Savenko as least popular, 39 percent gave Gorbenko that designation.[33] Political commentators in Kaliningrad said Savenko possessed another asset: at one point in his career he attended school with Putin. Furthermore, it was alleged that he had Primakov's support as well. Western diplomats said that he "looked Western" but one indicated off the record that in a private meeting with Savenko, the mayor said, "Democracy was bullshit!" He made several other jarring comments that indicated that on the outside he might be "Western," but lurking within was the "soul of a Soviet apparatchik."

Meanwhile, on the economic front the news was mixed. In contrasting industrial output in the last quarter of 1999 with 1998, Kaliningrad grew by 20.7 percent—a growth rate higher than most regions.[34] Further good news was that in 1999 Kaliningrad demonstrated its attractiveness to foreign investment when BMW began constructing cars in the oblast. The bad news was that by the fall of that year, the Liberal Democratic Party introduced a bill in the Russian Duma that would essentially abolish Kaliningrad's free-trade zone and undermine BMW's profits there. Valery Ustyugov, the chairman of the Kaliningrad Duma, claimed that the bill materialized because BMW car dealers in Moscow were behind it. The BMWs manufactured in Kaliningrad cost less to make than those manufactured in Germany and they were the ones that car dealers in Moscow sold in their showrooms.[35] Here was further reason why the federal government had to take measures to prevent Moscow-based economic barons from undercutting economic activities in Kaliningrad.

Meanwhile, Gorbenko continued to focus on how he could enhance his private economy. In February 2000, *The Moscow Times* ran a story that demonstrated how Gorbenko used his position to enrich himself. It revealed that

Gorbenko signed a deal with two Israeli firms that gave them a monopoly over Kaliningrad's oil and amber deposits. What's more, he gave them exclusive rights to build a rest and recreation center in the oblast. The deal was characterized as a "golden parachute" for him.[36]

In spite of such revelations, some political pundits in Russia believed that Gorbenko could win reelection later that year. Some polls showed him in the lead against his potential opponents, and besides, he had the means to deliver monetary and other favors to his voters that his competitors could not match. Like his compatriot in Minsk, Lukashenko, Gorbenko was very popular among Kaliningrad's rural folk, who were even more dependent upon the government's largesse than were city dwellers.

Gorbenko supported Putin in his bid to become president and Putin got proportionally more votes in Kaliningrad than in Russia at large. Putin captured 60.7 percent of Kaliningrad's votes in contrast to 57.5 percent in the rest of Russia, while his opponent Zyuganov got 23.5 percent and 29.4 percent respectively.[37]

After Putin's inauguration, however, Gorbenko's reelection prospects took a turn for the worse. By this time, most all-influential politicians in Kaliningrad had declared their support for Admiral Vladimir Yegorov, the former commander of the Baltic Sea Fleet. A poll indicated that Yegorov had a 23 percent favorable rating, Savenko a 20 percent positive rating, and Gorbenko was third with a 9 percent favorable rating.[38] Rumors were that Gorbenko's political opponents favored the admiral and not the mayor because the latter had a drinking problem.

In the summer, Lukoil announced that Yegorov was their choice for governor. In conversations with diplomats and TACIS experts who knew the man, Yegorov was characterized as intelligent, honest, and liberal minded. Some pundits indicated that he was not all that happy about running for office but he was convinced that it was in the interest of Kaliningrad that he do so.

Yegorov's prospects improved dramatically after Putin announced that he supported the admiral in his bid to replace Gorbenko. Also, during his July trip to Kaliningrad commentators there said the Russian president made an effort to snub the governor. In October, the party of Putin and the Kremlin, Unity, announced that it favored Yegorov in his race against Gorbenko.

The polls were right about the outcome of the gubernatorial race. During the first round on November 5, Yegorov led with 37 percent and Gorbenko came in second with 21.5 percent. In the second round conducted two weeks later, Yegorov defeated Gorbenko by 56.32 percent to 33.83 percent. About 8.5 percent of the votes cast indicated "none of the above."[39]

After Yegorov's election, the expectation of regional and foreign commentators was that the political situation in Kaliningrad would improve dramatically. For the first time since 1996, the governor and Kaliningrad Duma enjoyed a normal relationship that promised to provide the oblast with the prerequisite to Kaliningrad's coming to grips with its daunting economic and social problems—political stability. Also it appeared that real political parties were beginning to form and political discourse was less a matter of personalities than of policies.

But some Kaliningrad watchers indicated off the record that there were causes for a more pessimistic assessment. Among other things, some powerful economic barons were wielding influence in the new administration, and their presence suggested that the oblast would continue to be subjected to the scourge of widespread corruption. Second, there was the issue of competence. Yegorov was said to have little idea about how to attack Kaliningrad's problems, and he was looking to Moscow to provide the answers. But third, Moscow did not appear ready to provide them.

Angry Kaliningraders took to the streets, however, after the Federal State Customs Committee announced a change in the tax code that nullified what remained of SEZ. This action amounted to a 20 percent price hike for consumers in the oblast. In January 2001, university students marched in protest with signs that read: "Do you want us, Russia?" and "Hands off our special zone." Also, according to *Nezavisimaya Gazeta*, one businessman in Kaliningrad said: "If Moscow does not want to facilitate the problems of Kaliningrad, then it will be necessary to secede from Russia and to create on the territory of the Kaliningrad Oblast a Baltic republic."[40]

Several weeks later, Kaliningraders were delighted to learn that their protests bore fruit as Moscow announced that the tax changes that had nullified SEZ had been scrapped. Here was proof that the Kremlin was paying more attention to Kaliningrad. Clearly both Russian and foreign stories on Kaliningrad appeared with greater frequency at this time. In one of them, Boris Nemtsov, a reformer who still had private consultations with Putin, proclaimed the Kremlin should "do with Kaliningrad what the Chinese have done with Hong Kong."[41]

Meanwhile, Gorbenko was not leaving the scene quietly. He announced that, as provided for under the law, he planned to return to his former job as port master for the civilian and military ports in Kaliningrad City. It appeared that the Russian State Fishing Committee had originally supported him in his quest. Yegorov opposed the move and said that Gorbenko had tried to privatize it piece by piece. The new governor wanted to maintain it as a single entity.[42] After he was blocked from returning to his old job, Gorbenko said that he was a victim of human rights violations and would fight for his job. Meanwhile, his old crony Mikhail Karentnyi was accused of money laundering and misappropriating public funds.

In spite of reservations that many commentators in Kaliningrad had about Yegorov's ability to address the region's problems and uncertainty about the Kremlin's providing help, long-time Kaliningrad watchers had reason to be cautiously optimistic.

For example, in a February 2001 conference—"Russia, Kaliningrad Oblast and the Baltic Sea Region"—Stephen Dewar noted, "Several speakers have commented that Moscow is absent from our discussions. This is not new, Moscow is always absent from occasions such at this." Dewar was referring to authorities from Moscow choosing not to participate in the gathering. "However, what is new is that, for the first time since the gubernatorial election in 1996, Kaliningrad is here. For the first time in years, we have seen the highest levels of the Regional Administration participating and engaging alongside the leadership of the Regional Duma, and both these groups listening to, and working with, the many experts, scientists, and researchers from the region."[43]

Was the absence of representatives from Moscow at this meeting an indication that the Kremlin was disinterested in the oblast or was there another explanation for their nonparticipation? In light of the Kremlin leadership's propensity to play down the influence of regional officials, one might conclude that their absence was not driven by disinterest, but rather that they felt they were the ones to discuss the future of the oblast with foreigners, not regional politicians.

One thing was clear at this time; Russian authorities continued to display interest in how EU enlargement might affect Kaliningrad. In the spring of 2001, both representatives of the EU and Lithuania received messages from Moscow containing "requirements" that both had to comply with after Lithuania joined the EU. Moscow requested that residents of Kaliningrad be given annual Schengen-type visas allowing them to travel to Lithuania and Poland and the right to ship cargo by road and rail through these countries without border checks. Moscow also demanded the right to lay oil and gas pipelines and power grids through these countries and the option of Kaliningrad fishing interests to fish in the EU zone of the Baltic Sea. Moreover, travelers between Kaliningrad and Russia would not need visas, and special permits would be provided for those who traveled by car.[44]

What Role Can the United States Play?

Relations between Washington and Moscow had cooled during the last year of the Clinton administration. During the presidential campaign, the Republicans fingered Vice President Al Gore, in particular, for failing to acknowledge this gross misuse of funds. After all, he had worked closely with Russian prime ministers to coordinate U.S.–Russian relations.

As a presidental candidate, George W. Bush and his foreign-policy team indicated that it would build NMD even if the Russians strongly opposed it. Moreover, Condoleeza Rice, who would become his national security adviser, indicated that unlike the Clinton administration, a Bush administration would not meddle in Russian affairs. Most pointedly, she said it made little sense for the United States to provide economic aid to Russia as long as corrupt politicians and their friends in the Mafia were misusing such assistance. But what really angered Moscow were comments she reportedly made in an interview in the French newspaper *Le Figaro:* "I believe that Russia is a threat to the West in general and to our European allies in particular."[45]

U.S.–Russian relations became even cooler when Bush, within a month after entering office, ordered U.S. aircraft to bomb communications and antiaircraft targets in Iraq. U.S. intelligence sources indicated that Saddam Hussein's military was about to enhance those systems and place U.S. and British pilots who monitored the "no-fly" zones at risk.

Russian authorities characterized the strikes as a further example of a U.S. president doing what he wanted to—in spite of international reaction— because the United States was the world's only superpower. Vladimir Lukin, a deputy in the Duma and former Russian ambassador to the United States, deemed the strike a message from Bush: "Russia look out."[46] Weeks later, the climate became even cooler when the U.S. government expelled fifty Russian "spies" from the United States.

Meanwhile, early in January 2001, while Clinton was enjoying his last days in office, Kaliningrad became a hot topic when the *Washington Times* ran a story that began: "Russia is moving tactical nuclear weapons into a military base in Eastern Europe for the first time since the Cold War ended in an apparent effort to step up military pressure on the expanded NATO alliance."

Later in the article the author, Bill Gertz, identified Kaliningrad as the site where the CIA reputedly claimed that Russia had deployed tactical nuclear weapons. He wrote, "The precise type of new tactical weapons could not be learned. Some defense officials said they are probably for use on a new short-range missile known as the Tockha. A Tockha was test-fired on April 18 (2000) in Kaliningrad. It has a range of about 44 miles."

After I read the piece, I contacted Gertz and asked him if the allegation had been confirmed. He responded: "It's true. Pentagon officials have confirmed my story to the AP (the Associated Press) and the Russian military is denying it."[47]

The next day, while President Putin was walking across Red Square with

German Chancellor Gerhard Schroeder, he was asked by a reporter about the claim and he responded: "It's rubbish!"

In spite of Putin's assertion, the Polish government called for inspections to determine whether the charge was true. Polish Defense Minister Bronislaw Komorowski said, "Poland needs to monitor in Kaliningrad on a day-to-day basis, and it is doing that." Lithuania's president Valdas Adamkus said he supported the Polish president's request.[48]

Meanwhile, U.S. officials refused publicly to comment upon the charge but the independent Russian defense analyst Pavel Felgenhauer provided an insightful analysis of the allegation. He said that he understood why no one would accept the word of the Russian Navy, but in asserting that there were no nukes in Kaliningrad they probably were telling the truth. Under Russian defense doctrine, Moscow would not deploy tactical nukes in Kaliningrad because they anticipated that such weapons would be destroyed in a preemptive NATO strike. To avoid this, Russian military planners were prepared to deploy them just prior to an expected attack and at that point would transport them to Kaliningrad.[49]

On February 15, Gertz wrote: "Satellite photographs first revealed the transfers June 3 when the weapons were spotted aboard a Russian military train at a seaport near St. Petersburg, according to U.S. intelligence officials."[50]

Other news sources such as Reuters indicated that U.S. officials, in private, had confirmed the report. They reasoned it was in reaction to NATO plans to enlarge eastward. The U.S. government would not confirm the charge, although that did not mean it was untrue, since U.S. officials do not comment on intelligence reports.[51]

Some U.S. defense analysts speculated that perhaps some tactical nuclear weapons that had been deployed earlier in Kaliningrad remained there and had never been removed for economic or logistical reasons, not because of Russian military planning. The source of the story, of course, was deemed relevant to the charge. The Korean cult leader Reverend Moon owns *The Washington Times*. It has a reputation among liberals as a right-wing newspaper, and critics claim that it, at times, is more concerned about running provocative stories than with their accuracy.

Whatever the merits of the charge, a related question was what the motives were for those who leaked the information. A number of plausible answers presented themselves.

Conceivably some proponents of NATO enlargement hoped to cite it as cause for the Baltic democracies gaining membership in the alliance. But one could make just the opposite case: here was proof that the Russians were serious about deploying nuclear weapons in Kaliningrad once NATO crossed the Red Line and admitted Lithuania into the club. Was it in the U.S. interest to provoke the Russians while we were negotiating vital strategic nuclear arms reduction matters with them and seeking their acceptance of the NMD?

Of course, one might reason that if Moscow was sending a warning to the West then it would confirm, not deny the charge. But one could also plausibly argue that authorities in Moscow would not have to admit to their deployment because the audience they were attempting to reach (the U.S. Senate) would "get the message."

Perhaps the most powerful argument against Moscow's deploying new tactical nuclear weapons to Kaliningrad in June 2000 was Putin's campaign to drive a wedge between the Americans and their European allies. To deploy nukes there would create problems for Putin with the British, French, and Germans and undercut his campaign to court them. But one could provide a counterargument: European disenchantment with Washington only gained momentum in the second half of 2000 after the nuclear weapons had been deployed. Besides, the generals might have deployed the nukes without Putin's knowing about the action.

In spite of widespread skepticism about the merits of the charge, it would not go away. One thing was clear, the dispute over nukes in Kaliningrad demonstrated that the oblast could become a source of friction between Russia and NATO as the next round of enlargement moved toward the 2002 deadline. Consequently, neither the Americans nor the Russians could ignore the Kaliningrad Question; it had to be addressed to prevent that from happening.

There was another incentive for addressing it, of course. Western–Russian cooperation in Kaliningrad might promote greater harmony between the Euro-Atlantic democracies and Russia.

By the fall of 2001, Lithuanian authorities concluded that Putin was ready to cooperate fully with the EU and Kaliningrad's neighbors in addressing the exclave's problems. Early in the summer, Lithuanian authorities had noted with concern that their Russian counterparts no longer expressed interest in providing a special visa regime for Kaliningrad's residents. This led some in Vilnius to the conclusion that hard-liners in Moscow, who wanted to reduce and not expand relations between the exclave and its neighbors, had convinced Putin of the wisdom of their position.

But on July 26, Putin met with his Security Council to discuss Kaliningrad, and he supported those who had counseled that Russia fully cooperate with the EU in addressing the Kaliningrad Question.[52] Here was evidence that those around Putin, who were urging him to be proactive and take concrete measures to demonstrate that he wanted to join the West, and not to turn inward, had scored a victory.

The 11 September 2001 terrorist attacks on New York City and the Pentagon, and Putin's response to it, provided even more powerful evidence that the Russian president had categorically supported those who favored Russia throwing its lot in with the West.

In a telephone call to President Bush, Putin was the first major world leader to express his condolences. And after two-weeks of relative silence, Putin offered via a TV address to the Russian people to assist the United States in its campaign to topple the Taliban government and root-out Osama bin Laden and those responsible for the atrocities in America. In keeping with offer of help, Putin endorsed Washington's request to the governments of Tajikistan and Uzbekistan to use former Soviet ground and air bases in both countries and make it possible for the United States to begin the war against the Taliban on 7 October.

Putin not only overruled the communists and neofascists in the Duma, but his own defense minister, Sergei Ivanov and the Russian general staff who had advocated Russia restore its international position through the CIS. As a consequence, the U.S. Secretary of State Colin Powell said U.S.–Russian relations had experienced "a seismic change of historic proportions." And President Bush's national security advisor, Condoleezza Rice characterized Putin's offer of help as the true "end of the Cold War."[53]

Only time will tell whether or not a new era of protracted American–Russian harmony has begun; as the U.S.-led antiterrorist campaign unfolded in the fall of 2001, there was reason to be optimistic about future relations between the two countries.

Of course, in any assessment of the major issues that entangle Washington and Moscow, the Kaliningrad Question is of minor importance. But given Kaliningrad's small size and unique situation, joint projects not feasibly tested in Russia can be tested there. Modestly funded American programs implemented in cooperation with the EU might provide insight into how the West can help Russia build a free-market economy.

Stephen Dewar contends that both legal and political reasons prevent the EU from creating a special development fund for Kaliningrad. He calculates that an investment of forty million Euro must be provided from 2001 to 2006 to avoid the "black hole" scenario from materializing. But if the EU did not provide this funding, who would? "I propose that countries that are concerned about this situation should consider establishing a development fund for Kaliningrad that would be analogous to the programs for the candidate neighboring states, but customized to Kaliningrad's particular features and needs."[54] The funding would be canalized through, or run parallel, to the EU's Northern Dimension initiative.

The American contribution to this effort would be modest but worthwhile if it contributed to warmer relations with Moscow, and provided insight into how the West might help Russia build a free and prosperous economy. Help of this kind, of course, would be predicated upon Moscow allowing regional authorities to cooperate with foreign donors without hampering them with legal barriers. Officials in Kaliningrad must also make sure that corruption and bureaucratic red tape does not hamper such efforts.

Government programs aside, U.S. business interests would like to see evidence that the federal government can indeed make it safe for foreign investors by providing the appropriate legal and administrative infrastructure. A development program in Kaliningrad might serve this purpose for private sector skeptics.

Finally, can Kaliningrad once again become a point of conflict between Russia and the West? Should there be a regime change in Moscow or should Putin turn his back on the West? The answer to that question could be yes. But insofar as Baltic membership in NATO has been cited by most analysts as a catalyst for such conflict, there is reason to be optimistic on this front as well. For in the aftermath of the terrorist attacks on the United States, President Putin's suggestion that Russia be included in NATO no longer was considered by Moscow, or many in the West, as ludicrous.

The German Chancellor Gerhard Schroeder brought up the subject when Putin visited Germany in the fall of 2001, and so did NATO's secretary general, Lord Robertson. Meanwhile, among American analysts one found a growing consensus that the West had to include Russia in building a new security architecture for the Euro-Atlantic community whatever form that might take. This was predicated upon the expectation, of course, that the American-led war on terrorism would further enhance American-Russian relations and not undermine them.

Notes

1. See Stephen E. Hanson, "Ideology, Interests, and Identity," in *Center Periphery Conflict in Post-Soviet Russia,* ed. Mikhail Alexseev (New York: St. Martin's Press, 1999), 15–46.

2. RFE/RL, *Russian Federation Report,* 23 February 2000.

3. Conference on "The U.S.–Baltic Charter at Age Two: Achievements, Problems and Prospects," Washington, D.C., 10 February 2000.

4. "Germany Conducts Secret Talks with Russia," *Sunday* (London) *Telegraph,* 21 January 2001.

5. Communication from the Commission to the Council, "The EU and Kaliningrad," Brussels: Commission on the European Community, 17 January 2001, 2.

6. Communication from the Commission, "The EU and Kaliningrad," 10.

7. Reuters, 15 January 2001.

8. James Baxendal et al., eds., *The EU and Kaliningrad* (London: The Federal Trust, 2001).

9. Communication from the Commission, "The EU and Kaliningrad," 7.

10. RFE/RL, *Russian Federal Report,* 5 January 2000.

11. Benjamin Barber, *Jihad vs. McWorld* (New York: Ballentine Books, 1996), 106.

12. Report by the Russian and Eurasian Program, "An Agenda for Renewal: U.S.– Russian Relations," (Washington, D.C.: Carnegie Endowment for International Peace, 2000), 3.

13. See Michael McFaul, "Getting Russia Right," *Foreign Policy* (winter 1999– 2000): 59 and *Washington Post,* 20 February 2000.

14. Amy Knight, "The Enduring Legacy of the KGB in Russian Politics," *Problems of Post-Communism* 47, no. 1 (July/August 2000): 14–15.

15. Andrei Piontkovsky, *The Russian Journal,* 23–29 December 2000.

16. Grigory Yavlinsky, "Sham Reform Leads to National Bolshevism," *The Moscow Times,* 30 January 2001.

17. Sophia Lambruschini, "Russia: Unity Bloc Holds Founding Conference," RFE/ RL, *Weekly Magazine,* 28 December 1999.

18. RFE/RL, *Russian Federal Report,* 20 December 2000.

19. EWI *Regional Report,* 10 November 1999.

20. Robert W. Ortung, EWI *Russian Regional Report* 6, no. 11 (21 March 2001).

21. Mikhail Alexseev, "Challenges to the Russian Federation," in *Center Periphery Conflict in Post-Soviet Russia,* ed. Alexseev, 169.

22. RFE/RL, *Baltic States Report* 2, no. 8 (2 April 2001).

23. John P. Willerton, "Russia and the New Regionalism—A Review Article," in *Europe-Asia Studies* 51, no. 1 (spring 1999): 143.

24. Dmitri Gorenburg, "Regional Separatism in Russia: Ethnic Mobilization or Power Grab?" *Europe-Asia Studies* 51, no. 2 (summer 1999): 245–74.

25. These remarks were made at a Roundtable on Kaliningrad in Vilnius in January 1999, but because of the roundtable's ground rules, no direct attributions are permitted.

26. Lithuanian Foreign Ministry memo, January 2000.

27. Press release from Lithuanian Foreign Ministry, 10 February 2000. For a detailed assessment of how Lithuania's membership in the EU might affect Kaliningrad, see Pertti Joenniemi, Ramunas Lopata, Vladas Sirutavicius, and Ramunas Vilpisauskas, "Impact Assessment of Lithuania's Integration into the EU on Relations between Lithuania and Kaliningrad Oblast Russian Federation," Institute of International Relations and Political Science, Vilnius University (October 2000).

28. Communication from the Commission, "The EU and Kaliningrad," 10.

29. *Kaliningradskya Pravda,* 1 August 2000.

30. Ian Traynor, "Putin Shuns the US in Favour of Europe," *Guardian,* 3 April 2001.

31. Yuri Matochkin, interview, May 2000.

32. "TV Report Suggests High Level Corruption in Kaliningrad," EWI *Regional Report,* 14 December 1999.

33. Lithuanian Foreign Ministry undated memo.

34. RFE/RL, *Russia Federal Report,* 12 January 2000.

35. EWI, *Russian Regional Report,* 10 November 1999.

36. *The Moscow Times,* 14 February 2000.

37. RFE/RL, *Newsline,* 20 August 2000.

38. *TheMoscowTimes.com,* special report Kaliningrad, 9 September 2000.

39. RFE/RL, *Newsline,* 25 January 2001.

40. RFE/RL, *Newsline,* 25 January 2001.

41. *Financial Times,* 14 February 2001.

42. RFE/RL, *Federal Report,* 20 December 2000.

43. Stephen Dewar, "Presentation on Cross Border Cooperation in the Baltic Sea Region," delivered at conference on Russia, Kaliningrad, and the Baltic Sea region, Kaliningrad, 8–10 February 2001, 2.

44. RFE/RL, *Baltic States Report,* 24 April 2001.

45. *Pravda Ru,* 12 February 2001.

46. *Itar-Tass,* 17 February 2001.

47. Bill Gertz, "Russia Transfers Nuclear Arms to Baltics," *Washington Times,* and e-mail communication, 3 January 2001.

48. Bill Gertz, "Poland Wants Inspectors to Kaliningrad," *Washington Times,* 5 January 2001.

49. Pavel Felgenhauer, "Read for the Worse," *Moscow Times,* 11 January 2001.

50. Bill Gertz, "Satellites Pinpoint Russian Nuclear Arms in Baltics," *Washington Times,* 15 February 2001.

51. Conversation with official at State Department. Some analysts think that the United States might have played the Kaliningrad card here. See the Stratfor.com *Intelligence Report,* 5 January 2001, 1. Here we read, "Uneasy with Russia's apparent disregard for U.S. concerns, Washington likely leaked the story in an attempt to undermine Russia's strengthening economic relations with Europe."

52. Interview with Lithuanian diplomats in summer and fall of 2001.

53. See *Deutsche Press Agentur,* 3 October 2001 and *Reuters,* 4 October 2001.

54. Dewar, "Presentation on Cross Border Cooperation," 4.

Index

About the Author

Richard J. Krickus is a Distinguished Professor Emeritus of Political Science at Mary Washington College, and he has held the H. L. Oppenheimer Chair for Warfighting Strategy at the U.S. Marine Corps University. In 1990 he served as an international monitor to the elections in Soviet Lithuania. His books include, *Pursuing the American Dream, The Superpowers in Crisis,* and *Showdown: The Lithuanian Rebellion and the Breakup of the Soviet Empire.* He writes a column on world affairs for Lithuania's leading daily, *Lietuvos rytas,* and he has written for the *Washington Post, Los Angeles Times,* and *Wall Street Journal* as well as academic journals.